Second Workshop on Computational Approaches to Code Switching 2016

Held at the Conference on Empirical Methods in
Natural Language Processing (EMNLP 2016)

Austin, Texas, USA
1 November 2016

ISBN: 978-1-5108-3147-6

Introduction

Code-switching (CS) is the phenomenon by which multilingual speakers switch back and forth between their common languages in written or spoken communication. CS is pervasive in informal text communications such as news groups, tweets, blogs, and other social media of multilingual communities. Such genres are increasingly being studied as rich sources of social, commercial and political information. Apart from the informal genre challenge associated with such data within a single language processing scenario, the CS phenomenon adds another significant layer of complexity to the processing of the data. Efficiently and robustly processing CS data presents a new frontier for our NLP algorithms on all levels. The goal of this workshop is to bring together researchers interested in exploring these new frontiers, discussing state of the art research in CS, and identifying the next steps in this fascinating research area.

The workshop program includes exciting papers discussing new approaches for CS data and the development of linguistic resources needed to process and study CS. We received a total of 12 regular workshop submissions of which we accepted nine for publication four of them as workshop talks and five as posters. The accepted workshop submissions cover a wide variety of language combinations from languages such as English, Hindi, Swahili, Mandarin, Dialectical Arabic and Modern Standard Arabic. The majority of the papers focus on social media data such as Twitter, and discussion fora.

Another component of the workshop is the Second Shared Task on Language Identification of CS Data. The shared task focused on social media and included two language pairs: Modern Standard Arabic-Dialectal Arabic and English-Spanish. We received a total of 14 system runs from nine different teams. All teams except one submitted a shared task paper describing their system. All shared task systems will be presented during the workshop poster session and two of them will also present a talk. We would like to thank all authors who submitted their contributions to this workshop and all shared task participants for taking on the challenge of language identification in code switched data. We also thank the program committee members for their help in providing meaningful reviews. Lastly, we thank the EMNLP 2016 organizers for the opportunity to put together this workshop.

See you all in Austin, TX at EMNLP 2016!

Workshop co-chairs,

Mona Diab
Pascale Fung
Mahmoud Ghoneim
Julia Hirschberg
Thamar Solorio

Publications & Shared Task Chairs,

Fahad AlGhamdi
Mahmoud Ghoneim
Giovanni Molina

Workshop Co-Chairs:

Mona Diab, George Washington University
Pascale Fung, Hong Kong University of Science and Technology
Mahmoud Ghoneim, George Washington University
Julia Hirschberg, Columbia University
Thamar Solorio, University of Houston

Publications & Shared Task Chairs:

Fahad AlGhamdi, George Washington University
Mahmoud Ghoneim, George Washington University
Giovanni Molina, University of Houston

Program Committee:

Constantine Lignos, University of Pennsylvania
Elabbas Benmamoun, University of Illinois at Urbana-Champaign
Agnes Bolonyia, NC State University
Cecilia Montes-Alcala, Georgia Institute of Technology
Yves Scherre, Université de Genève
Björn Gambäck, Norwegian Universities of Science and Technology
Amitava Das, University of North Texas
Younes Samih, Dusseldorf University
David Vilares, Universidade da Coruña
Sunayana Sitaram, Microsoft Research India
Almeida Jacqueline Toribio, University of Texas at Austin
Fahad AlGhamdi, The George Washington University
Giovanni Molina Ramos, University of Houston
Nicolas Rey Villamizar, University of Houston
Victor Soto, Columbia University
Borja Navarro Colorado, Universidad de Alicante
Rabih Zbib, BBN Technologies
Barbara Bullock, University of Texas at Austin

Invited Speakers:

Monojit Choudhury, Microsoft Research Lab India.
Kalika Bali, Microsoft Research Lab India

Table of Contents

This page intentionally left blank.

Workshop Program

Tuesday, November 1, 2016

Session 1: Opening Session

08:45–09:00 *Welcome Remarks*

09:00–10:00 *Keynote Talk*
NLP for Code-switching: Why more data is not necessarily the solution
Monojit Choudhury and Kalika Bali

10:00–10:30 *Challenges of Computational Processing of Code-Switching*
Özlem Çetinoğlu, Sarah Schulz and Ngoc Thang Vu

10:30–11:00 **Coffee Break**

Session 2: Workshop Talks

11:00–11:30 *Simple Tools for Exploring Variation in Code-switching for Linguists*
Gualberto A. Guzman, Jacqueline Serigos, Barbara E. Bullock and Almeida Jacqueline Toribio

11:30–12:00 *Word-Level Language Identification and Predicting Codeswitching Points in Swahili-English Language Data*
Mario Piergallini, Rouzbeh Shirvani, Gauri S. Gautam and Mohamed Chouikha

12:00–12:30 *Part-of-speech Tagging of Code-mixed Social Media Content: Pipeline, Stacking and Joint Modelling*
Utsab Barman, Joachim Wagner and Jennifer Foster

12:30–14:00 **Lunch**

Session 3: Shared Task

14:00–14:30 *Overview for the Second Shared Task on Language Identification in Code-Switched Data*
Giovanni Molina, Fahad AlGhamdi, Mahmoud Ghoneim, Abdelati Hawwari, Nicolas Rey-Villamizar, Mona Diab and Thamar Solorio

Challenges of Computational Processing of Code-Switching

Özlem Çetinoğlu and **Sarah Schulz** and **Ngoc Thang Vu**
IMS, University of Stuttgart
Germany
`{ozlem,schulzsh,thangvu}@ims.uni-stuttgart.de`

Abstract

This paper addresses challenges of Natural Language Processing (NLP) on non-canonical multilingual data in which two or more languages are mixed. It refers to *code-switching* which has become more popular in our daily life and therefore obtains an increasing amount of attention from the research community. We report our experience that covers not only core NLP tasks such as normalisation, language identification, language modelling, part-of-speech tagging and dependency parsing but also more downstream ones such as machine translation and automatic speech recognition. We highlight and discuss the key problems for each of the tasks with supporting examples from different language pairs and relevant previous work.

1 Introduction

Data that includes mixing of two or more languages finds more place in the Natural Language Processing (NLP) tasks over the last few years. This changing picture induces its own challenges as well.

The analysis of mixed language is not a new field, and has been extensively studied from several sociological and linguistic aspects (Poplack, 1980; Myers-Scotton, 1993; Muysken, 2000; Auer and Wei, 2007; Bullock and Toribio, 2012). This has also brought different perspectives on the definition and types of mixed language. Switching between sentences (*inter-sentential*) is distinguished from switching inside of one sentence (*intra-sentential*). Poplack (1980) defines *code-switching* as 'the alternation of two languages within a single discourse, sentence or constituent'. Muysken (2000) avoids this term arguing that it suggests alternation but not insertion, and prefers *code-mixing* for intrasentential switching. Myers-Scotton (1993) employs the cover term *code-switching* for the use of two languages in the same conversation, sentence, or phrase. In this paper we use code-switching (CS) as a cover term for all types of mixing. The terminology is still controversial among researchers, but there is no doubt that all types pose challenges for computational systems built with monolingual data.

Computational approaches in the analysis of CS data are quite recent as compared to linguistic studies. The first theoretical framework to parse code-switched sentences dates back to the early 1980s (Joshi, 1982), yet few studies are done in the 2000s (Goyal et al., 2003; Sinha and Thakur, 2005; Solorio and Liu, 2008a; Solorio and Liu, 2008b). With the beginning of the last decade, this picture has changed due to increasingly multi-cultural societies and the rise of social media. Supported with the introduction of annotated data sets on several language pairs, different tasks are applied on CS data.

The characteristics of mixed data affect tasks in different ways, sometimes changing the definition (e.g. in language identification, the shift from document-level to word-level), sometimes by creating new lexical and syntactic structures (e.g. mixed words that consist of morphemes from two different languages). Thus, it is clear that mixed data calls for dedicated tools tailored to the specific problems and contexts encountered. In order to take these specialties into account, these different cases have to be understood. This way, differences in techniques for

1

Proceedings of the Second Workshop on Computational Approaches to Code Switching, pages 1–11,
Austin, TX, November 1, 2016. ©2016 Association for Computational Linguistics

monolingual and mixed language processing can be unfolded to yield good results.

In this paper, we view CS processing from a variety of perspectives, and discuss the unique challenges that one encounters. We redescribe NLP tasks under the assumption that the data contains more than one language. For tasks that are studied more compared to others we compile approaches taken by previous work. Examples from different language pairs highlight the challenges, supporting the need for awareness about the nature of mixed data for successful automatic processing.

2 Data

Nature of the data Annotated CS corpora, that are designed for computational purposes, center around three sources so far: spoken data (Solorio and Liu, 2008b; Lyu et al., 2015; Yılmaz et al., 2016), social media (Nguyen and Doğruöz, 2013; Barman et al., 2014; Vyas et al., 2014; Solorio et al., 2014; Choudhury et al., 2014; Jamatia et al., 2015; Çetinoğlu, 2016; Samih and Maier, 2016), and historical text (Schulz and Keller, 2016). All these data sources are challenging on their own even if they do not exhibit CS. They are non-canonical in their orthography, lexicon, and syntax, thus the existing resources and tools should be adapted, or new ones should be created to handle domain-specific issues in addition to the challenges of CS itself.

Accessing the data Although CS is prominent in every day life, especially in countries with a high percentage of multilingual communities, accessing it is still problematic. Speech as one of the main sources requires consent prior to recording. One way to keep recordings as natural as possible is to not mention the goal as capturing CS instances to participants. Being recorded however raises self-awareness, and could possibly change how the language is used. Many bilinguals are not keen on mixing languages, e.g. human annotators comment "we shouldn't code-switch" (Solorio and Liu, 2008a).

On this point, social media has an advantage: users of Facebook, Twitter, forums, or blogs, are not aware that their data will be used for analysis, which therefore makes it a more naturalistic setting. They give their consent after, once the content is created. Among social media sites, Twitter has its disadvantages like license issues, and limited characters per tweet. Other media that does not have these advantages remain popular sources.

3 Normalisation

Text normalisation is the task of standardising text that deviates from some agreed-upon (or canonical) form. This can e.g. refer to normalising social media language to standard language ("newspaper language") (cf. e.g. Schulz et al. (2016) and Aw et al. (2006)) or historical language to its modern form (Bollmann et al., 2011). Since mixed text often occurs in spoken language or text close in nature to spoken language like social media, normalisation is a highly relevant task for the processing of such text. In the case of mixed text there are two languages embedded into each other. Defining a canonical form is a challenge because each of the languages should be standardised to its own normal form.

Normalisation of text has started out as a task mainly solved on token-level. Most of the recent approaches are based on context e.g. in character-based machine translation (Liu et al., 2012; Schulz et al., 2016). This results from the fact that normalisation requires a certain degree of semantic disambiguation of words in context to determine if there is a normalisation problem. These problems can appear on two levels: a) The word is an out-of-vocabulary (OOV) word (which are the easy cases), thus it does not exist in the lexicon. b) The word is the wrong word in context (often just the wrong graphematic realisation e.g. *tree* instead of *three*).

This context dependency results in issues for mixed text. The presence of CS increases the number of possible actions regarding an erroneous word. The word could be incorrect in one language and not in the other, or incorrect in both. Either way, the intended language should be decided as well as the usage. (1) emphasises the need for semantic understanding in context (Çetinoğlu, 2016) in which Turkish (in italics) is mixed with German (in bold).

(1)   **meisten**   *kıyımıza*
Meis.Abl(TR)/mostly(DE) shore.P1pl.Dat
vurmuş   *olmasi muhtemel* :)
hit.EvidPast be.Inf possible

'It is possible that it hit our shore from Meis.'/'Mostly it is possible that it hit our shore.'

The first word in the example can be interpreted in two different ways. In Turkish it could be an orthographically incorrect form of *Meis'ten* 'from Meis' which refers to the Greek island Kastellorizo. Or it could be a typo where the *s* of German *meistens* 'mostly' is missing. Such uncertainty might be observed more when language pairs are from similar languages, and share identical and similar words.

Another example is taken from a corpus of Facebook chats (Androutsopoulos, 2015). In this example, three languages, Greek (in italics), German (in bold) and English, are used within one sentence:

(2)   hahahahaha ***ade***
      hahahahaha come on(GR)/goodbye(DE)
      ok   **tanz** *zebekiko* **aber bei**
      okay(GR/DE/EN) dance zebekiko but   on
      billy jean please
      Billy Jean please
      'hahahahaha come on ok dance zebekiko but on
      Billy Jean please'

Androutsopoulos (2015) explains that the post starts with a bilingual discourse marker that indexes concessiveness (*ade ok* 'come on, ok'). The Greek vernacular item *ade* is combined with *ok*, which could be assigned to any of the three languages whereas the preceding *hahahahaha* is not a word in any of them. *Ade* 'goodbye', however, is an existing German word and without larger context of the sentence it is hard to determine if the German *Ade* is intended, in which case a normalisation action (capitalisation) is required, or indeed the Greek vernacular *ade*. Semantic contextualisation is aggravated due to the trilingual context.

One solution is the approach by Zhang et al. (2014). They use a neural net based translation architecture for Chinese-English text normalisation. It includes a Chinese language model and a Chinese-English translation model as well as user history-based context. Since training material for such systems might be sparse for some language pairs, methods for mixed text tend to return to smaller context windows as done by Dutta et al. (2015). They suggest to use two monolingual language models with context windows depending on the neighbouring words using language identification information. In case of a high density of switch points between languages, the context window might be small.

As another normalisation challenge, Kaur and Singh (2015) describe issues emerging from mixing different scripts in Punjabi-English and Sarkar (2016) for Hindi-English and Bengali-English social media text. Since text is often realised in Roman script, in order to utilise resources from other writing systems, the text has to be mapped back to the system of the respective language. Due to this problem Barman et al. (2014) do not use existing Bengali and Hindi resources in their dictionary-based approach. Das and Gambäck (2014) Romanised the resources whereas Vyas et al. (2014) go in the opposite direction and develop a back-transliteration component.

4   Language Modelling

A statistical language model assigns a probability to a given sentence or utterance. Models such as n-gram models (Brown et al., 1992), factored language models (Bilmes and Kirchhoff, 2003) and neural language models (Bengio et al., 2003) are used in many NLP applications such as machine translation and automatic speech recognition. One can consider mixed text as an individual language and use existing techniques to train the model. Tokenisation and normalisation are the first steps to prepare the training data. Hence, one will face the problems presented in Section 3 first. Another serious problem is the lack of CS training data which makes statistical language models unreliable. We consider three kinds of CS to identify challenges of code-switching language modelling (LM).

Inter-sentential CS In addition to the CS data corpus, we can use monolingual data to train several language models and interpolate them. Under the assumption that we can find monolingual data which has the same domain as the CS data, there is no obvious problem in this case.

Intra-sentential CS The only available data resource is the code-switching training data. Previous work suggests to add syntactic and semantic information into the original statistical model to first predict the CS points and then the current word. It shows improvement when integrating additional resources such as language identification and POS tags into the recurrent neural language model (Adel et al., 2013a), the factored language model (Adel et al., 2015) and their combination (Adel et al., 2013b).

Their statistical analysis in Table 1 on the Mandarin-English CS data set (Lyu et al., 2015) gives some insights on how accurate one can predict CS points based on POS tags. Additional information such as

Tag	Meaning	Frequency	CS-rate
DT	determiner	11276	40.44%
MSP	other particle	507	32.74%
NN	noun	49060	49.07%
NNS	noun (plural)	4613	40.82%
RP	particle	330	36.06%
RB	adverb	21096	31.84%

Table 1: Mandarin and English POS tags that trigger a code-switching (First two columns: Man → En, rest: En → Man)

language identification and POS tags might not be accurate due to problems presented in Section 5 and Section 6. In their work, they propose to combine Stanford Mandarin and English POS taggers to generate POS tags. There is, however, no report on POS tagger performance due to the lack of gold data.

Li and Fung (2012;2014) propose another research direction which assembles syntactic inversion constraints into the language model. Instead of learning to predict the CS points alone, they suggest to learn the permission probabilities of CS points from a parallel corpus as to not violate the grammatical rules of both languages. This information is then integrated in a language model to constrain the CS points. It appears to be a promising approach if a large amount of parallel data of the two language exists and if the assumption holds that people do not change the grammatical rules of the mixed languages.[1]

Intra-word CS In addition to challenges presented in the previous paragraphs, one has to face the out-of-vocabulary problem when CS appears within a word. This word has a high potential to be an unknown word. For example in the German-Turkish corpus (Çetinoğlu, 2016), 1.16% of the corpus are mixed words. 93.4% of them appear only once which indicates a big challenge not only for language modelling but also for other tasks.

---

[1]This assumption is quite controversial among CS researchers, even Section 7 has counter-examples that show grammar changes. The assumption, however, could still be useful in statistical systems if the majority of switches follow the rules.

5 Language Identification

Identifying the language of a text as one of the given languages is considered to be a solved task (McNamee, 2005). Simple n-gram approaches (Cavnar and Trenkle, 1994), character encoding detection (Dunning, 1994) or stop word lists (Grefenstette, 1995) can lead to a recognition accuracy of up to 100% on benchmark data sets.

Discriminating between closely related languages that show a significant lexical and structural overlap, like Croatian and Serbian, already poses a bigger problem. Stop word list approaches are problematic in such language pairs. N-gram approaches show an accuracy of up to 87% (Tan et al., 2014).

However, all these techniques rely on the assumption that the input text is encoded in exactly one language. As soon as different languages are mixed inside a text or further within a sentence, a more fine-grained detection is needed. CS reduces the minimum unit of detection to a token.

Language identification (LID) is the most well-studied task among computational CS approaches: there is relatively more annotated data; it is one of the preprocessing steps for more complex tasks; and shared tasks (Solorio et al., 2014; Choudhury et al., 2014) attract more research.

Language identifiers with good performance on monolingual input (Cavnar and Trenkle, 1994; Lui and Baldwin, 2012) encounter accuracy loss due to shorter and/or unobserved context (Nguyen and Doğruöz, 2013; Volk and Clematide, 2014). Thus researchers have chosen to build new tools tailored to CS, using simple dictionary-based methods or machine learning techniques such as Naive Bayes, CRF, and SVM (Lignos and Marcus, 2013; Nguyen and Doğruöz, 2013; Voss et al., 2014; Das and Gambäck, 2014; Barman et al., 2014 and cf. Solorio et al., 2014). While they outperform language identifiers trained on monolingual data, they reach accuracies in the mid-90s. Shared task results (Solorio et al., 2014) report even lower F-scores (80-85%), for some language pairs (Modern Standard Arabic- Egyptian Arabic, and surprise data sets for Nepalese-English, Spanish-English).

Some of the challenges CS poses are inherent to the languages involved, which then propagate to language annotation and identification. One of the language-specific challenges is language annotation when the mixed languages are closely related either linguistically or historically, e.g., Modern Standard Arabic and dialects (Elfardy and Diab, 2012; Samih and Maier, 2016) and Frisian-Dutch (Yılmaz et al., 2016). In such cases it is hard to find a clear distinction between code-switching and borrowing, thus deciding the language ID of a particular token. For English-Hindi, Das and Gambäck (2014) give the word 'glass' as an example. The concept was borrowed during the British colonisation in India, and Indian dictionaries contain the transliterated version. Yet, annotators sometimes labelled it as English.

The opposite is also observed. Both Vyas et al. (2014) and Barman et al. (2014) propose to label English borrowings in Hindi and Bengali as English. However, Barman et al. (2014) report that some annotators still annotated them as Hindi and Bengali. In the end almost 7% of the unique tokens were labelled in more than one language during annotation, which demonstrates that it is challenging to decide language IDs even for humans.

Vague division between CS and borrowing partially affects the language pairs when one or both are influenced by another language, e.g. English in present day. For instance in the Turkish-German corpus (Çetinoğlu, 2016), the word *leggings* was controversial among annotators, as some think it is English while others believe it is already integrated in the German language. This phenomenon could be challenging for statistical systems too, if the monolingual resources contain those controversial words inconsistently or in the opposite label of gold data.

Another big challenge for LID is mixing two languages inside one single word. These mixed words are treated differently among researchers. While many do not specify a special tag for intra-word mixing due to very infrequent representation in their corpus, Das and Gambäck (2014) propose 10 tags that mark the combinations of root and suffix languages. The CodeSwitch Workshop 2014 Shared Task (Maharjan et al., 2015), Barman et al. (2014), and Çetinoğlu (2016) use a Mixed tag.

This pattern is e.g. very productive in German-Turkish code-switching where the suffixes of Turkish, as an agglutinating language, are attached to German words.[2] This can result in words like *Aufgabeler* 'assignments' in (3) where the Turkish plural suffix *-ler* is appended to the German word *Aufgabe* 'assignment' and poses problems not only for LID but also for existing tools for POS tagging and morphological analysis.

6 POS Tagging

POS tagging assigns a category from a given set to each input token. It has a popular use as a stand-alone application or as part of a preprocessing step for other tasks, e.g., parsing. It is the second most popular task after language identification in the current state of CS research. Unlike LID, CS does not change the definition of the task. Nevertheless, the task gets harder compared to tagging monolingual text. While state-of-the-art models reach over 97% accuracy on canonical data[3], in work on CS data scores mostly around 70% are reported.

One problem, as expected, is the lack of large annotated data. Table 2 shows all the POS-annotated CS corpora to our knowledge and their sizes. CS POS tagging requires more annotated data compared to monolingual tagging, as CS increases the possible context of tokens.

Corpus	Language	Tokens	Tag set
S&L'08	En-Es	8k	PTB[4] + 75 Es
V'14	En-Hi	4k	12 UT + 3 NE
J'15	En-Hi	27k	34 Hi + 5 Twitter
ICON'15[5]	En-Hi	27k	34 Hi + 5 Twitter
	En-Bn	38k	34 Hi + 5 Twitter
	En-Ta	7k	17 UD
Ç&Ç'16	De-Tr	17k	17 UD
S'16	En-Hi	11k	12 UT
S&K'16	midEn-La	3k	12 UT

Table 2: Overview of POS-annotated CS corpora. S&L'08:Solorio and Liu (2008b), V'14:Vyas et al. (2014), J'15:Jamatia et al. (2015), Ç&Ç'16:Çetinoğlu and Çöltekin (2016), S'16:Sharma et al. (2016), S&K'16:Schulz and Keller (2016). UT: Google Universal Tags (Petrov et al., 2012). UD: Universal Dependencies tag set (Nivre et al., 2016).

---

[2]The Turkish-German CS tweets (Çetinoğlu, 2016) have 1.16% Mixed tokens as compared to 0.32% Mixed in En-Bn-Hi (Barman et al., 2014) and 0.08-0.60% in Ne-En and 0.04-0.03% in Es-En (Maharjan et al., 2015) corpora.

[3]https://aclweb.org/aclwiki/index.php?
title=POS_Tagging_(State_of_the_art)

The last column of Table 2 shows the tag sets used in annotating POS. Only one corpus uses language-specific tags (Solorio and Liu, 2008b), which pre-dates universal tag sets. With the introduction of Google Universal Tags (UT) (Petrov et al., 2012) and later, its extended version Universal Dependencies (UD) tag set (Nivre et al., 2016) preference has moved to using a common tag set for all tokens. Vyas et al. (2014) employ 3 additional tags for named entities. Jamatia et al. (2015) and ICON 2015 Shared Task use a Hindi tag set that is mappable to UT. They also adopt 5 Twitter-specific tags.

Solorio and Liu (2008b) show that high accuracy English and Spanish taggers achieve only 54% and 26% accuracy respectively on their data, indicating that off-the-shelf monolingual taggers are not suitable for CS text. Common methods applied to overcome this problem in several experiments (Solorio and Liu, 2008b; Vyas et al., 2014; Jamatia et al., 2015; Sharma et al., 2016; Schulz and Keller, 2016) are to choose between monolingual tagger outputs based on probabilities, utilising monolingual dictionaries and language models, and applying machine learning on the annotated CS data. One feature that deviates from standard POS tagging is language IDs, which are shown to be quite useful in previous work. Thus another challenge that comes with CS is predicting language IDs as a prior step to POS tagging.

Solorio and Liu (2008b) achieve a high score of 93.48% with an SVM classifier, but this could be partly due to monolingual English sentences that constitute 62.5% of the corpus. In corpora with higher level of mixing, e.g. (Vyas et al., 2014; Jamatia et al., 2015; Sharma et al., 2016) best scores drop to 65.39%, 72%, and 68.25% respectively. Schulz and Keller (2016) have an accuracy of 81.6%. At the ICON 2015 Shared Task, the best system has an average of 76.79% accuracy. These scores show POS-tagging on CS data has room for improvement.

7 Parsing

Parsing, the task of determining syntactic relations between words and phrases of a given sentence, has

---

[4] Solorio and Liu (2008b) report the tagset is a slightly modified version of PTB, but do not give the exact number of tags.

[5] Data from the ICON 2015 Shared Task on *Pos Tagging For Code-mixed Indian Social Media Text*. It is available at `http://amitavadas.com/Code-Mixing.html`

advanced substantially over the last decade. With the current rise of deep learning, a lot of parsers are developed, that, e.g. go above 93% unlabelled attachment score in dependency parsing of English (cf. Kiperwasser and Goldberg (2016) for a recent comparison of various high-performing parsers).

While theories on parsing CS text have started quite early (Joshi, 1982) and a rule-based HPSG prototype is available (Goyal et al., 2003), there are no statistical parsers developed to handle CS. The main reason is the lack of treebanks that contain CS instances. Nevertheless, two recent works signal that research is moving in this direction.

Sharma et al. (2016) build a pipeline for Hindi-English social media text. They create a corpus with four layers of annotation: language IDs, normalisation, POS tags, and for the first time, chunk boundaries and labels. Each component of their pipeline predicts one layer with data-driven approaches. When all steps are predicted the accuracy for chunking is measured as 61.95%.

Vilares et al. (2016) train lexicalised bilingual parsers by merging the training sets of two languages into one. They compare these models to monolingual ones on 10 Universal Dependencies treebanks (Nivre et al., 2016). The authors also apply their approach on English-Spanish code-switching data in a toy experiment. They have annotated 10 tweets exhibiting CS according to UD rules. They train an English-Spanish POS tagger by merging the training sets of both languages. Their experiments show that using the bilingual tagger and parser is a promising direction for parsing CS.

Challenges in parsing CS stem from error propogation in previous steps, but also from the syntactic constructions that are not native to monolingual languages. (3) is such an example from an ongoing corpus collection.

(3) birkaç *Aufgabe*ler   yaptık
     a few assignment(DE).Pl(TR) make.Past.1Pl
     arkadaşla
     friend.Sg.Ins
     'We made a few assignments with a friend.'

The sentence above contains a German-Turkish mixed word *Aufgabeler* (German portion in italics) as explained in Section 5 and the rest of the words are Turkish. The whole sentence employs Turkish syntax, except that in the NP *birkaç Aufgabeler*, the noun modified by *birkaç* should be singular to be grammatical in Turkish. Perhaps the speaker utilises the German syntax where the noun is expected to be plural for this construction.

(4) is a similar example from Broersma (2009) where the word order is from the embedded language (English, in italics), and shows how the syntactic and lexical systems of the two languages are combined during production: lexical items of one language are ordered according to the syntax of the other.

(4)   *Later* ik naaide voor mensen.
Later I sewed for people.
'Later I sewed for people.'
correct: 'Later naaide ik voor mensen.'

Although not explicitly CS, code-switching bilinguals produce monolingual instances that do not follow the syntax of the uttered language. (5) and (6) show such instances where German syntax interferes with English (Albrecht, 2006, p.130) and Dutch syntax interferes with Turkish (Doğruöz and Backus, 2009). We include them into parsing challenges as the CS corpora to be parsed is likely to contain similar monolingual constructions.

(5)   Daniel: but me too not
Faye: no, no, that goes not
correct: 'Daniel: but me neither
Faye: no, no, that does not go'

(6)   Beyimin ailesi hep o da burda.
Husband.Gen family.Poss all it also here
'My husband's family is also all here.'
correct: 'Beyimin ailesi de hep burda.'

Repeating a word or a whole clause in both languages in a loose or direct translation is a common CS phenomenon, especially in speech or historical documents, and it might pose syntactic challenges e.g. when repetitive subordinate clauses exist which lead to complex coordinations (7) (Lodge and Wood, 2008, p.259). In this example the French portion (in italics) affirmatively translates and completes the Latin *Pater Noster* verse.

(7)   Sed libera nos, *mais livre nous, Sire*, a
But deliver us, but deliver us, God, from
malo, de tout mal et de cruel martire
evil, of all evil and of cruel martyrdom
'But deliver us, God, of all evil and martyrdom'

All these examples demonstrate that, in addition to the solutions that would improve preprocessing steps of parsing, new models and methods should be developed to handle parsing-specific problems.

8 Machine Translation

Machine translation (MT) explores methods to translate text from one language to another. Like all other tasks that rely on large amounts of data for training, MT quality decreases when encountering CS text. Not only the parallel text used for compiling phrase tables and translation probabilities but also the language models included are trained on monolingual data. Mixed text results in a high number of words unknown to the system and low probabilities for translations. Training dedicated translation systems for mixed text is, however, often not feasible due to the insufficient availability of data.

Moreover, translation quality increases with increasing context lengths (cf. phrase-based MT). CS, however, leads to limited accessibility of context (in form of phrases included as such in the phrase table) and thus leads to a decrease in translation quality.

A solution is to detect foreign words and then translate them into the matrix language before translating into a third language (Sinha and Thakur, 2005). Identifying foreign material and translating them into the fitting word in context poses similar problems as described in Sections 3 and 5. The lexical translations of inserted parts can be considered as a normalisation approach. In addition, an underlying assumption of this approach is the availability of a bilingual lexicon for the mixed language pairs which is not always a given. Even in a perfect foreign word translation scenario, it is questionable if the "monolingualised" text syntactically and lexically behaves like any other monolingual text so that a conventional MT system can handle it.

Another challenge is intra-word CS due to morphological binding of one language to a stem from another language as often observed in e.g. Hindi-English text (Sinha and Thakur, 2005) or Turkish-German (Çetinoğlu, 2016) which is shown in (8) .

(8)   Lehrerzimmer*de* schokolade
staff room(DE).Loc(TR) chocolate
dağıtıyorlar
distribute.Prog.3Pl
'They give away chocolate in the staff room.'

(9)   Handing schokolade Lehrerzimmer

Google translate[6] returns (9) as a translation from Turkish to English. The Turkish morpheme *de* is correctly recognised as an inflectional suffix and severed from the base word *Lehrerzimmer* 'staff room'. Yet, it is not translated as the preposition *in* as expected. The German word is present, but without a translation. Moreover, the subject of the sentence (which should be *they*) is not translated at all even though the information is contained in the purely Turkish word *dağıtıyorlar* 'they distribute'. Another word oblivious to the translation is *schokolade* 'chocolate'. When the same sentence is input to Google Translate, all in German and all in Turkish, both cases receive a fully-translated output.[7] Thus, the mixed context seems to harm the correct translation of the sentence.

Manandise and Gdaniec (2011) describe a way to deal with morphological bindings in the context of MT. They use a morphological analyser to first separate the base word from its morphological affixes. Those are then analysed and translated according to the morphology of the target base. They give Example (10), an English-Spanish mixed word *anticooldad* 'anti-coolness':

(10)   a. anticooldad
       b. anticool: dad
       c. cooldad:anti
       d. cool: anti, dad
       e. dummy: anti, dad

The analyser returns all possible base terms (shown as the string before the colon in (10)) along with the possible morphemes (shown as the strings after the colon in (10)). Since the word *cool* appears in the English dictionary and the other suggested base terms do not, the translation of the morphemes along with the correct morphological analysis and language-specific rules lead to the translation *anti-coolness*.

Even though there might be suggested solutions for token-based translations of embedded words as a preprocessing step, translation of the monolingualised sentence might still pose problems due to syntactic specificities as described in Section 7. In

---

case the sentence is monolingualised into one language and uses the syntax of the other original language, MT faces the problem of two separate combined systems: the lexical system of one language and the syntax of another.

9 Automatic Speech Recognition

For automated processing of spoken communication, an automatic speech recognition (ASR) system, which transforms speech signal to text, is an essential component. In the context of CS, ASR is important because CS appears mainly in conversational speech. To develop an ASR system, three major components need to be built: a pronunciation dictionary, a language model and an acoustic model (AM) (Young, 1996). In general, there are two possible ways to build an ASR system for CS speech (Vu et al., 2012). In the first approach, a LID system is used to split the CS speech into monolingual parts and, afterwards, monolingual recognisers are applied to the corresponding speech segments. This method is straightforward since the monolingual systems are already available. We lose, however, the semantic information between the segments and the mistakes of the LID system cannot be recovered especially if speech segments are short (e.g. < 3s). The second approach is building an integrated system with a multilingual AM, dictionary and language model. Compared to the first approach, it allows handling of CS within a word and the semantic information can be used between languages. Therefore, we focus only on identifying challenges of developing pronunciation dictionaries and acoustic models for multilingual ASR.

Pronunciation dictionary A pronunciation dictionary is a collection of words and phoneme sequences which describe how a word is pronounced. A straightforward implementation of a dictionary is to combine pronunciations of the mixed languages. This is often not suitable because pronunciation often changes in a CS context due to the articulation effect when speakers switch from one language to another. Another challenge is how to automatically create the pronunciation for CS words. To our best knowledge, this is a difficult task which has never been addressed so far.

Acoustic modelling An AM estimates the probability of sound state given a speech frame. The most crucial problem is again the lack of transcribed CS data. Another one is the phonetic transfer phenomenon which occurs even when the speaker is proficient in both languages. Hence, most recent proposed approaches focus on bilingual acoustic models which combine the properties of both languages and to some extent overcome the sparsity problem. Vu et al. (2012) merge the phoneme sets based on the International Phonetic Alphabet (IPA) manual mapping to share training data between phonemes across languages. Furthermore, their system allows to ask language specific questions during the context dependent decision tree building process. They achieve an improvement over the baseline with concatenated phoneme sets. Li and Fung (2013) propose an asymmetric AM which automatically derives phone clusters based on a phonetic confusion matrix. In the decision tree building process, they identify similar context dependent tree states across languages. The new output distribution is a linear interpolation of the pretrained monolingual state models. Their proposed approach outperforms the baseline with a large margin.

Another direction is to integrate LID prediction into ASR during testing. The LID gives the probability of a language given a speech frame which can be combined directly with the acoustic score for testing. Weiner et al. (2012) show good improvement when the LID system is sufficiently accurate. It is, however, a challenging task to develop a LID system on the acoustic frame level.

10 Conclusion

In this paper, we discuss the challenges that surface when well-established NLP tasks deal with CS data. Some of these challenges are language-pair dependent e.g. Romanisation and back-translation in Hindi or Bengali. Others are recurring throughout various tasks regardless of the language such as the increased amount of unseen constructions caused by combining lexicon and syntax of two languages.

Working on NLP for mixed data yields the advantage that resources and tools for the respective languages can be beneficial. Although we do not have to start from scratch, the tasks and required techniques are significantly different from those for monolingual data. Context-sensitive methods suffer due to increased combinatoric possibilities crossing syntactic and lexical systems of different languages.

In addition, CS is a phenomenon that appears in data with hard-to-process factors other than mixing. CS-typical genres are often close to spoken text and thus have to deal with problems that colloquial text poses from non-canonicity to incomplete syntactic structures to OOV-words. Although this would already suggest that a higher number of training instances are needed, there are just small amounts of annotated data available. So far there are annotated bilingual training resources for just three of the tasks (LID, POS and ASR) for specific language pairs. Since each mixed language comes with its own challenges, each pair requires a dedicated corpus.

To alleviate the data sparsity problem, some approaches work by generating artificial CS text based on a CS-aware recurrent neural network decoder (Vu and Schultz, 2014) or a machine translation system to create CS data from monolingual data (Vu et al., 2012). Such techniques would benefit from better understanding of the characteristics of code-switching data. This is why we enriched our paper with examples from data sets covering different language pairs. So far, very little NLP research makes use of linguistic insights into CS patterns (cf. Li and Fung (2014)). Such cues might improve results in the discussed tasks herein.

Another recurring and not yet addressed issue[8], is the inter-relatedness of all these tasks. Features required for one task are the output of the other. Pipeline approaches cannot take advantage of these features when task dependencies are cyclic (e.g., normalisation and language identification). Moreover pipelines cause error propagation. This fact asks for attention on joint modelling approaches.

Acknowledgments

We thank our anonymous reviewers for their helpful comments. This work was funded by the Deutsche Forschungsgemeinschaft (DFG) via SFB 732, projects D2 and A8, and by the German Federal Ministry of Education and Research (BMBF) via CRETA Project.

---

[8]Vyas et al. (2014) discuss joint modelling in the conclusion.

References

H. Adel, N. T. Vu, F. Kraus, T. Schlippe, T. Schultz, and H. Li. 2013a. Recurrent neural network language modeling for code switching conversational speech. In *Proceedings of ICASSP*.

H. Adel, N. T. Vu, and T. Schultz. 2013b. Combination of recurrent neural networks and factored language models for code-switching language modeling. In *Proceedings of ACL*.

H. Adel, N. T. Vu, K. Kirchhoff, D. Telaar, and T. Schultz. 2015. Syntactic and semantic features for code-switching factored language models. *IEEE/ACM TASL*, 23(3).

E. Albrecht. 2006. *I can speak German-und Deutsch: The development and use of code-switching among simultaneous and successive English-German bilingual children*. Rombach Druck- und Verlagshaus.

J. Androutsopoulos. 2015. Networked multilingualism: Some language practices on facebook and their implications. *International Journal of Bilingualism*, 19:185–205.

P. Auer and L. Wei. 2007. *Handbook of multilingualism and multilingual communication*, volume 5. Walter de Gruyter.

A. Aw, M. Zhang, J. Xiao, and J. Su. 2006. A phrase-based statistical model for sms text normalization. In *Proceedings COLING/ACL*.

U. Barman, A. Das, J. Wagner, and J. Foster. 2014. Code mixing: A challenge for language identification in the language of social media. In *Proceedings of the CodeSwitch Workshop*.

Y. Bengio, R. Ducharme, P. Vincent, and C. Jauvin. 2003. A neural probabilistic language model. *Journal of machine learning research*, 3.

J. Bilmes and K. Kirchhoff. 2003. Factored language models and generalized parallel backoff. In *Proceedings of NAACL*.

M. Bollmann, F. Petran, and S. Dipper. 2011. Rule-Based Normalization of Historical Texts. In *Proceedings of LaTeCH*.

M. Broersma. 2009. Triggered codeswitching between cognate languages. *Bilingualism: Language and Cognition*, 12:447–462.

P. Brown, P. de Souza, R. Mercer, V. Della Pietra, and J. Lai. 1992. Class-based n-gram models of natural language. *Computational Linguistics*, 18(4).

B. E. Bullock and A. J. Toribio. 2012. *The Cambridge handbook of linguistic code-switching*. Cambridge University Press.

W. B. Cavnar and J. M. Trenkle. 1994. N-gram-based text categorization. In *In Proceedings of SDAIR-94*.

Ö. Çetinoğlu and Ç. Çöltekin. 2016. Part of speech tagging of a turkish-german code-switching corpus. In *Proceedings of LAW-X*.

Ö. Çetinoğlu. 2016. A Turkish-German code-switching corpus. In *Proceedings of LREC*.

M. Choudhury, G. Chittaranjan, P. Gupta, and A. Das. 2014. Overview of fire 2014 track on transliterated search. In *Proceedings of FIRE*.

A. Das and B. Gambäck. 2014. Code-mixing in social media text: the last language identification frontier. *Traitement Automatique des Langues (TAL): Special Issue on Social Networks and NLP*, 54(3).

S. Doğruöz and A. Backus. 2009. Innovative constructions in dutch turkish: An assessment of ongoing contact-induced change. *Bilingualism: language and cognition*, 12(01).

T. Dunning. 1994. Statistical identification of language. Technical report.

S. Dutta, T. Saha, S. Banerjee, and S. K. Naskar. 2015. Text normalization in code-mixed social media text. In *Recent Trends in Information Systems (ReTIS)*.

H. Elfardy and M. Diab. 2012. Simplified guidelines for the creation of large scale dialectal arabic annotations. In *Proceedings of LREC*.

P. Goyal, M. R. Mital, A. Mukerjee, A. M. Raina, D. Sharma, P. Shukla, and K. Vikram. 2003. A bilingual parser for hindi, english and code-switching structures. In *Proceedings of EACL*.

G. Grefenstette. 1995. Comparing two language identification schemes. In *Proceedings of JADT*.

A. Jamatia, B. Gambäck, and A. Das. 2015. Pos tagging for code-mixed english-hindi twitter and facebook chat messages. In *Proc. of RANLP*.

A. K. Joshi. 1982. Processing of sentences with intra-sentential code-switching. In *Proc. of COLING*.

J. Kaur and J. Singh. 2015. Toward normalizing romanized gurumukhi text from social media. *Indian Journal of Science and Technology*, 8(27).

E. Kiperwasser and Y. Goldberg. 2016. Simple and accurate dependency parsing using bidirectional LSTM feature representations. *TACL*, 4.

Y. Li and P. Fung. 2012. Code-switch language model with inversion constraints for mixed language speech recognition. In *Proceedings of COLING*.

Y. Li and P. Fung. 2013. Improved mixed language speech recognition using asymmetric acoustic model and language model with code-switch inversion constraints. In *Proceedings of ICASSP*.

Y. Li and P. Fung. 2014. Language modeling with functional head constraint for code switching speech recognition. In *Proceedings of EMNLP*.

C. Lignos and M. Marcus. 2013. Toward web-scale analysis of the codeswitching. In *Proceedings of of LSA*.

F. Liu, F. Weng, and X. Jiang. 2012. A broad-coverage normalization system for social media language. In *Proceedings of ACL*.

D. Lodge and N. Wood. 2008. *Modern Criticism and Theory: A Reader*. Pearson Longman.

M. Lui and T. Baldwin. 2012. langid. py: An off-the-shelf language identification tool. In *Proc. of ACL*.

D.-C. Lyu, T.-P. Tan, E.-S. Chng, and H. Li. 2015. Mandarin–english code-switching speech corpus in south-east asia: Seame. *LRE*, 49(3):581–600.

S. Maharjan, E. Blair, S. Bethard, and T. Solorio. 2015. Developing language-tagged corpora for code-switching tweets. In *Proceedings of LAW-9*.

E. Manandise and C. Gdaniec. 2011. Morphology to the rescue redux: Resolving borrowings and code-mixing in machine translation. In *Proceedings of SFCM*.

P. McNamee. 2005. Language identification: A solved problem suitable for undergraduate instruction. *J. Comput. Sci. Coll.*, 20(3).

P. Muysken. 2000. *Bilingual Speech: A Typology of Code-Mixing*.

C. Myers-Scotton. 1993. *Duelling languages: Grammatical structure in codeswitching*. Oxford University Press.

D. Nguyen and A. S. Doğruöz. 2013. Word level language identification in online multilingual communication. In *Proceedings of EMNLP*.

J. Nivre, M.-C. de Marneffe, F. Ginter, Y. Goldberg, J. Hajič, C. Manning, R. McDonald, S. Petrov, S. Pyysalo, N. Silveira, R. Tsarfaty, and D. Zeman. 2016. Universal dependencies v1: A multilingual treebank collection. In *Proceedings of LREC*.

S. Petrov, D. Das, and R. McDonald. 2012. A universal part-of-speech tagset. In *Proceedings of LREC*.

S. Poplack. 1980. Sometimes I'll start a sentence in Spanish y termino en Espanol: toward a typology of code-switching. *Linguistics*, 18(7-8).

Y. Samih and W. Maier. 2016. An arabic-moroccan darija code-switched corpus. In *Proceedings of LREC*.

K. Sarkar. 2016. Part-of-speech tagging for code-mixed indian social media text at ICON 2015. *CoRR*, abs/1601.01195.

S. Schulz and M. Keller. 2016. Code-switching ubique est - language identification and part-of-speech tagging for historical mixed text. In *Proc. of LaTeCH*.

S. Schulz, G. De Pauw, O. De Clercq, B. Desmet, V. Hoste, W. Daelemans, and L. Macken. 2016. Multimodular text normalization of dutch user-generated content. *ACM Trans. Intell. Syst. Technol.*, 7(4).

A. Sharma, S. Gupta, R. Motlani, P. Bansal, M. Shrivastava, R. Mamidi, and D. M. Sharma. 2016. Shallow parsing pipeline - hindi-english code-mixed social media text. In *Proceedings of NAACL*.

R.M.K. Sinha and A. Thakur. 2005. Machine translation of bi-lingual hindi-english (hinglish) text. In *Proceedings of the MT Summit*.

T. Solorio and Y. Liu. 2008a. Learning to predict code-switching points. In *Proceedings of EMNLP*.

T. Solorio and Y. Liu. 2008b. Part-of-Speech tagging for English-Spanish code-switched text. In *Proceedings of EMNLP*.

T. Solorio, E. Blair, S. Maharjan, S. Bethard, M. Diab, M. Ghoneim, A. Hawwari, F. AlGhamdi, J. Hirschberg, A. Chang, and P. Fung. 2014. Overview for the first shared task on language identification in code-switched data. In *Proceedings of the CodeSwitch Workshop*.

L. Tan, M. Zampieri, and J. Tiedemann. 2014. Merging comparable data sources for the discrimination of similar languages: The dsl corpus collection. In *Proceedings of BUCC*.

D. Vilares, M. A. Alonso, and C. Gómez-Rodríguez. 2016. One model, two languages: training bilingual parsers with harmonized treebanks. In *Proc. of ACL*.

M. Volk and S. Clematide. 2014. Detecting code-switching in a multilingual alpine heritage corpus. In *Proceedings of the CodeSwitch Workshop*.

C. Voss, S. Tratz, J. Laoudi, and D. Briesch. 2014. Finding romanized arabic dialect in code-mixed tweets. In *Proceedings of LREC*.

N. T. Vu and T. Schultz. 2014. Exploration of the impact of maximum entropy in recurrent neural network language models for code-switching speech. In *Proceedings of the CodeSwitch Workshop*.

N. T. Vu, D. Lyu, J. Weiner, D. Telaar, T. Schlippe, F. Blaicher, E.-S. Chng, T. Schultz, and H. Li. 2012. A first speech recognition system for mandarin-english code-switch conversational speech. In *Proc. of ICASSP*.

Y. Vyas, S. Gella, J. Sharma, K. Bali, and M. Choudhury. 2014. Pos tagging of english-hindi code-mixed social media content. In *Proceedings of EMNLP*.

J. Weiner, N. T. Vu, D. Telaar, F. Metze, T. Schultz, D.g Lyu, E.-S. Chng, and H. Li. 2012. Integration of language identification into a recognition system for spoken conversations containing code-switches. In *Proceedings of SLTU*.

E. Yılmaz, M. Andringa, S. Kingma, J. Dijkstra, F. Van der Kuip, H. Van de Velde, F. Kampstra, J. Algra, H. van den Heuvel, and D. van Leeuwen. 2016. A longitudinal bilingual frisian-dutch radio broadcast database designed for code-switching research. In *Proceedings of LREC*.

S. Young. 1996. A review of large-vocabulary continuous-speech. *IEEE SPM*, 13(5).

Q. Zhang, H. Chen, and X. Huang. 2014. Chinese-english mixed text normalization. In *Proc. of WSDM*.

Simple Tools for Exploring Variation in Code-Switching for Linguists

Gualberto A. Guzman Jacqueline Serigos Barbara E. Bullock Almeida Jacqueline Toribio
University of Texas at Austin
{gualbertoguzman, jserigos}@utexas.edu
{bbullock, toribio}@austin.utexas.edu

Abstract

One of the benefits of language identification that is particularly relevant for code-switching (CS) research is that it permits insight into how the languages are mixed (i.e., the level of integration of the languages). The aim of this paper is to quantify and visualize the nature of the integration of languages in CS documents using simple language-independent metrics that can be adopted by linguists. In our contribution, we (a) make a linguistic case for classifying CS types according to how the languages are integrated; (b) describe our language identification system; (c) introduce an Integration-index (I-index) derived from HMM transition probabilities; (d) employ methods for visualizing integration via a language signature (or switching profile); and (e) illustrate the utility of our simple metrics for linguists as applied to Spanish-English texts of different switching profiles.

1 Introduction

Sociolinguists who focus on CS have been reluctant to adopt automatic annotation tools in large part because of the Principle of Accountability (Labov, 1972), which demands an exhaustive and accurate report for every case in which a phenomenon (e.g., a switch) occurs or could have occurred. Thus, in order to encourage linguists to move beyond slow but accurate manual coding and to take benefit of computational methods, the tools need to be precise and intuitive and consistent with linguistic concepts pertaining to CS. Herein, we provide a means of quantifying language integration and of

visualizing the language profile of documents, allowing researchers to isolate events of single-word other-language insertions (borrowing, nonce borrowing) versus spans of alternating languages (code-switching) versus lengthy sequences of monolingual text (translation, author/speaker change). Our methods differ from existing NLP approaches in attending to some issues that are relevant for linguists but neglected in other approaches, e.g., in classifying the language of Named Entities as they can trigger CS (Broersma & De Bot, 2006) , in using ecologically valid training data, and in not assuming that each text or utterance has a main language.

2 Related Work

2.1 Mixed Texts

Multilingual documents may comprise more than one language for various reasons, including translation, change of author/speaker, use of loanwords, and code-switching (CS). For this reason, the term bilingual (or multilingual) as applied to corpora can be ambiguous, referencing a parallel corpus such as Europarl (Koehn, 2002) as well as a speech corpus in which more intimate language mixing is present (e.g., the *BilingBank Spanish-English Miami Corpus* (Deuchar, 2010)). King & Abney (2013) have noted that it is desirable that a language identification annotation system operate accurately irrespective of whether it is processing a document that contains monolingual texts from different languages or texts in which single authors are mixing different languages (Das & Gambäck, 2013; Gambäck & Das, 2014, Gambäck & Das, 2016; Nguyen & Doğruöz, 2013; Chittaranjan et al., 2014) . For lin-

Proceedings of the Second Workshop on Computational Approaches to Code Switching, pages 12–20,
Austin, TX, November 1, 2016. ©2016 Association for Computational Linguistics

guists with interests in patterns of CS there is also a need to be able to classify types of mixed multilingual documents. CS is not monolithic—it can range from switching for lone lexical items and multi-word expressions to alternation of clauses and larger stretches of discourse within an individual's speech or across speech turns—and different types of CS invite different types of analyses and reflect different social conditions and types of grammatical integration.

2.2 Mixing Typology

There is consensus that 'classic' or intrasentential code-switching, of all mixing phenomena, is most revealing of the interaction of grammatical systems (Joshi 1982, Muysken 2000, Myers-Scotton 1993, Poplack 1980). Muysken (2000) presents a typology of mixing, identifying three processes—insertion, alternation, and congruent lexicalization—each reflecting different levels of contributions of lexical items and structures from two (or more) languages and each associated with different historical and cultural embedding. Insertional switching, (Example 1, Rampton et al. 2006:1) involves the grammatical and lexical properties of one language as the Matrix Language (Myers-Scotton, 1993) which supplies the morphosyntactic frame into which chunks of the other language are introduced (e.g., borrowing and small constituent insertion). Insertion is argued to be prevalent in postcolonial and immigrant settings where there is asymmetry in speakers' competence of both languages. In alternational switching (Example 2, Nortier 1990: 126) the participating languages are juxtaposed and speakers are said to draw on 'universal combinatory' principles in building equivalence between discrete language systems while maintaining the integrity of each (MacSwan, 2000; Sebba, 2009). Alternation is purported to be most common among proficient bilinguals in situations of stable bilingualism. In a third type, congruent lexicalization (Example 3, Van Dulm, 2007:7; cited in Muysken 2014), the syntax of the languages are aligned and speakers produce a common structure using words from both languages; it is claimed to be attested among bilinguals who are fluent in typologically similar languages of equal prestige as well as in dialect/standard and post-creole/lexifier mixing. Muysken (2013) augments this tripartite

taxonomy by incorporating a fourth strategy, back-flagging (Example 4, DuBois & Horvath, 2002: 276), in which the grammatical and lexical properties of the majority language serve as the base language into which emblematic minority elements are inserted (e.g., greetings, kinship terms); speakers may select this strategy to signal ethnic identities once they have shifted to the majority language.

- Example 1, English/Punjabi
  I don't mix with <kɑʅe:> ('black boys')

- Example 2, Moroccan Arabic/Dutch
  <Maar 't hoeft niet> li-?anna ida seft ana ('But it need not be, for when I see, I . . . ')

- Example 3, English/Afrikaans
  You've got no idea how <vinnig> I've been <slaan-ing> this <by mekaar> ('You have no idea how quickly I've been throwing this together')

- Example 4, English/French in Louisiana
  <Ça va>. Why don't you rewire this place and get some regular light switches? ('It's okay.')

2.3 Mixing types as correlates of social differences

Social factors are the source of variation in CS patterns (Gardner-Chloros, 2009). The same language pairings can be combined in various ways and with varying frequency depending on a range of social variables. Post (2015) found gender to be a significant predictor of both frequency and type of switching among Arabic-French bilingual university students in Morocco. Vu, Adel & Schultz (2013) showed that syntactic patterns of Mandarin-English CS differ according the regional origin of the speaker (Singapore vs. Malaysia). Poplack (1987) observed that CS patterns reflected the differential status of French and English in the adjacent Canadian communities of Ottawa and Hull. Larsen (2014) demonstrated that there are significant differences in the frequency of English unigram and bigram insertions in Argentine newspapers destined for distinct social classes of readerships. In contrast, Bullock, Serigos & Toribio (2016) report that in Puerto Rico, where degree of language contact is stronger, it is the presence of longer spans of English (3+gram but not uni- and bigram) that correlates with higher social prestige.

2.4 Matrix language

In linguistic CS research, the Matrix Language (ML) refers to the morphosyntactic frame provided by the grammar of one of the contributing languages as distinct from lexical items or spans (islands) from embedded languages (Myers-Scotton, 1993). The ML cannot be assumed to be the most frequent language, instead it must be discovered via grammatical analysis.

2.5 Multilingual Indexes

For sociolinguists, Barnett et al. (2000) created a mixing index M to calculate the relative distribution of languages within a given document. Values range from 0 (a monolingual text) to 1 (a text with even distribution of languages). The M-index is valuable in that it indicates the degree to which various languages are represented in a text; its limitation is that it does not show how the languages are integrated and, as a consequence, cannot provide an index of CS versus the wholesale shift from one monolingual text to another in a document. Methods of estimating the proportion of languages in large corpora like Wikipedia have been proposed by Lui, Lau & Baldwin (2014) and by Prager (1999).

2.6 Integration Index

Gambäck & Das (2014) created an initial Code-Mixing Index (CMI) based on the ratio of language tokens that are from the majority language of the text, which they call the matrix language. Like the M-index, CMI does not take account of the integration of CS, thus Gambäck & Das (2016) present a more complex formulation that enhances the CMI with a measure of integration that is applied first to the utterance level and then at the corpus level.

2.7 Language Signature of a document

In their description of the Bangor Autoglosser, a multilingual tagger for transcriptions of Welsh, Spanish, and English conversations in which languages are manually annotated, Donnelly & Deuchar (2011) underline the utility of their system for visualizing the shifting of languages during the course of a conversation, but they make no attempt to quantify language integration, a central point of interest for linguists and one we address here.

2.8 Language Identification

Language identification in multilingual documents continues to present challenges (Solorio et al. 2014 for the first shared task on language identification in CS data). Researchers have tested a combination of methods (dictionaries, n-grams, and machine learning models) for identifying language or for predicting switching, mostly at the word level, with varying degrees of accuracy (Elfardi & Diab, 2014; King & Abney, 2013; Solorio & Liu, 2008a, 2008b; Nguyen & Doğruöz, 2013; Rodrigues, 2012). Because transcriptions of spoken CS are rare, researchers have drawn on social media, particularly Twitter (Bali et al., 2014; Vilares, Alonso, & Gómez-Rodríguez, 2016; Çetinoglu, 2016; Jurgens, Dimitrov & Ruths, 2014; Samih & Maier, 2016), as well as artificially generated texts to develop NLP tools that support the processing of mixed-language data (Lui, Lau & Baldwin, 2014; Yamaguchi & Tanaka-Ishii, 2012) .

3 Language Model

Our language model produces two tiers of annotation: language (Spanish, English, Punctuation, or Number) and Named Entity (yes or no). For the language tier, two heuristics are applied first to identify punctuation and number. For tokens that are not identified as either, a character n-gram (5-gram) and first order Hidden Markov Model (HMM) model, trained on language tags from the gold standard, are employed to determine whether the token is Spanish or English. Two versions of the character n-gram model were tested. One is trained on the CALLHOME American English and CALLHOME Spanish transcripts. The second n-gram model is trained on two subtitle corpora: the SUBTLEX$_{US}$ corpus representing English and the ACTIV-ES representing Spanish. Though in its entirety, the SUBTLEX$_{US}$ corpus contains 50 million words, only a 3 million-word section was used to remain consistent with the ~3 million words in the ACTIV-ES corpus. Both these corpora provide balanced content as they include subtitles from film and television covering a broad range of genres. The validity of film and television subtitle corpora to best represent word frequency has been successfully tested by Brysbaert & New (2009). For the Named Entity tier, we use the Stanford Named Entity recognizer with both the English and Spanish parameters. If either Entity recognizer identified the token as a named entity, it was tagged as a named entity. Unlike other taggers where named entities are viewed as language neutrals, our named entities retained their language identification from their first tier of annotation (Çetinoglu, 2016).

4   Integration Index

In order to quantify the amount of switching between languages in a text, we offer the I-Index, which serves as a complement to the M-index (Barnett et al., 2000). It is a computationally simpler version of the revised CMI index of Gambäck & Das (2016) and one which does not require the segmentation of the corpus into utterances or require computing weights. Consistent with principles of CS, our approach does not assume a matrix language. Consider the two examples below.

- Example 5 (Spanish-English, KC)
  Anyway, al taxista right away le noté un acentito, not too specific.

- Example 6 (Spanish-English, YYB)
  Sí, ¿y lo otro no lo es? Scratch the knob and I'll kill you.

Ex.	1	2	3	4	5	6
Lg. 1	4	4	8	2	6	7
Lg. 2	1	5	4	12	6	7
CS	1	1	5	1	4	1
M	0.47	0.98	0.8	0.32	1	1
I	0.25	0.125	0.45	0.08	0.36	0.08

Table 1: Spans for Examples

Examples 5 and 6 contain perfectly balanced Spanish/English usage, reflected in their M-index of 1. However, the two languages are much more integrated in the first sentence, with four switch points, when compared to the second sentence, with just one switch point. Their respective integration, or I-index, captures this difference. Additionally, Example 2 and 3 each have high M-index values but differ

in the I-index values in ways that might be predicted by social context: English-Afrikaans contact lends itself to congruent lexicalization, while Moroccan-Arabic-Dutch shows low integration insertion common of immigrant settings. The I-index is calculated as follows. Given a corpus composed of tokens tagged by language $\{l_i\}$ where i ranges from 1 to n, the size of the corpus, the I-index is calculated by the following expression:

$$\frac{1}{n-1} \sum_{1 \leq i < j \leq n} S(l_i, l_j),$$

where $S(l_i, l_j) = 1$ if $l_i \neq l_j$ and 0 otherwise. The factor of $1/(n-1)$ reflects the fact that there are $n-1$ possible switch sites in a corpus of size n. The I-index can also be calculated using the transition probabilities generated from a first-order Hidden Markov Model on an annotated corpus (ignoring the language independent tags) by summing only the probabilities where there has been a language switch. The I-index is an intuitive measure of how much CS is in a document, where the value 0 represents a monolingual text with no switching and 1 a text in which every word switches language, a highly unlikely real-world situation. For a 10-word sentence in which each word is contributed by a different language, Gämback & Das's (2016) maximum integration is .90 rather than 1.

5   Language Signature

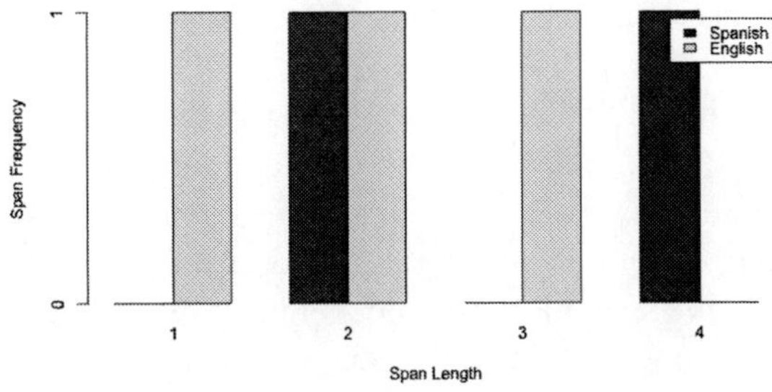

Figure 1: Example 5 Span Distribution

In order to visualize the level of language integration along with language spans, we offer the concept of a language signature that takes into account span length and frequency to derive a unique pattern per document. For Example 5,

	ACTIV-ES & SUBTLEX$_{US}$			CALLHOME		
Language	Accuracy	Precision	Recall	Accuracy	Precision	Recall
English	0.9507	0.9332	0.9729	0.9343	0.8931	0.9893
Spanish	0.9479	0.9021	0.9853	0.9442	0.9286	0.9422

Table 2: Accuracy of language detection on KC using different training corpora

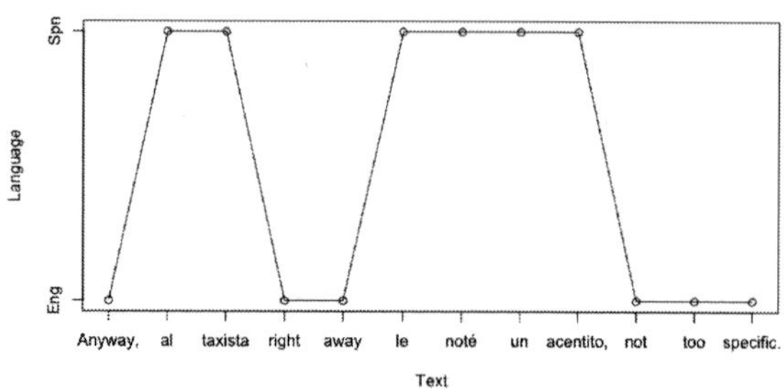

Figure 2: Example 5 Span Plot

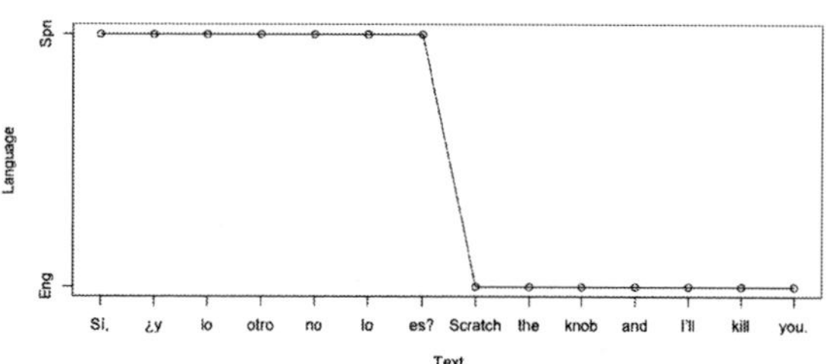

Figure 3: Example 6 Span Plot

there are spans in English of length one, two and three words. In Spanish, there are language spans of length two and four words. Although not particularly revealing with such a short segment, these distributions result in a histogram plot as shown (Figure 1).

In combination with the I-indices, these plots (Figures 1, 2, and 3) display a unique insight into the nature of language mixing and the extent of integration. In contrast to the singular data point of the I-index, the span plots provide a multi-level view of how and to what extent CS occurs in the text.

6 Experiments

6.1 Dataset

Because our interest here is in exploiting language identification for the purpose of detecting variable CS patterns, we draw on two literary texts that we know to employ extensive Spanish-English CS but in two distinctly different styles. Killer Crónicas: Bilingual Memoires (KC), by the Jewish Chicana writer Susana Chávez-Silverman (2004), is a 40,469-word work of creative nonfiction that chronicles the author's daily life through a series of letters that began as email messages written entirely in 'Spanglish'. Yo-Yo Boing! (YYB), by the Puerto Rican writer Giannina Braschi (1998), is a 58,494-word hybrid of languages and genres, incorporating Spanish, English, and 'Spanglish' monologues, dialogues, poetry, and essays. These popular press texts are available online and were used with the permission of the authors.

6.2 Evaluation

The effectiveness of our model was evaluated on a gold standard of 10k words from KC. The segment was selected from the middle of the text, beginning at token 10,000. It was tagged for language by a Spanish-English bilingual professional linguist and 10% was inspected by a second bilingual professional linguist for accuracy. The annotators agreed on all but 2 of the 1000 tokens. The gold standard includes the following tags: Spanish, English, Punctuation, Number, Named Entity, Nonstandard Spanish, Nonstandard English, Mixed along with three other language tags (French, Italian, Yiddish). The Nonstandard tags included forms such as *cashe ~ calle* 'street' to represent dialectal differences, and the Mixed tags included any tokens with morphology from two or more languages such as *hangueando ~ hanging out*. Since Spanish, English, Punctuation, Number and Named Entity account for over 98% of the gold standard, only those tags were used in our model. For the evaluation, we relabel the nonstandard tags to their respective languages and the other languages were ignored.

6.3 Results

As seen in Table 3, despite the close similarity in M-index for the two corpora, the I-index demonstrates

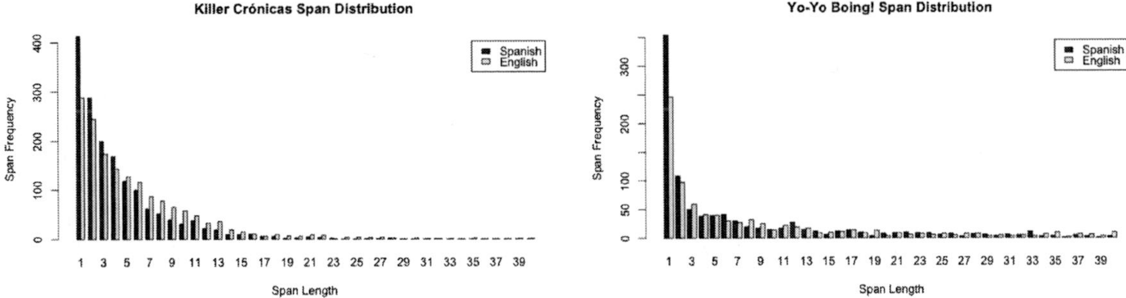

Figure 4: Span Distributions

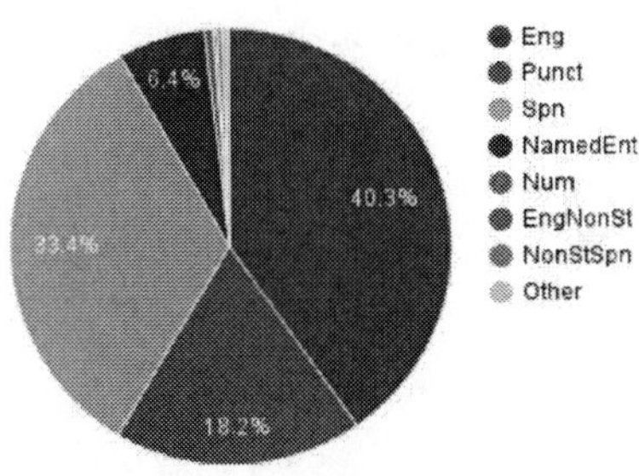

Figure 5: Distribution of Tags

	Accuracy	Precision	Recall
Same	96.72%	79.19%	65.30%
Opposite	88.92%	33.24%	74.85%
English	96.65%	83.94%	58.08%
Spanish	89.00%	34.42%	82.06%

Table 4: NER Classification Performance

the difference in CS between them; KC has a higher integration of languages than YYB. In Figure 4, we see that even though both corpora contain switches, KC has a much higher incidence of short, switched spans in both languages, increasing its I-index relative to YYB.

As shown in Figure 4, KC displays a rapid exponential decay in span length vs. frequency, whereas YYB does not. In addition, YYB displays a heavy tail, indicating a higher frequency of large spans in both languages compared to KC, which has very few spans longer than twenty words.

Table 2 shows our model's performance on language tagging the 10k gold standard of KC using two separate sets of training corpora.

However, as shown in Table 2, our original results

Corpus	M-index	I-index
Killer Crónicas	0.96	0.197
Yo-Yo Boing!	0.95	0.034
EN-ES	0.72	0.067

Table 3: Language Integration and Mixing

using the CALLHOME corpus reflect a lower performance due to the disparity in size of the corpora (3.1M Eng, 976K Mex). Using these corpora resulted in recurring mistakes such as identifying the word "ti" as English due to the overabundance of the acronym "TI" in the English CALLHOME corpus relative to the Mexican Spanish corpus. Additionally, common words in both languages such as "a" or "me" were initially tagged as English for similar reasons. In contrast, changing to equal-size corpora of 3.5M words (ACTIV-ES and SUBTLEX$_{US}$) resulted in a quantitative increase of 1% in language accuracy for both languages as seen in Table 2 and better tagging of "ti", "me" and "a" in mixed contexts.

Furthermore, we chose four different methods of classifying named entities as shown in Table 4: using the classifier in the same language as the token, the opposite language, only the English classifier, and only the Spanish classifier. The Stanford Named Entity Recognizer clearly over identifies named entities, reflected in its low precision scores. We found that using only the English classifier in all cases recognized named entities with the highest precision, but the Spanish classifier resulted in the highest recall rate. Finally, using the classifier in the same language as the token is only marginally better in

17

accuracy than relying purely on the English classifier.

7 Conclusion

In this paper we provided an intuitively simple and easily calculated measure—the I-index—for quantifying language integration in multilingual texts that does not require weighting, identification of a matrix language, or dividing corpora into utterances. We also presented methods of visualizing the language profile of mixed-language documents. To illustrate the I-index and how it differs from a measure that shows the ratio of languages mixed in a text (the M-index), we created an automatic language-identification system for classifying Spanish-English bilingual documents. Our annotation system is similar to that of Solorio & Liu (2008a, 2008b), which includes an n-gram method and a bi-gram HMM model for probabilistically assigning language tags at the word level. We improved accuracy by 1% in our model by using training corpora that reflected natural dialogue and we used different methods of classifying Named Entities in an attempt to reduce the greediness of the Named Entity Recognizer. Our automatic procedure achieves high accuracy in language identification, and although the texts examined proved to be equally bilingual, our analysis demonstrated that the languages are integrated very differently in the two data sets, a distribution that can be intuitively depicted visually.

The implication is that though texts might be mixed, only some texts are suitable for the study of intrasentential CS. For instance, the I-index metric indicates that any random selection from KC, but not YYB, would likely contain intersentential CS. As linguists move to exploit larger multilingual datasets to examine language interaction (Jurgens et al., 2014; Bali et al., 2014), it is crucial to have an uncomplicated metric of how the languages are integrated because different types of integration correlate with different social contexts and are of interest for different domains of linguistic inquiry.

References

Kalika Bali, Yogarshi Vyas, Jatin Sharma, and Monojit Choudhury. 2014. 'i am borrowing ya mixing?' an analysis of English-Hindi code mixing in Facebook. In *Proceedings of the First Workshop on Computational Approaches to Code Switching, EMNLP.* pages 116–126.

R. Barnett, E. Codo, E. Eppler, M. Forcadell, P. Gardner-Chloros, R. van Hout, M. Moyer, M. C. Torras, M. T. Turell, M. Sebba, M. Starren, and S. Wensing. 2000. The LIDES Coding Manual: A document for preparing and analyzing language interaction data Version 1.1–July, 1999. *International Journal of Bilingualism*, 4(2):131–132, June.

Giannina Braschi. 1998. *Yo-yo boing!* Latin American Literary Review Press.

Mirjam Broersma and Kees De Bot. 2006. Triggered codeswitching: A corpus-based evaluation of the original triggering hypothesis and a new alternative. *Bilingualism: Language and cognition*, 9(01):1–13.

Marc Brysbaert and Boris New. 2009. Moving beyond Kučera and Francis: A critical evaluation of current word frequency norms and the introduction of a new and improved word frequency measure for American English. *Behavior Research Methods*, 41(4):977–990, November.

Barbara E. Bullock, Jacqueline Serigos, and Almeida Jacqueline Toribio. 2016. The stratification of English-language lone-word and multi-word material in Puerto Rican Spanish-language press outlets: A computational approach. In Rosa Guzzardo Tamargo, Catherine M. Mazak, and M. Carmen Parafita Cuoto, editors, *Spanish-English code-switching in the Caribbean and the U.S.*, pages 171–189. Benjamins, Amsterdam ; Philadelphia.

Ozlem Cetinoglu. 2016. A Turkish-German Code-Switching Corpus. *Proceedings of the Tenth International Conference on Language Resources and Evaluation (LREC 2016)*, pages 4215–4220.

Susana Chávez-Silverman. 2004. *Killer crónicas: bilingual memories*. Univ of Wisconsin Press.

Gokul Chittaranjan, Yogarshi Vyas, Kalika Bali, and Monojit Choudhury. 2014. Word-level language identification using crf: Code-switching shared task report of msr india system. In *Proceedings of The First Workshop on Computational Approaches to Code Switching*, pages 73–79.

Amitava Das and Björn Gambäck. 2013. Code-mixing in social media text: the last language identification frontier. *Traitement Automatique des Langues (TAL): Special Issue on Social Networks and NLP*, 54(3).

Amitava Das and Björn Gambäck. 2014. Identifying languages at the word level in code-mixed indian social media text. *11th International Conference on Natural Language Processing*.

Margaret Deuchar. 2010. BilingBank Spanish-English Miami Corpus.

Kevin Donnelly and Margaret Deuchar. 2011. The Bangor Autoglosser: a multilingual tagger for conversational text. *ITA11, Wrexham, Wales.*

Sylvie Dubois and Barbara M. Horvath. 2002. Sounding Cajun: The Rhetorical Use of Dialect in Speech and Writing. *American Speech*, 77(3):264–287.

Heba Elfardy, Mohamed Al-Badrashiny, and Mona Diab. 2014. A hybrid system for code switch point detection in informal Arabic text. *XRDS: Crossroads, The ACM Magazine for Students*, 21(1):52–57, October.

Björn Gambäck and Amitava Das. 2014. On Measuring the Complexity of Code-Mixing. In *Proceedings of the 11th International Conference on Natural Language Processing, Goa, India*, pages 1–7.

Björn Gambäck and Amitava Das. 2016. Comparing the level of code-switching in corpora. *Proceedings of the Tenth International Conference on Language Resources and Evaluation (LREC 2016)*, pages 1850–1855.

Penelope Gardner-Chloros. 2009. Sociolinguistic factors in code-switching. In Barbara E. Bullock and Almeida Jacqueline Toribio, editors, *The Cambridge handbook of linguistic code-switching*, pages 97–113. Cambridge University Press, Cambridge, UK.

Aravind K. Joshi. 1982. Processing of sentences with intra-sentential code-switching. In *Proceedings of the 9th conference on Computational linguistics-Volume 1*, pages 145–150. Academia Praha.

David Jurgens, Stefan Dimitrov, and Derek Ruths. 2014. Twitter users# codeswitch hashtags!# moltoimportante# wow. *EMNLP 2014*, pages 51–61.

Ben King and Steven Abney. 2013. Labeling the languages of words in mixed-language documents using weakly supervised methods. In *Proceedings of NAACL-HLT*, pages 1110–1119.

Philipp Koehn. 2002. *Europarl: A multilingual corpus for evaluation of machine translation.*

William Labov. 1972. Some Principles of Linguistic Methodology. *Language in Society*, 1(1):97–120, April.

Jacqueline Rae Larsen. 2014. *Social stratification of loanwords: a corpus-based approach to Anglicisms in Argentina*. Masters Thesis, University of Texas at Austin.

Marco Lui, Jey Han Lau, and Timothy Baldwin. 2014. Automatic detection and language identification of multilingual documents. *Transactions of the Association for Computational Linguistics*, 2:27–40.

Jeff MacSwan. 2000. The architecture of the bilingual language faculty: Evidence from intrasentential code switching. *Bilingualism: Language and Cognition*, 3(1):37–54, April.

Pieter Muysken. 2000. *Bilingual speech: a typology of code-mixing*. Cambridge University Press, Cambridge.

Pieter Muysken. 2013. Language contact outcomes as the result of bilingual optimization strategies. *Bilingualism: Language and cognition*, 16(04):709–730.

Pieter Muysken. 2014. DÉJÀ VOODOO OR NEW TRAILS AHEAD? *Linguistic Variation: Confronting Fact and Theory*, page 242.

Carol Myers-Scotton. 1993. *Duelling languages: grammatical structure in codeswitching*. Oxford University Press (Clarendon Press), Oxford.

Dong-Phuong Nguyen and A. Seza Dogruoz. 2013. Word level language identification in online multilingual communication. Association for Computational Linguistics.

Jacomine Nortier. 1990. *Dutch-Moroccan Arabic code switching among Moroccans in the Netherlands*. Foris, Dordrecht.

Shana Poplack. 1980. Sometimes I'll Start a Sentence in Spanish Y TERMINO EN ESPAÑOL: Toward a Typology of Code-Switching. *Linguistics*, 18(7-8):581–618.

Shana Poplack. 1987. Contrasting patterns of code-switching in two communities. In Erling Wande, Jan Anward, Bengt Nordberg, Lars Steensland, and Mats Thelander, editors, *Aspects of multilingualism: Proceedings from the Fourth Nordic Symposium on Bilingualism, 1984*, pages 51–77. Borgströms, Uppsala.

Rebekah Elizabeth Post. 2015. *The impact of social factors on the use of Arabic-French code-switching in speech and IM in Morocco*. Ph.D. thesis, University of Texas at Austin.

John M. Prager. 1999. Linguini: Language identification for multilingual documents. *Journal of Management Information Systems*, 16(3):71–101.

Ben Rampton, Roxy Harris, and Lauren Small. 2006. The meanings of ethnicity in discursive interaction: Some data and interpretations from ethnographic sociolinguistics. *ESRC Identities and Social Action Programme*, pages 1–14.

Paul Rodrigues. 2012. *Processing highly variant language using incremental model selection*. Ph.D. thesis, Indiana University.

Younes Samih and Wolfgang Maier. 2016. An Arabic-Moroccan Darija Code-Switched Corpus. *Proceedings of the Tenth International Conference on Language Resources and Evaluation (LREC 2016)*, pages 4170–4175.

Mark Sebba. 2009. On the notions of congruence and convergence in code-switching. In Barbara E. Bullock and Almeida Jacqueline Toribio, editors, *The Cambridge handbook of linguistic code-switching*, pages

40–57. Cambridge University Press, Cambridge, UK ; New York.

Thamar Solorio and Yang Liu. 2008. Learning to predict code-switching points. In *Proceedings of the Conference on Empirical Methods in Natural Language Processing*, pages 973–981. Association for Computational Linguistics.

Thamar Solorio, Elizabeth Blair, Suraj Maharjan, Steven Bethard, Mona Diab, Mahmoud Ghoneim, Abdelati Hawwari, Fahad AlGhamdi, Julia Hirschberg, Alison Chang, and others. 2014. Overview for the first shared task on language identification in code-switched data. In *Proceedings of The First Workshop on Computational Approaches to Code Switching*, pages 62–72. Citeseer.

Ondene van Dulm. 2007. *The grammar of English-Afrikaans code switching: A feature checking account.* Utrecht: LOT.

David Vilares, Miguel Alonso, and Carlos Gómez-Rodríguez. 2016. EN-ES-EC: An English-Spanish code-switching twitter corpus for multilingual sentiment analysis. *Proceedings of the Tenth International Conference on Language Resources and Evaluation (LREC 2016)*, pages 4149–4153.

Ngoc Thang Vu, Heike Adel, and Tanja Schultz. 2013. An investigation of code-switching attitude dependent language modeling. *Statistical Language and Speech Processing*, pages 297–308.

Hiroshi Yamaguchi and Kumiko Tanaka-Ishii. 2012. Text segmentation by language using minimum description length. In *Proceedings of the 50th Annual Meeting of the Association for Computational Linguistics: Long Papers-Volume 1*, pages 969–978. Association for Computational Linguistics.

Word-Level Language Identification and Predicting Codeswitching Points in Swahili-English Language Data

Mario Piergallini, Rouzbeh Shirvani, Gauri S. Gautam, and **Mohamed Chouikha**
Howard University Department of Electrical Engineering and Computer Science
2366 Sixth St NW, Washington, DC 20059
`mario.piergallini@howard.edu, Rouzbeh.asgharishir@bison.howard.edu`
`gaurishankar.gaut@bison.howard.edu, mchouikha@howard.edu`

Abstract

Codeswitching is a very common behavior among Swahili speakers, but of the little computational work done on Swahili, none has focused on codeswitching. This paper addresses two tasks relating to Swahili-English codeswitching: word-level language identification and prediction of codeswitch points. Our two-step model achieves high accuracy at labeling the language of words using a simple feature set combined with label probabilities on the adjacent words. This system is used to label a large Swahili-English internet corpus, which is in turn used to train a model for predicting codeswitch points.

1 Introduction

Language technology has progressed rapidly in many applications (speech recognition and synthesis, parsing, translation, sentiment analysis, etc.), but efforts have been focused mainly on large, high-resource languages and on monolingual data. Many tools have not been developed for low-resource languages nor can they be applied to mixed-language data containing codeswitching. In many cases, dealing with low-resource languages requires the ability to deal with codeswitching. For example, it is quite common to codeswitch between the lingua franca and English in many former English colonies in Africa, such as Kenya, Zimbabwe and South Africa (Myers-Scotton, 1993b). Thus, expanding the reach of language technologies to users of these languages may require the ability to handle mixed-language data, depending on which domains it is intended for.

Codeswitching produces additional challenges for NLP due to the simple fact that monolingual tools cannot be applied to mixed-language data. Beyond that, codeswitching also has its own peculiarities and can convey meaning in and of itself, and these aspects are worthy of study as well. Codeswitching can be used to increase or decrease social distance, indicate something about a speaker's social identity or their stance towards the subject of discussion, or to draw attention to particular phrases (Myers-Scotton, 1993b). Sometimes, of course, it may simply indicate that the speaker does not know the word in the other language, or is not able to recall it quickly in this instance. Computational approaches to discourse analysis will require tools specific to codeswitching in order to be able to make use of these social meanings.

Multiple theories propose grammatical constraints on codeswitching (Myers-Scotton, 1993a), and computational approaches may contribute to providing stronger evidence for or against these theories (Solorio and Liu, 2008). These grammatical constraints also can inform the social interpretation of codeswitching. If a codeswitch occurs in a position that is less expected, it may be more likely to have been used for effect. Similarly, when a codeswitch occurs in a less likely context based on features of the discourse, this also affects the interpretation. The longer a discussion is carried out in a single language, the more likely it would seem that a switch indicates a change in the discourse. For example, Carol Myers-Scotton (1993b) analyzes a conversation where a switch to Swahili and then to English after small talk in the local language adds

Proceedings of the Second Workshop on Computational Approaches to Code Switching, pages 21–29,
Austin, TX, November 1, 2016. ©2016 Association for Computational Linguistics

force to the speaker's rejection of a request. This type of switch could also be precipitated by a change in conversation topic, task (e.g. pre-class small talk transitioning into the beginning of lessons), location, etc. By contrast, in conversations where participants switch frequently between languages, each individual switch carries less social meaning. In those situations, it is the overall pattern of codeswitching that conveys meaning (Myers-Scotton, 1993b). A model should be able to see this pattern and adjust the likelihood of switches accordingly. Being able to predict how likely a switch is to occur in a particular position may thus provide information to aid in the social analysis of codeswitching behavior.

In this paper, we will be introducing two corpora of Swahili-English data. One is comprised of live interviews from Kenya, while the other was scraped from a large Tanzanian/Kenyan Swahili-language internet community. We will be analyzing codeswitching in both data sets. Human-annotated interviews and a small portion of human-annotated internet data are used to train a language identification model, which is then applied to the larger internet corpus. The interview data and this automatically-labeled data are then used in training a model for predicting codeswitch points.

There are few NLP tools for Swahili and we could find no prior computational work on Swahili that addressed codeswitching. Additionally, available corpora in Swahili are monolingual, so the creation of two sizable corpora of mixed Swahili-English data will be valuable to research in this area.

2 Prior Research

2.1 Language Identification

Until recent years, most work on automatic language identification focused on identifying the language of documents. Work on language identification of very short documents can be found, for example, in Vatanen et al. (2010). But language identification at the word level in codeswitching data has begun to receive more attention in recent years, particularly with the First Workshop on Computational Approaches to Codeswitching (FWCAC). The workshop had a shared task in language identification, with eight different teams submitting systems on the four language pairs included (Spanish-English, Nepali-English, Mandarin-English and Modern Standard Arabic-Egyptian Arabic) (Solorio et al., 2014). Additionally, prior to this workshop, some work had been done on word-level language identification in Turkish-Dutch data (Nguyen and Doğruöz, 2013) and on language identification on isolated tokens in South African languages (Giwa and Davel, 2013), both with an eye towards analyzing codeswitching.

Most, if not all, of the previous approaches to word-level language identification utilized character n-grams as one of the primary features (Nguyen and Doğruöz, 2013; Giwa and Davel, 2013; Lin et al., 2014; Chittaranjan et al., 2014; Solorio et al., 2014). Those focused on intrasentential codeswitching also utilized varying amounts of context. Nguyen and Doğruöz (2013) and all but one of the systems submitted to the shared task at FWCAC used contextual features. A number of other types of features have been utilized as well, including capitalization, text encoding, word embedding, dictionaries, named entity gazetteer, among others (Solorio et al., 2014; Volk and Clematide, 2014). Significant variation in the difficulty of the task has been found between language pairs. More closely related languages can be more difficult if they also share similar orthographic conventions, as was found with the MSA-Egyptian Arabic language pair (Solorio et al., 2014). In the FWCAC shared task, notable declines in system performance were found when introduced to out-of-domain data.

2.2 Codeswitch Point Prediction

There has been significantly less work done on the task of predicting codeswitch points. We could only find two articles that deal precisely with this task, Solorio and Liu (2008) and Papalexakis, Nguyen and Doğruöz (2014). The two groups take fairly different approaches to feature design and performance evaluation, while both groups use naïve Bayes classifiers. Solorio and Liu also explore Voting Feature Intervals.

Solorio and Liu look at English-Spanish codeswitching in a relatively small conversational data set created for the study. They use primarily phrase constituent position and part-of-speech tagger outputs as features. The word, its language and its human-annotated POS were also used. These

	Interviews	JamiiForums
# Utterances/Posts	10,105	220,434
# Words (tokens)	188,188	16,176,057
Avg. words/item	18.6	73.4
% English words	84.5%	45.8%
% Swahili words	15.4%	54.1%
% Mixed words	<0.1%	<0.1%
% Other words	<0.1%	<0.1%

Table 1: Data set Stats

were tested both with and without the features for the previous word. Initial evaluation was done using F1-scores, but as noted in the paper, codeswitching is never a forced choice. As such, the upper-bound on this task should be relatively low. To get around this issue, Solorio and Liu came up with a novel approach to test performance by artificially generating codeswitched sentences. These sentences were scored for naturalness by bilingual speakers and compared to naturally-occurring codeswitched sentences. Their model achieved scores not far from the natural examples. This approach seems well-justified but requires significant human input.

Papalexakis et al. use simpler features focused on the context of the word. These include the language of the word and the two previous words, whether there was codeswitching previously in the document, the presence of emoticons in the previous two words and the following words, and whether the word is part of a common multi-word expression. These features are applied on a large data set from a Turkish-Dutch internet forum. The language of tokens in this data was labeled automatically using the system in Nguyen and Doğruöz (2013). They find that these features are useful, particularly the language sequence features. The exception is that the emoticon-based features actually reduced performance when combined with other features.

3 Data Sets

The two data sets we use in this paper come from very different domains. The first is comprised of live interviews, and as such is spoken conversation. The second is from a large internet forum, and so is casual, written data with use of emoticons and other behaviors specific to computer-mediated communication. The use of data from two linguistic domains also provides a test of the robustness of our model.

Some descriptive statistics about the two data sets can be seen in Table 2.2. The forum data set is a couple of orders of magnitude larger than the interview data set. Our utterances are similar in length to the posts analyzed in Nguyen and Doğruöz (2013). JamiiForums posts are considerably longer than both.

3.1 Kenyan Interviews

The interviews in this data set were conducted in Kenya. The participants were students at a Kenyan university and the interviewers were a combination of other students and professors at the same university. Most of the participants were interviewed twice, once by a student and once by a professor. This provides two social contexts, one in which the participant and interviewer have the same social status, and one in which the interviewer has a higher social status. In our examination of the data, some differences can be seen in codeswitching behavior in these two situations, but this is beyond the scope of this paper.

The interviews were transcribed, translated, and the words were tagged by language by native speakers of Swahili who are fluent in English. Words were labeled as either English, Swahili, mixed, or other. Some words were originally labeled as Sheng, which is a term used in Kenya for a register of heavy codeswitching with urban street slang (Mazrui, 1995). The annotators were not instructed to use this label. Since most Sheng words clearly originate in either Swahili or English, they were relabeled accordingly. In contrast to the FWCAC shared task (Solorio et al., 2014), we did not label named entities or ambiguous words. Words that might have been labeled that way were instead labeled according to the context – a proper name was labeled as English if it was surrounded by English, or Swahili if it was surrounded by Swahili. Such words that occurred at language boundaries were labeled with the following words or the words within the same sentence (if it occurred at the end of a sentence). There were relatively few instances of this.

3.2 JamiiForums Internet Data

The internet data comes from a large Tanzania-based internet forum named JamiiForums[1]. It was scraped

---

[1]https://www.JamiiForums.com

by a Python script, but due to changes in the forum software and increased security, scraping was not completed. Thus the data only comprises a small fraction of the entire forum. As we already had a large amount of data, we did not feel it necessary to continue immediately[2]. Since our interview data came from Kenya, we prioritized scraping the entire Kenyan subforum first.

During scraping, full URLs, embedded images and email addresses were replaced with placeholder terms. Bare hostnames[3] were left alone since they can double as the name of an organization or website. Emoticons were replaced with the name of the emoticon as defined by the hover text or image file name. Text within quotation boxes was separated from text in the main body of the post. However, given that users do not always format their posts correctly, some improperly formatted forum code will inevitably have been included in our data.

Language labels for 22,592 tokens of the Jamii-Forums data were annotated by a native English speaker. These were annotated according to the same rules as the interview data. Annotation was done after applying the initial language identification model to the forum data, with only disagreements being labeled by the annotator. This significantly increased the speed that annotation could be done.

4 Language Identification Task

4.1 Methodology

For the language identification task, we applied some additional preprocessing to the data. First, the data was tokenized to split words from punctuation marks other than word-internal periods, apostrophes and hyphens. Then all punctuation except for periods, question and exclamation marks were removed. Prior work has explored whether emoticons have any influence on codeswitching behavior (Papalexakis et al., 2014), but did not find them to be significantly useful. Therefore other symbols with no lexical content such as emoticons and the placeholders for embedded images, etc. were also removed.

After this, we experimented with a few different features before settling on the final set. The first type

of feature we used was character n-grams (unigrams, bigrams and trigrams), filtered to exclude n-grams that occurred less than 25 times. The symbol # was appended to the beginning and end of the word to enable the n-gram features to capture prefixes and suffixes. Additionally, we used a capitalization feature, English and Swahili dictionary features and a regular expression feature. The capitalization feature categorized words by whether the first letter only was capitalized and if so, whether it occurred at the beginning of a sentence. Otherwise, words were categorized as either all lower case, all upper case, or all numbers and symbols. Words which did not match any of those patterns were labeled as "other". The dictionary-type features were generated using the English and Swahili models using the TreeTagger tool (Schmid, 1994). They were binary features based on whether the word was recognized by the English tagger or the Swahili tagger. The final feature we explored was a regular expression designed to match Swahili phonology. Since Swahili orthography is highly regular and native Bantu vocabulary conforms strictly to certain phonological constraints, it was possible to write a regular expression that matches >95% of Swahili words, with the primary exceptions being words borrowed from Arabic.

We found that the Swahili regular expression was redundant with the use of character n-grams. Additionally, the English TreeTagger was highly overinclusive, marking many Swahili words as recognized, while the Swahili TreeTagger was underinclusive, making those features relatively weak. So we settled on using only the n-gram features along with the capitalization feature.

We then used the LIBLINEAR algorithm (Fan et al., 2008) with L2-regularization to generate context-free predictions over the words from the interview data. Punctuation tokens were excluded from this model since classifying them would be trivially easy. This context-free model was then used to expand the feature vector for each word. In addition to the original features, the generated probabilities for each class (English, Swahili, mixed, other) on the previous and following word were added to the feature vector. Punctuation was included as part of the context for generating these features. This achieved a high performance within our training set

---

[2]We discuss other aspects of the site in Section 6

[3]For example, Pets.com

| Train / | Interview | | Interview | | Intvw & JF Small | |
| Test Set | 10-fold CV | | JF Small | | JF Large | |
Context Features	None	Word±1	None	Word±1	None	Word±1
English Precision	94.2%	99.4%	41.6%	87.6%	90.1%	99.2%
Recall	99.0%	99.7%	95.9%	96.6%	96.5%	98.8%
F1 Score	96.5%	99.5%	58.0%	91.9%	93.2%	99.0%
Swahili Precision	92.1%	97.9%	98.1%	99.0%	83.7%	95.3%
Recall	67.0%	97.2%	62.4%	96.2%	64.1%	97.7%
F1 Score	77.6%	97.5%	76.3%	97.6%	72.6%	96.5%
Accuracy	94.0%	99.3%	69.7%	96.5%	89.0%	98.4%
Cohen's Kappa	0.74	0.98	0.40	0.92	0.66	0.96

Table 2: Performance of Word-Level Language Identification Models

over a 10-fold cross-validation.

Next, we applied this model to a subset of the JamiiForums data. These labels were used to aid in annotating a portion of the forum data (JF Small). The 6,118 words annotated were then added to the training set and the resulting model was applied to an additional 16,475 words which were then hand-labeled (JF Large). The final model used all of the annotated data and was applied to the full 16+ million word JamiiForums data set.

4.2 Results

The results of the various iterations of the model are summarized in Table 3.2. We used Cohen's Kappa in addition to the measures of accuracy, precision, recall and F1 scores. Cohen's Kappa is used to measure inter-annotator agreement and is suitable for measuring performance across multiple classes and unbalanced label distributions. Effectively, we consider the model as one annotator and our annotators as the other. This measure is more robust across test sets with different label distributions, as is the case with the interview data, which is mostly English, and the JamiiForums data, which is balanced between English and Swahili.

As can be seen, the language probability scores of the word context improve performance significantly. Error analysis suggests that it primarily reduces the errors on named entities and numbers. Since we consider named entities and numbers as belonging to the language they're embedded in, it makes sense that these can sometimes only be correctly labeled using information about the context. But it also reduces errors on other words. For example, "wake" can be a word in both English and Swahili and context is necessary to disambiguate which language it is.

Overall, performance within the training set was highly accurate. The greater test was applying it to the out-of-domain forum data. As expected, performance decreased noticeably, with the context-dependent model going from 99.3% to 96.5% accuracy, and 0.98 Cohen's Kappa to 0.92. Nevertheless, this performance compares favorably to the performance of the systems in the FWCAC shared task on the out-of-domain "surprise" data (Solorio et al., 2014). There are several potential explanations for this. One obvious hypothesis is that the Swahili-English language pair is simply easier to distinguish than the language pairs in the shared task. English and Swahili are quite distinct phonologically; for example, Swahili words of Bantu stock universally end in vowels, so a final consonant is a strong indicator that a word is not Swahili. Another potential explanation is that our language label set was different and so the fact that we did not attempt to label named entities or ambiguous words explains the difference in performance. A final hypothesis is that using fewer features made our model more robust across domains. These explanations are difficult to disambiguate without direct comparisons of systems on similar data.

Error analysis on the JF Small set suggested that many of the errors were simply due to out-of-vocabulary *n*-grams. Our interview data included very few numerals and no symbols such as '&', since transcribers were instructed to write only the words as spoken. However, these characters are common in written communication. Rather than adjusting our feature set, we decided to add this annotated data to the training set and see how this im-

	Interviews	JamiiForums
# Codeswitches	8,508	922,547
Codeswitch %	4.5%	5.7%

Table 3: Codeswitch Point Statistics

proved performance. Adding the JF Small set to the interview data and testing on the JF Large set cut the error rate by over half and brought the Cohen's Kappa up to 0.96, almost as high as the performance within the training set. The accuracy of over 98% made us feel confident in applying this model to the full JamiiForums set, which would be used for the codeswitch point prediction task, discussed below.

5 Predicting Codeswitch Points

The second task was to explore how well we could predict whether a speaker or writer would codeswitch based on the language behavior prior to the current word. In this task, if the current word is $word_i$, then $word_i$ is labeled as a codeswitch point if $word_{i+1}$ is of a different language. Otherwise it is a non-switch point.

(1) Okay, *na unafikiria ni* important *kujua* native language?
(**Translation**: Okay, *and do you think it is* important *to know* native language?)

Consider example (1) from our interview data. At each word in the sentence, we want to predict whether a codeswitch will occur in the next word. The words "okay", "*ni*", "important" and "*kujua*" would all be codeswitch points. If the current word is "*ni*", we want to be able to predict that the next word "important" would be in English. For this, we use only the evidence available in the utterance to that point: "Okay, *na unafikiria ni*". This task is obviously more difficult with less evidence, as would be the case for the word "okay".

5.1 Methodology

As mentioned, we labeled the 16,176,057 words in the full JamiiForums data set using the language identification system we described above. The data used to train the language identification model was excluded from this set. In generating these labels for codeswitch points, we ignored punctuation. We then experimented with predicting codeswitch points using the Kenyan interview data and this much larger internet forum data set. The distribution of codeswitch points in our data sets can be seen in Table 5. The amount of codeswitching appears to be fairly similar, despite the difference in language distribution.

Previous approaches to this problem have used naïve Bayes classifiers trained using contextual and POS features (Solorio and Liu, 2008; Papalexakis et al., 2014). We explored a similar set of features, but additionally tried to represent a few other intuitions. The set of features for a potential codeswitch point at $word_i$ are shown in Table 5. In total, we explored eleven features. For features 6-10, we used binning to make the values more appropriate for the naïve Bayes algorithm. Features 1-3 and 11 were previously used in either Solorio and Liu (2008), Papalexakis et al. (2014), or both and found to have predictive value. Features 4 and 5 are meant as alternative versions of 2 and 3. The idea was that this can reduce sparsity in the data since a three-word sequence of Swahili generates the same values as a three-word sequence of English. Features 6-9 represent the intuition that the longer a speaker continues in a single language, the less likely a switch is at any particular point. We explored using a logarithmic scale since it seemed that after a long stretch of words in the same language, the likelihood of a codeswitch would not decrease much after a few more. The documents in our data have a large variation in length, as can be seen in Table 2.2. There are a number of very long documents in the JamiiForums data, which increases the range of values for these features. Finally, feature 10 is similar to features 6-9, but is not influenced by the length of the document. We had also explored using the POS taggers, as POS had been a useful feature in Solorio and Liu (2008). It did not provide an increase in performance on the interview data, and since applying the TreeTagger algorithm to 16 million words would have been very time-consuming, we did not explore it further. Other free POS taggers are not available for Swahili, nor could we find any large, easily accessible and POS-annotated Swahili corpus available to train our own.

Using these features, a naïve Bayes model was trained on the two data sets. In the unbalanced condition, this was done with a 10-fold cross-validation

Feature #	Feature Name	Description
1	lang_i	Language of word_i
2	lang_{i-1}	Language of word_{i-1}
3	lang_{i-2}	Language of word_{i-2}
4	$\text{match}(\text{lang}_{i-1})$	Are lang_i and lang_{i-1} the same?
5	$\text{match}(\text{lang}_{i-2})$	Are lang_i and lang_{i-2} the same?
6	# same lang words	# of words of lang_i in $\text{words}_{[0..i]}$
7	# diff lang words	# of words *not* of lang_i in $\text{words}_{[0..i]}$
8	*log* # same lang words	$log_2(1+\text{value(feature 6)})$
9	*log* # diff lang words	$log_2(1+\text{value(feature 7)})$
10	% same lang words	% of words of lang_i in $\text{words}_{[0..i]}$
11	Previous codeswitch	Did a codeswitch occur before word_i?

Table 4: Classification features for codeswitch point at word_i

on the full set. In the balanced condition, random samples of approximately 10,000 switch points and 10,000 non-switch points were taken from the data sets in a manner similar to Papalexakis et al. (2014). This allows a more direct comparison to both previous papers.

5.2 Results

The results of our prediction experiments are summarized in Table 5.2. The precision, recall and F1 score are for the codeswitch point class. Since our data is highly unbalanced, you could achieve an accuracy of 94% and 95% on our data sets by never predicting a codeswitch, so we also provide Cohen's Kappa which accounts for the label distribution.

The combination of features that worked best on our data was (1, 4, 5, 6, 9, 11). Reducing sparsity by making features 2 and 3 relative to the language of word_i appears slightly better. It is less clear why using the raw number of same language words worked better in combination with the logarithmic scale on different language words.

Performance on the two data sets is fairly similar despite the differing language distribution, the spoken vs. written domain, and the human-annotated vs. automatic language labels. This could indicate that English-Swahili codeswitching conventions are similar across these two domains. Relative to previous work on codeswitch prediction, our F1 score is similar but higher than in Solorio and Liu (2008) in the unbalanced condition. In the balanced condition, our F1 scores are similar to those reported in Papalexakis et al. (2014) on the interview data.

As mentioned earlier, codeswitching is never a forced choice (Solorio and Liu, 2008), so it would not be expected that these types of features could fully predict codeswitching behavior. In many sentences, there are multiple valid points at which one could codeswitch, and whether one does is informed by social considerations as well as grammatical constraints (Myers-Scotton, 1993a; Myers-Scotton, 1993b).

Given the important social component of codeswitching behavior, another avenue we would like to explore is the use of conversational features. Who someone is communicating with and why can also influence codeswitching behavior (Myers-Scotton, 1993b). Our interview data has a structure of questions and replies, making it possible to examine the influence of previous utterances. The JamiiForums data also has structure in the forum threads, although who is talking to whom is not always obvious since it does not use a nested reply structure. We discuss some of these future directions in the next section.

6 Discussion & Future Directions

As mentioned in our introduction, one of the motivations for predicting codeswitch points is that it could be used to aid in a social analysis of codeswitching behavior. Knowledge of when a decision to codeswitch – or not to – is more or less likely can mark such a decision as more or less meaningful. If the other participant in a conversation has been engaging in frequent codeswitching, this may generally lead the speaker to engage in more codeswitching. If the speaker does not accommodate to their interlocutor, it can give insight into the

Measure	Interviews		JamiiForums	
	unbal	bal	unbal	bal
Model accuracy	97.5%	74.4%	96.9%	67.4%
Precision	28.5%	78.3%	27.4%	81.4%
Recall	52.2%	72.6%	51.3%	58.1%
F1 Score	36.8%	75.3%	35.7%	67.8%
Cohen's Kappa	0.327	0.524	0.306	0.448

Table 5: Codeswitch point prediction performance

social relationship between the participants. For example, Myers-Scotton (1993b) noted that power relations can be reflected in codeswitching behavior. If one participant is more powerful, they may be able to control the language of the interaction and how much language mixing is allowed within it. Other computational studies of linguistic accommodation have found correlations between with power relations (Danescu-Niculescu-Mizil et al., 2012). It is likely that accommodation in codeswitching behavior would follow similar patterns.

The data sets we have collected have metadata that can be used for such social analyses. The Kenyan interview data set has, in addition to conversational structure, pairs of interviews of the same students conducted by another student and by a professor, creating a difference in power across those conditions. The JamiiForums data has less explicit power relations to exploit, with the only easily recognizable hierarchy being between regular users, moderators and administrators, and only a handful of members fall into the latter categories. However, social closeness can be represented by certain interactions between users, such as quotation replies, "liking" each others posts, and following other users. Exploiting these social relations to inform our analysis could yield improvements in our prediction of codeswitching behavior. It would also be possible to track changes in behavior over time, given the decade-long history of the site. An important note about this data set is that while we have approximately 220,000 posts in our collection, the full JamiiForums site has over 17 million posts and an estimate of over 1 billion words. Gaining access to the full data set would increase the scale of the corpus by a couple of orders of magnitude.

Finally, going beyond analyzing patterns of codeswitching to interpreting individual instances of codeswitching will require a finer-grained analysis.

For example, differentiating between quotative, parenthetical and emphatic uses of codeswitching requires not merely an estimate of how expected a codeswitch is in that position, but some understanding of the semantics of the language used. While some uses may be easier to distinguish (codeswitching to quote someone is likely to be preceded by a quotative verb, for example), interpreting the sociopragmatic meaning of codeswitching will generally be far more difficult. Distinguishing between what Myers-Scotton (1993b) refers to as "codeswitching as the unmarked choice" and marked uses of codeswitching is an important first step in that direction.

7 Conclusion

In this paper, we built models for language identification and to predict codeswitching using Swahili-English data. This is, to our knowledge, the first computational paper addressing Swahili codeswitching. We achieved a high accuracy on the language identification task, and modest improvement on the codeswitch point prediction task.

Future directions of study will focus on social analyses of codeswitching behavior, such as the connection between power and linguistic accommodation, or codeswitching and social solidarity. Further work can be done on the Kenyan interview data, while the language identification model will enable analysis of other aspects of codeswitching within the large JamiiForums corpus.

References

Gokul Chittaranjan, Yogarshi Vyas, Kalika Bali, and Monojit Choudhury. 2014. Word-level language identification using CRF: Code-switching shared task report of MSR India system. In *Proceedings of The First Workshop on Computational Approaches to Code*

Switching, pages 73–79. Association for Computational Linguistics.

Cristian Danescu-Niculescu-Mizil, Lillian Lee, Bo Pang, and Jon Kleinberg. 2012. Echoes of power: Language effects and power differences in social interaction. In *Proceedings of the 21st International Conference on World Wide Web*, WWW '12, pages 699–708, New York, NY, USA. ACM.

Rong-En Fan, Kai-Wei Chang, Cho-Jui Hsieh, Xiang-Rui Wang, and Chih-Jen Lin. 2008. LIBLINEAR: A library for large linear classification. *Journal of Machine Learning Research*, 9:1871–1874.

Oluwapelumi Giwa and Marelie H. Davel. 2013. N-gram based language identification of individual words. In *Proceedings of the Twenty-Fourth Annual Symposium of the Pattern Recognition Association of South Africa*, pages 15–22. Association for Computational Linguistics.

Chu-Cheng Lin, Waleed Ammar, Lori Levin, and Chris Dyer. 2014. The CMU submission for the shared task on language identification in code-switched data. In *Proceedings of The First Workshop on Computational Approaches to Code Switching*, pages 80–86. Association for Computational Linguistics.

Alamin Mazrui. 1995. Slang and codeswitching: The case of Sheng in Kenya. *Afrikanistische Arbeitspapiere*, 42:168–179.

Carol Myers-Scotton. 1993a. *Duelling Languages: Grammatical Structure in Codeswitching*. Oxford University Press, Oxford, UK.

Carol Myers-Scotton. 1993b. *Social Motivations for Codeswitching: Evidence from Africa*. Oxford University Press, Oxford, UK.

Dong Nguyen and A. Seza Doğruöz. 2013. Word level language identification in online multilingual communication. In *Proceedings of the 2013 Conference on Empirical Methods in Natural Language Processing*, pages 857–862. Association for Computational Linguistics.

Evangelos E. Papalexakis, Dong Nguyen, and A. Seza Doğruöz. 2014. Predicting code-switching in multilingual communication for immigrant communities. In *Proceedings of The First Workshop on Computational Approaches to Code Switching*, pages 42–50. Association for Computational Linguistics.

Helmut Schmid. 1994. Probabilistic part-of-speech tagging using decision trees. In *Proceedings of International Conference on New Methods in Language Processing*.

Thamar Solorio and Yang Liu. 2008. Learning to predict code-switching points. In *Proceedings of the 2008 Conference on Empirical Methods in Natural Language Processing*, pages 973–981. Association for Computational Linguistics.

Thamar Solorio, Elizabeth Blair, Suraj Maharjan, Steve Bethard, Mona Diab, Mahmoud Ghoneim, Abdelati Hawwari, Fahad AlGhamdi, Julia Hirshberg, Alison Chang, and Pascale Fung. 2014. Overview for the first shared task on language identification in codeswitched data. In *Proceedings of The First Workshop on Computational Approaches to Code Switching*, pages 62–72. Association for Computational Linguistics.

Tommi Vatanen, Jaakko J. Väyrynen, and Sami Virpioja. 2010. Language identification of short text segments with n-gram models. In *Proceedings of the Seventh conference on International Language Resources and Evaluation (LREC'10)*, pages 3423–3430. European Language Resources Association (ELRA).

Martin Volk and Simon Clematide. 2014. Detecting code-switching in a multilingual Alpine heritage corpus. In *Proceedings of The First Workshop on Computational Approaches to Code Switching*, pages 24–33. Association for Computational Linguistics.

Part-of-speech Tagging of Code-mixed Social Media Content: Pipeline, Stacking and Joint Modelling

Utsab Barman, Joachim Wagner and Jennifer Foster
ADAPT Centre, National Centre for Language Technology
School of Computing, Dublin City University, Dublin, Ireland
{ubarman, jwagner, jfoster}@computing.dcu.ie

Abstract

Multilingual users of social media sometimes use multiple languages during conversation. Mixing multiple languages in content is known as code-mixing. We annotate a subset of a trilingual code-mixed corpus (Barman et al., 2014) with part-of-speech (POS) tags. We investigate two state-of-the-art POS tagging techniques for code-mixed content and combine the features of the two systems to build a better POS tagger. Furthermore, we investigate the use of a joint model which performs language identification (LID) and part-of-speech (POS) tagging simultaneously.

1 Introduction

Automatic processing of code-mixed social media content is an emerging topic in NLP (Solorio et al., 2014; Choudhury et al., 2014). Code-mixing is a linguistic phenomenon where language switching occurs at a sentence boundary (inter-sentential), or within a sentence (intra-sentential) or within a word (word-level). This phenomenon can be observed among multilingual speakers and in many languages. Additionally, non-English speakers often use Roman script to write something in social media. This is known as Romanisation. The following comment taken from a Facebook group of Indian students is an example of trilingual code-mixed content:

Original: *Yaar tu to*, GOD *hain*. **tui** JU **te ki korchis**? Hail u man!

Translation: Buddy you are GOD. What are you doing in JU? Hail u man!

Three languages are present in this comment: English, Hindi (italics) and Bengali (bold). Bengali and Hindi words are written in romanised forms. These phenomena (code-mixing and Romanisation) can occur simultaneously and increase the ambiguity of words. For example, in the previous comment, 'to' could be mistaken as an English word but it is a romanised Hindi word. Moreover, the romanised form of a native word may vary according to the user's preference. In such situations automatic processing is challenging.

POS tagging in code-mixed data (Solorio and Liu, 2008; Vyas et al., 2014) is an interesting problem because of its word-level ambiguity. Traditional NLP systems trained in one language perform poorly on such multilingual code-mixed data. In this paper, we present a data set manually annotated with part of speech and language[1]. We implement and explore two state-of-the-art methods for POS tagging in code-mixed data, i.e. (1) a stacked system (Solorio and Liu, 2008)[2] and (2) a pipeline system (Vyas et al., 2014). To our knowledge, a comparison between these two POS tagging methods for code-mixed content, i.e. (1) and (2), has not been carried out before. In our study we compare these two POS tagging approaches which is an important contribution of this paper.

In romanised and code-mixed text, words of different languages may take the same lexical form. As a result, language and POS ambiguity are in-

---

[1]This is a subset of the romanised English-Bengali-Hindi code-mixed corpus described by Barman et al. (2014).

[2]In a stacking approach one learner is used to perform a certain task and the output of this learner is used as features for a second learner performing the same task (in our case POS tagging).

30

Proceedings of the Second Workshop on Computational Approaches to Code Switching, pages 30–39,
Austin, TX, November 1, 2016. ©2016 Association for Computational Linguistics

creased. POS labels often depend on the language in code-mixed content. Thus, modelling the interaction between language labels and POS labels may be useful. Furthermore, joint modelling avoids error propagation. We compare our joint model for LID and POS tagging to the stacked model and the pipeline system. We use Factorial Conditional Random Fields (FCRF) (Sutton et al., 2007) as the joint model in our study.

The rest of the paper is organised as follows: in Section 2, we discuss related work. In Section 3 we describe our data for this task. Our experiments are described in Section 4. Section 5 contains analysis of the results. Finally, we conclude and suggest ways to extend this work in Section 6.

2   Related Work

POS tagging with code-mixed social media content is attracting much attention these days (Das, 2016). Different machine learning solutions are being proposed, e.g. Hidden Markov Models (Sarkar, 2015), Conditional Random Fields (Sharma and Motlani, 2015), Decision Trees (Jamatia and Das, 2014; Pimpale and Patel, 2015) and Support Vector Machines (SVM) (Solorio and Liu, 2008). Combining monolingual taggers in a pipeline (Vyas et al., 2014) is also another approach. The POS tagging methods used in these studies can be divided into the following approaches: (i) using a single machine learning classifier (Sarkar, 2015; Sharma and Motlani, 2015; Jamatia and Das, 2014; Pimpale and Patel, 2015), (ii) stacking (Solorio and Liu, 2008) and (iii) pipeline architectures (Vyas et al., 2014).

POS tagging with Spanish-English code-mixed data is first explored by Solorio and Liu (2008). They use two monolingual POS taggers (Spanish and English) to extract the lemma, POS tag and POS confidence scores for each word according to both taggers. First they investigate heuristic methods. These methods are based on handcrafted rules and use the prediction confidence, the predicted tag and the lemma for a particular word from each POS tagger as well as language information of the word generated from a LID system to select the tag from one of the (English or Spanish) POS taggers. Further, they employ an SVM classifier with the extracted information as features and achieve higher accuracy

than their heuristic methods.

Vyas et al. (2014) implement a pipeline approach for POS tagging in English-Hindi code-mixed data. They divide the text into contiguous maximal word chunks which are in the same language according to the language identifier. These chunks are further processed through normalisation and transliteration modules. Normalisation is carried out if the chunk is in English, otherwise transliteration is performed to convert the non-English romanised chunk to its Hindi transliterated form. Afterwards, language-specific POS taggers are applied to predict the POS labels of the word chunks. They identify that normalisation and transliteration are two challenging problems in this pipeline approach.

Our inspiration behind the joint modelling of LID and POS tagging comes from the work of Sutton et al. (2007). They use Factorial Conditional Random Fields (FCRF) to jointly model POS tagging and noun-phrase chunking. In their work the FCRF achieves better accuracy than a cascaded CRF approach. FCRF is also found to be useful in joint labelling of sentence boundaries and punctuations (Lu and Ng, 2010).

3   Data

We use a subset[3] of 1,239 code-mixed posts and comments from the English-Bengali-Hindi corpus (a trilingual code-mixed corpus of 12K Facebook posts and comments) of Barman et al. (2014). This corpus contains word-level language annotations. Each word in the corpus is tagged with one of the following labels: (1) English, (2) Hindi, (3) Bengali, (4) Mixed, (5) Universal, (6) Named Entity and (7) Acronym. The label *Universal* is associated with symbols, punctuation, numbers, emoticons and universal expressions (e.g. *hahaha* and *lol*).

We manually annotate POS using the universal POS tag set [4] (Petrov et al., 2012). These annotations were performed by an annotator who is proficient in all three languages of the corpus. As we had no second annotator proficient in all three languages,

---

[3]We are preparing to release the data set. For more information please contact the first author.

[4]An alternative tag set is the one introduced for code-mixed data by Jamatia and Das (2014). However, we prefer the universal tag set because of its simplicity, its applicability to many languages and its popularity within the NLP community.

we cannot present the inter-annotator agreement for the annotations.

The language and POS label distributions for our data set are shown in Table 1 and 2. In terms of tokens, Bengali (47.9%) is the majority language. 23.2% tokens are English but the amount of Hindi tokens is low, only 6.3%. We analyse the ambiguity of word types in this subset. Our subset contains 7,959 word types, among which only 297 (3.7%) types are ambiguous according to language labels and 569 types (7.1%) are ambiguous according to POS labels.

Label	Count
English	6,383
Bengali	13,171
Hindi	1,746
Universal	5,209
Name Entity	712
Acronym	229
Mixed	69

Table 1: Language label distribution.

Label	Count
NOUN	8,376
PRT	1,332
VERB	4,422
ADV	754
DET	893
ADP	1,358
CONJ	745
ADJ	1,999
PUNCT	4,321
PRON	2,484
NUM	164
X	671

Table 2: POS label distribution.

4   Experiments and Results

We divide the experiments into four parts. We implement baselines for POS tagging in Section 4.1. In Section 4.2 we implement pipeline systems. In Section 4.3 we present our stacking systems and in Section 4.4 we present our joint model.

We perform five fold cross-validation with the data and report average cross-validation accuracy. We investigate the use of handcrafted features and features that can be obtained from monolingual POS taggers (stacking). We perform experiments with different combinations of these feature sets. The following are the features used in our experiments.

1. **Handcrafted Features:** Following Barman et al. (2014), we use prefix and suffix character-n-grams (n = 1 to 5), presence in dictionaries, length of the word, capitalisation information and the previous and the next word as handcrafted features.

2. **Stacking Features:** These features are obtained from the output of a POS tagging system. These features are tokens, predicted labels, and prediction confidence of a POS tagging system.

3. **Combined Features:** This feature set is a union of the previous two feature sets.

Following Barman et al. (2014) we train an LID SVM classifier using handcrafted features. Its predictions are used in the POS tagging experiments below. The LID classifier achieves 91.52% average accuracy in 5-fold cross-validation.

4.1   Baseline

This method only uses the *code-mixed romanised data* and handcrafted features. We try an linear kernel SVM and a linear chain CRF classifier (see Tabble 3). In terms of average cross-validation accuracy, the SVM classifier (85.00% for $C = 0.00097$) performs better than the CRF classifier (83.89%) in optimised settings.

4.2   Pipeline

Following Vyas et al. (2014), we design a pipeline system. The training data for this method is *monolingual non-romanised*. First, it uses an LID system (trained on romanised data) to identify language-specific chunks. After that it applies monolingual POS taggers to the relevant language chunks to produce the output. The component POS taggers are trained on monolingual non-romanised data.

In this system, code-mixed romanised data passes through a pipeline of LID, transliteration and POS tagging modules. For example, for Bengali-English romanised code-mixed content, the LID module produces Bengali and English chunks, and the Bengali chunks are transliterated into Bengali script and are sent to a Bengali tagger. The English chunks are sent to an English tagger as they are. The final output combines the results from the individual taggers. To implement this method we carry out the following steps:

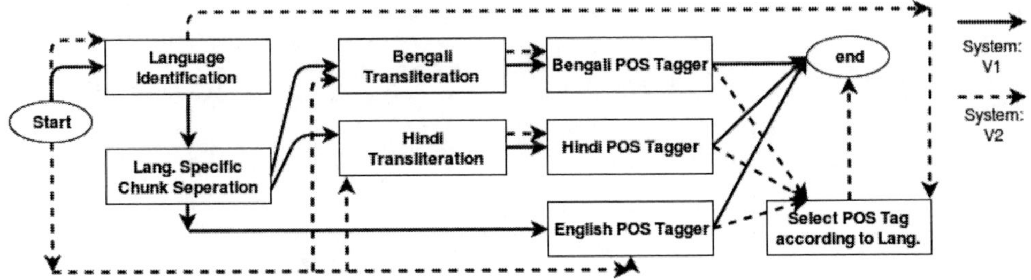

Figure 1: Pipeline systems: system V1 and V2 (Section 4.2).

1. We perform transliteration based on language using Google Transliteration[5] for Hindi and Bengali tokens. (Vyas et al. (2014) use an in-house tool).

2. For the next step of the pipeline, we train monolingual POS taggers for Bengali and Hindi using the SNLTR Bengali and Hindi corpus[6] with TreeTagger[7] (Schmid, 1994). For English we use the default English model which is available with the TreeTagger package[8]. We also use a lightweight Bengali and Hindi stemmer (Ganguly et al., 2012) to provide a stemmed lexicon to TreeTagger during training. We use these taggers to make predictions on English, transliterated Bengali and transliterated Hindi chunks.

The black lines in Figure 1 shows the pipeline of this method (V1). The three training data sets for the three POS taggers follow different tag sets, we map these tags to the universal POS tags after prediction.[9] We achieve 71.12% average cross-validation accuracy with this method (V1) (third row of Table 3).

In method V1, the TreeTagger models are trained on full monolingual sentences. If language-specific text fragments are presented to such monolingual taggers, the taggers may treat these fragments as full

sentences. At the start and at the end of the input, the prediction of such taggers may become biased to some specific patterns (e.g. NOUN + PUNCT) that have been observed frequently as a start and an end tag sequence of sentences during training. To avoid this problem we implement a variant (V2) of this system in which we present full sentences (that may contain junk transliteration) to each POS tagger. We perform transliteration as the first component of the system. We present the transliterated content in Bengali script to the Bengali tagger, original romanised content to the English tagger and transliterated content in Hindi script to the Hindi tagger. Finally, we choose from the outputs of these three taggers based on the language prediction by the SVM classifier for the original (romanised) content. The pipeline of this system (V2) is shown by the dotted lines in Figure 1. We achieve 71.27% average cross-validation accuracy in this method (V2) (fourth row of Table 3).

4.3 Stacking

This method uses *non-romanised monolingual and romanised code-mixed data* with handcrafted, stacking and combined features. This method follows the approach of Solorio and Liu (2008) with necessary adjustments. In this method, romanised code-mixed content is transliterated blindly in all languages and is presented to different POS taggers (trained with non-romanised monolingual data) as in method V2. The romanised words and the output from the monolingual taggers are used as features to train an SVM classifier on romanised code-mixed content. To keep our methodology as similar as possible to Solorio and Liu (2008) we follow the steps described below:

1. We train a Bengali and a Hindi TreeTagger (Schmid, 1994) using the SNLTR corpus with

---

[5]https://developers.google.com/transliterate

[6]http://nltr.org/snltr-software/

[7]http://www.cis.uni-muenchen.de/ schmid/tools/TreeTagger/

[8]We use the English TreeTagger module to keep our setup as similar as possible to Solorio and Liu (2008). Other taggers such as the CMU ARK tagger (Owoputi et al., 2013) could also be tried.

[9]We also implement a system where all the tags in the SNLTR corpus are converted to universal POS tags before training. This variant does not outperform the current system.

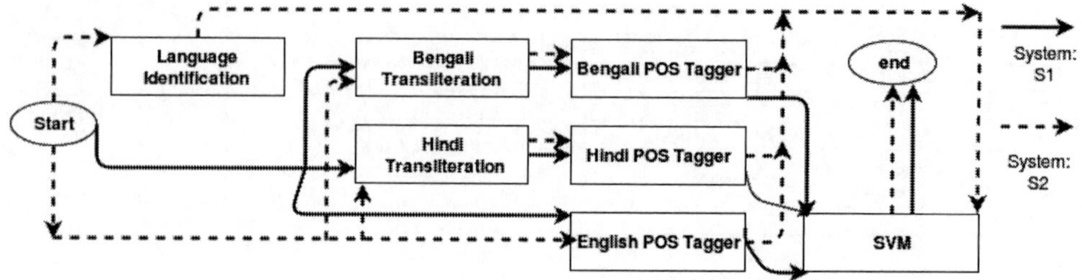

Figure 2: Stacked systems: system S1 and S2 (Section 4.3).

default settings as described in Section 4.2.

2. We transliterate each token of a sentence into Hindi and Bengali irrespective of its language using Google Transliteration as in system V2.

3. After transliteration we send each transliterated output to the respective TreeTagger, i.e. we send the original sentence to the English TreeTagger, Bengali transliterated output to the Bengali TreeTagger and the Hindi transliterated output to the Hindi TreeTagger.

After that we follow the stacking approach of Solorio and Liu (2008). Here, we stack an SVM classifier on top of the predictions generated by the TreeTaggers. We train a linear kernel SVM with stacking features and optimise parameter C in five fold cross-validation. The black lines in Figure 2 show the pipeline of this system (S1). The average cross-validation accuracy of this system is shown in the fifth row of Table 3 – 86.57% . Given the setup, we further experiment by using the combined features from romanised and transliterated tokens and also consider SVM language predictions as a feature. We observe that combining these features boosts the accuracy. After trying combinations of these features the best accuracy (87.59%) is achieved by adding all features together (S2) (sixth row of Table 3). The architecture of the system is shown by the dotted lines in Figure 2.

We also investigate the use of pipeline systems in stacking. The idea is to use all the predictions from a pipeline system and feed them into an SVM classifier. The stacked version of V1 (stacked-V1) achieves 85.99% and the stacked version of V2 (stacked-V2) achieves 85.83% average cross-validation accuracy with SVM using combined features. The black lines in Figure 3 show the

pipeline of S3, stacked-V1 and dotted lines show the pipeline of S4, stacked-V2. These methods do not outperform our implementation of Solorio and Liu (2008)'s method S1 or its extended version S2.

4.4 Joint Modelling

To reduce error propagation from the LID module to POS tagging, we jointly model these two tasks using a 2-level factorial CRF (FCRF). In a linear-chain CRF, there is only one input level ($x = x_{1:T}$) and one output level ($y = y_{1:T}$) (see Figure 4). The conditional probability in a linear-chain CRF is expressed by Equation 1:

$$p(y|x) = \frac{1}{z(x)} \prod_{t=1}^{T} \psi_t(y_t, y_{t-1}, x_t) \qquad (1)$$

$$\psi_t(y_t, y_{t-1}, x_t) = exp \sum_{k=1}^{K} \lambda_k f_k(y_t, y_{t-1}, x_t). \quad (2)$$

$$z(x) = \sum_y \prod_{t=1}^{T} \psi_t(y_{t,l}, y_{t-1,l}, x_t) \qquad (3)$$

$$p(y|x) = \frac{1}{z(x)} \prod_{t=1}^{T} \prod_{l=1}^{L} \psi_t(y_{t,l}, y_{t-1,l}, x_t)$$
$$\varphi_t(y_{t,l}, y_{t,l+1}, x_t)$$
$$\text{where, } y_{T,L+1} = 1. \quad (4)$$

where, ψ_t represents clique[10] potential functions and is expressed by Equation 2. Here, K is the number of feature functions (f_k). The denominator $z(x)$ is the partition function, which is the sum over all 'y's and it is expressed by Equation 3.

---

[10] A clique in an undirected graph is formed with two vertices if there exists an edge connection between them.

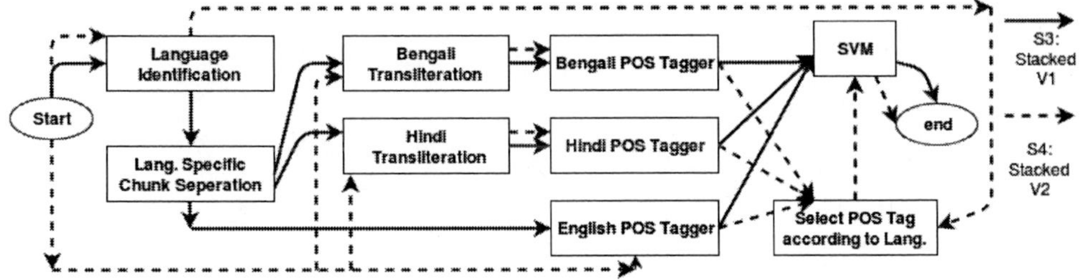

Figure 3: Pipeline systems in stacking: S3 (stacked-V1) and S4 (stacked-V2).

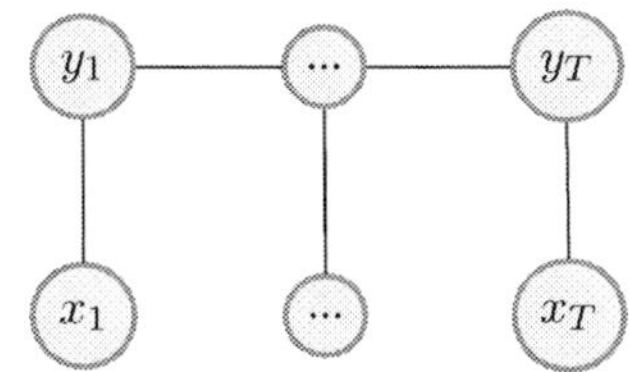

Figure 4: Graphical structure of a linear-chain CRF, where $(y_1, ..., y_T)$ represents language or POS labels and $(x_1, ..., x_T)$ is the observed sequence (tokens).

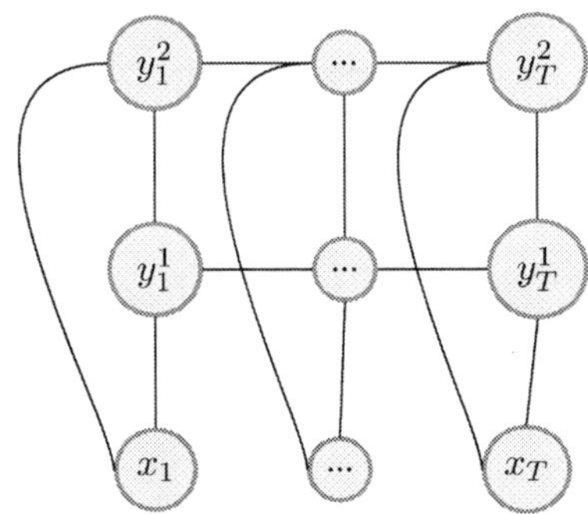

Figure 5: Graphical structure of the 2-Level factorial CRF, where $(y_1^1, ..., y_T^1)$ represents language labels, $(y_1^2, ..., y_T^2)$ represents POS labels and $(x_1, ..., x_T)$ is the observed sequence (tokens).

A factorial CRF (see Figure 5) combines multiple linear-chain CRFs, one for each output level. Unlike linear-chain CRFs, an FCRF deals with a vector of labels. In our case, the vector contains two labels, a language label $(y^1 = y_{1:T}^1)$ and a POS label $(y^2 = y_{1:T}^2)$. The inputs $(x = x_{1:T})$ are shared among these output labels (e.g. $y_{1:T}^1$ and $y_{1:T}^2$) and the output labels also have interconnections (y_i^1 and $y_i^2 \ \forall i = 1, 2, ..., T$). The conditional probability is expressed by Equation 4, where L is the number of levels (in our case $L = 2$), ψ_t represents transitions in each level (e.g. y_1^1 to y_2^1) and φ_t represents contemporal connections between two levels (e.g. y_1^1 to y_1^2). The denominator $z(x)$ is the partition function.

We implement this FCRF using the GRMM toolkit (Sutton, 2006). We use three different feature sets in our experiments. In cross-validation we find that, using handcrafted features, the average language tagging accuracy is 89.37% and average POS tagging accuracy is 81.77%. Use of stacked features gives 90.60% LID accuracy and 85.28% POS tagging accuracy. Finally, the combined feature set achieves 92.49% accuracy in LID and 85.64% in POS tagging (see Table 6 and the last row of Table 3).

5 Analysis and Discussion

We perform manual error analysis on the first test split of cross-validation. This split is a collection of 246 posts and comments with 5,044 tokens.

5.1 Effect of LID and Transliteration as Pre-processing modules

The most frequent error category for the SVM LID classifier is the confusion of Hindi words as Bengali words. We believe that the reason behind this is the small number of Hindi tokens in our training data. Most of these errors occur for tokens which are lexically identical in Hindi and Bengali, e.g. *'na'*, *'chup'*, *'sale'* and *'toh'*. All systems are trained with our SVM language classifier prediction. To quantify the error propagation from SVM language prediction we repeat the experiments of V1, V2 and S2 with the gold language labels and observe that the performance of each systems is slightly increased (Table 5).

We manually evaluate the accuracy of Google's transliterations for Bengali and Hindi. For Hindi,

Type	Systems	Acc.
Baseline	SVM	85.00%
	CRF	83.89%
Pipeline	V1: Vyas	71.12%
	V2: Extn. of V1	71.27%
Stacking	S1: Solorio	86.57%
	S2: Extn. of S1	**87.59%**
	S3: Stacked-V1	85.99%
	S4: Stacked-V2	85.83%
Joint Model	FCRF	85.64%

Table 3: Average cross-validation accuracy of POS tagging systems.

			% of Total Error		
Total	Gold	Pred.	V2	S2	FCRF
41	NUM	PRT	0.73	0.00	0.00
138	X	NOUN	0.57	0.10	0.00
138	X	ADJ	0.36	0.00	0.00
421	**ADJ**	**NOUN**	**0.32**	**0.26**	**0.29**
150	CONJ	NOUN	0.26	0.06	0.08
246	ADP	NOUN	0.15	0.08	0.12
147	ADV	NOUN	0.23	0.15	0.19
843	VERB	NOUN	0.26	0.12	0.14
246	ADP	PRON	0.09	0.09	0.10

Table 4: Top error categories produced by top three POS tagging systems.

Systems	Gold LID	SVM LID
V1	72.09	71.12
V2	72.07	71.27
S2	88.92	87.59

Table 5: POS tagging accuracy of V1, V2 and S2 with gold language labels and predicted (SVM) language labels.

Features	LID Accuracy	POS Accuracy
Handcrafted	89.37%	81.77%
Stacking	90.60%	85.28%
Combined	92.49%	85.64%

Table 6: Performance of FCRF with handcrafted, stacking and combined feature set. The detail of these features are described in Section 4.

transliteration accuracy is 82.63% and for Bengali it is 86.71%. Most of the transliteration errors occurs for those tokens which (i) have a single character (e.g. *'k'*, *'j'*, *'r'*), (ii) have digits (e.g. *'2mi'*, *'2make'*, *'as6e'*) and (iii) have shortened spellings (e.g. *'amr'*, *'tmr'*, *'hygche'*). Our inspection of transliteration errors reveals that the transliteration accuracy depends on the normalisation of romanised tokens.

5.2 Statistical Significance Testing

For statistical significance testing we use two-sided bootstrap re-sampling (Efron, 1979) by implementing the pseudo-code of Graham et al. (2014). We find that the small improvement of V2 over V1 is statistically significant ($p = 0.0313$). However, the 0.93% improvement of S1 over system FCRF is not. Among other systems, we find that FCRFs and

SVMs are significantly better than the monolingual tagger combinations (V1 and V2).

5.3 Stacked vs Pipeline Systems

A reason for the poor accuracy of V1 and V2 is the difference between training and test data. The Tree-Taggers are trained on monolingual non-romanised formal content while the test data is romanised code-mixed social media content. Secondly, error propagation through transliteration and LID also have a role to play. We find that the accuracy of Bengali transliteration is 86.71% and for Hindi it is 82.63%. This can be a reason for the poor performance of the Bengali and the Hindi TreeTagger. Furthermore, Table 5 shows that errors introduced by automatic LID cause an absolute loss of accuracy of 0.97% for V1 and 0.80% for V2. The accuracy of these systems improves (12.98% for V1 and 12.97% for V2) when we engage these systems in stacking using in-domain training data (see stacked-V1 and stacked-V2 in Table 3). We find that choosing the tagger(s) based on LID does not help in stacking approaches (e.g. stacked-V1 and stacked-V2) but using all taggers to generate features for the stacked classifier results in higher accuracy (e.g. S1 and S2). We find that the stacked system S2 outperforms other POS tagging systems in our experiments (see Table 3).

5.4 Effect of Joint Modelling

The accuracy of POS tagging in our joint modelling approach using romanised code-mixed data is higher than monolingual tagger combinations V1 and V2, but it is outperformed by S2 and other stacking ap-

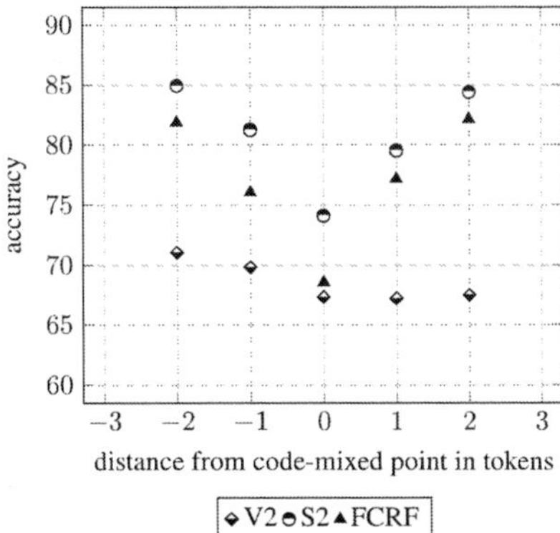

Figure 6: POS accuracy at code-mixed points and surroundings. The analysis is based on the first test split of cross-validation.

proaches. Table 6 shows the performance of FCRF with different feature sets. We find that combining handcrafted and stacking features achieves highest accuracy for both LID and POS tagging. In cross-validation FCRF with the combined feature set outperforms our SVM language classifier and achieves a reasonable cross-validation POS tagging accuracy of 85.64%, which is 2.05% less than the best stacking approach S2.

5.5 Monolingual vs Code-mixed Sentences

We choose the top POS tagging systems of each kind (V2, S2 and FCRF) and analyse the results in more detail on the first test split of cross-validation. First we test the accuracy on code-mixed sentences and on monolingual sentences. The results are depicted in Figure 7. V2 achieves 70.49% accuracy on code-mixed sentences and 72.20% on monolingual sentences. S2 achieves 83.42% on code-mixed sentences and 86.23% on the monolingual sentences. FCRF achieves 81.78% in code-mixed and 84.58% on monolingual sentences. All these systems perform better for monolingual sentences than their performance in code-mixed sentence. This result supports the hypothesis that performing POS tagging is harder on code-mixed sentences than it is on monolingual sentences.

5.6 Known and Unknown Words

Figure 7 also shows the performance of each system for known and unknown words based on the first training fold of romanised code-mixed data.

All systems perform better for known words than for unknown words, as expected. We find that S2 and FCRF perform very closely for unknown words. For known words, S2 achieves 2.82% better accuracy than FCRF. The known-unknown analysis for pipeline system, e.g. V2, differs from the stacking (S2) and the FCRF-based methods. All pipeline systems are trained on *non-romanised monolingual data* (SNLTR Bengali and Hindi corpus). On the other hand, stacking and FCRF based systems are trained on *romanised code-mixed data*. Hence, for V2, we compare tokens of the test split with the tokens of the SNLTR Bengali and Hindi corpus to complete the analysis. We find that 52% of test tokens (Bengali and Hindi) are present in the monolingual training data, these are known words to the systems. V2 achieves 78.30% accuracy for the known Bengali and Hindi words and 43.80% for the unknown Bengali and Hindi words. As we use the default English model (distributed with the TreeTagger package) and not an English corpus, we do not perform this analysis for English words for V2.

5.7 Code-mixing Points

We also observe that the POS tagger accuracy depends on the distance to the code-mixed points. We consider a token as a code-mixed point (token-0) if the language of the token has been changed compared to the language of the previous token. Figure 6 shows the result of our analysis, where +1 means one token to right of a code-mixed point and -1 means one token to the left. It can be seen that all tested methods perform poorly at code-mixed points. Performance of these systems increases by the distance to code-mixed points. Among these systems, the ranking is independent of the distance to the code-mixed point.

5.8 Error Categories

The top error categories produced by different systems are shown in Table 4. The most common error pattern produced by all three systems (see fourth row of Table 4) is ADJ-NOUN, i.e. English adjectives that are classified as NOUN. The number of these errors decreases with the better performing models, as expected. We observe that most of the chat-specific tokens (e.g. emoticons) are misclassified by V2. This system is trained with formal content. There-

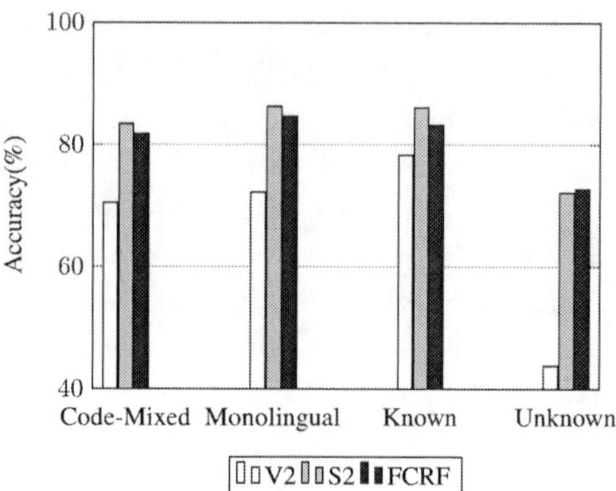

Figure 7: Some evaluation results of POS tagging. The analysis is based on the first test split of cross-validation.

fore, these tokens are misclassified as noun and adjectives by V2. These errors are rectified in S2 and FCRF. Other common error categories produced by the three systems are ADV-NOUN (adverb predicted as noun), VERB-NOUN (verb predicted as noun), CONJ-NOUN and ADP-NOUN.

6 Conclusion

We have presented a trilingual code-mixed corpus with POS annotation. We have performed POS tagging using state-of-the-art methods and also investigated the use of an FCRF-based joint model for this task. We find that the best stacking method (S2) that uses the combined features (see Section 4) performs better than the joint model (FCRF) and the pipeline systems. We also observe that joint modelling outperforms the pipeline systems in our experiments.

FCRF lags behind the best POS tagging system S2. Perhaps, using more training data would help FCRF to achieve better performance than S2. We consider this as a future work. The tagger combinations use either no context or junk context (transliterations) for POS tagger input. As a future work it would be interesting to modify these junk transliterations using a language model to provide meaningful context to the POS tagger.

Acknowledgement

This research is supported by the Science Foundation Ireland (Grant 12/CE/I2267) as part of CNGL (www.cngl.ie) at Dublin City University. The authors wish to acknowledge the DJEI/DES/SFI/HEA for the provision of computational facilities and support.

References

Utsab Barman, Amitava Das, Joachim Wagner, and Jennifer Foster. 2014. Code mixing: A challenge for language identification in the language of social media. In *Proceedings of the First Workshop on Computational Approaches to Code Switching. EMNLP 2014, Conference on Empirical Methods in Natural Language Processing*, pages 13–23, Doha, Qatar. Association for Computational Linguistics.

Monojit Choudhury, Gokul Chittaranjan, Parth Gupta, and Amitava Das. 2014. Overview of FIRE 2014 Track on Transliterated Search. http://www.isical.ac.in/~fire/working-notes/2014/MSR/2014-trainslit_search-track_over.pdf.

Amitava Das. 2016. Tool contest on POS tagging for code-mixed Indian social media (Facebook, Twitter, and Whatsapp) text. http://amitavadas.com/Code-Mixing.html, retrieved 2016-06-10.

B. Efron. 1979. Bootstrap Methods: Another Look at the Jackknife. *The Annals of Statistics*, 7(1):1–26.

Debasis Ganguly, Johannes Leveling, and Gareth J. F. Jones. 2012. DCU@ FIRE-2012: rule-based stemmers for Bengali and Hindi. In *FIRE 2012, Forum for Information Retrieval and Evaluation*, pages 34–42.

Yvette Graham, Nitika Mathur, and Timothy Baldwin. 2014. Randomized significance tests in machine translation. In *Proceedings of the ACL 2014 Ninth Workshop on Statistical Machine Translation*, pages 266–274.

Anupam Jamatia and Amitava Das. 2014. Part-of-speech tagging system for Indian social media text on Twitter. In *Social-India 2014, First Workshop on Language Technologies for Indian Social Media Text, at the Eleventh International Conference on Natural Language Processing (ICON-2014)*, volume 2014, pages 21–28.

Wei Lu and Hwee Tou Ng. 2010. Better Punctuation Prediction with Dynamic Conditional Random Fields. In *Proceedings of the 2010 Conference on Empirical Methods in Natural Language Processing*, pages 177–186, Cambridge, MA, October. Association for Computational Linguistics.

Olutobi Owoputi, Brendan O'Connor, Chris Dyer, Kevin Gimpel, Nathan Schneider, and Noah A. Smith. 2013. Improved part-of-speech tagging for online conversational text with word clusters. In *Proceedings of the 2013 Conference of the North American Chapter of the Association for Computational Linguistics:*

Human Language Technologies, pages 380–390, Atlanta, Georgia, June. Association for Computational Linguistics.

Slav Petrov, Dipanjan Das, and Ryan McDonald. 2012. A universal part-of-speech tagset. In *Proceedings of the Eight International Conference on Language Resources and Evaluation (LREC'12)*, Istanbul, Turkey, may. European Language Resources Association (ELRA).

Prakash B. Pimpale and Raj Nath Patel. 2015. Experiments with POS Tagging Code-mixed Indian Social Media Text. http://amitavadas.com/ICON2015/CDACM_ICON2015.pdf.

Kamal Sarkar. 2015. Part-of-Speech Tagging for Code-mixed Indian Social Media Text at ICON 2015. http://amitavadas.com/ICON2015/JU_ICON2015.pdf.

Helmut Schmid. 1994. Part-of-speech tagging with neural networks. In *Proceedings of the 15th Conference on Computational Linguistics - Volume 1*, COLING '94, pages 172–176, Stroudsburg, PA, USA. Association for Computational Linguistics.

Arnav Sharma and Raveesh Motlani. 2015. POS Tagging for Code-Mixed Indian Social Media Text : Systems from IIIT-H for ICON NLP Tools Contest. http://amitavadas.com/ICON2015/IIITH_ICON2015.pdf.

Thamar Solorio and Yang Liu. 2008. Part-of-speech tagging for English-Spanish code-switched text. In *Proceedings of the Conference on Empirical Methods in Natural Language Processing*, pages 1051–1060. Association for Computational Linguistics.

Thamar Solorio, Elizabeth Blair, Suraj Maharjan, Steve Bethard, Mona Diab, Mahmoud Gohneim, Abdelati Hawwari, Fahad AlGhamdi, Julia Hirshberg, Alison Chang, and Pascale Fung. 2014. Overview for the first shared task on language identification in code-switched data. In *Proceedings of the First Workshop on Computational Approaches to Code-Switching. EMNLP 2014, Conference on Empirical Methods in Natural Language Processing*, Doha, Qatar. Association for Computational Linguistics.

Charles Sutton, Andrew McCallum, and Khashayar Rohanimanesh. 2007. Dynamic conditional random fields: Factorized probabilistic models for labeling and segmenting sequence data. *The Journal of Machine Learning Research*, 8:693–723.

Charles Sutton. 2006. GRMM: Graphical Models in Mallet. http://mallet.cs.umass.edu/grmm, retrieved 2016-08-11.

Yogarshi Vyas, Spandana Gella, Jatin Sharma, Kalika Bali, and Monojit Choudhury. 2014. POS tagging of English-Hindi code-mixed social media content. In *Proceedings of the 2014 Conference on Empirical Methods in Natural Language Processing (EMNLP)*, pages 974–979, Doha, Qatar, October. Association for Computational Linguistics.

Overview for the Second Shared Task on Language Identification in Code-Switched Data

Giovanni Molina, Nicolas Rey-Villamizar, Thamar Solorio
Dept. of Computer Science
University of Houston
Houston TX, 77004
{gemolinaramos,nrey}@uh.edu solorio@cs.uh.edu

Fahad AlGhamdi, Mahmoud Ghoneim, Abdelati Hawwari, Mona Diab
Dept. of Computer Science
George Washington University
Washington DC, 20052
{fghamdi,mghoneim,abhawwari,mtdiab}@gwu.edu

Abstract

We present an overview of the second shared task on language identification in code-switched data. For the shared task, we had code-switched data from two different language pairs: Modern Standard Arabic-Dialectal Arabic (MSA-DA) and Spanish-English (SPA-ENG). We had a total of nine participating teams, with all teams submitting a system for SPA-ENG and four submitting for MSA-DA. Through evaluation, we found that once again language identification is more difficult for the language pair that is more closely related. We also found that this year's systems performed better overall than the systems from the previous shared task indicating overall progress in the state of the art for this task.

1 Introduction

With the First Shared Task on Language Identification in Code-Switched Data we managed to raise awareness and shine a spotlight on the difficult problem of automatic processing of Code-Switched (CS) text. This year our goal is not only to maintain research interest in the problem, but also to bring in new ideas to tackle it. With the continuing growth of social media usage, it is more likely to find CS text and thus the problem becomes more relevant.

Code-switching is a linguistic phenomenon where two or more languages are used interchangeably in either spoken or written form. It is important to study and understand CS in text because any advancement in solving the problem will positively contribute to other NLP tasks such as Part-of-Speech tagging, parsing, machine translation, among others. In order to achieve this, we organized this year's shared task with the intention of providing our peers with new annotated data, to further develop a universal annotation scheme for CS text and most significantly to motivate high quality research.

Language Pair	Example
MSA-DA	**Buckwalter:**[1] *hbt AlY AlmHAkm wAlnyAbAt fy Ehd mbArk HwAly 17mrp, EAyzyn nqflhm rqm mHtrm, xmsyn mvlA **English Translation:** *I went to courts in Mubark's era almost 17 times. I would like to reach a respectful number, for example 50 times.*
SPA-ENG	**Original:** Styling day trabajando con @username vestuario para #ElFactorX y soy hoy chofer. I will get you there in pieces im a Safe Driver. **English Translation:** *Styling day working with @username wardrobe for #ElFactorX and today I drive. I will get you there in pieces im a Safe Driver.*

Table 1: Twitter code-switched data examples.

This shared task covers two different language pairs and is focused on social media data obtained

---

[1] We use the Buckwalter encoding to present all the Arabic data in this paper: It is an ASCII only transliteration scheme, representing Arabic orthography strictly one-to-one.

Proceedings of the Second Workshop on Computational Approaches to Code Switching, pages 40–49,
Austin, TX, November 1, 2016. ©2016 Association for Computational Linguistics

from Twitter. The language pairs used this time are Spanish-English (SPA-ENG) and Modern Standard Arabic-Dialect Arabic (MSA-DA). These languages are widely used around the world and are good examples of language pairs that are easily interchanged by the speakers. Participants are tasked with predicting the correct language label for each token in the unseen test sets.

We provide a full description of the shared task in the following section and we talk about related work in section 3. The data sets used for the task are described in section 4, followed by an overview of the submitted systems in section 5. Finally, we show the results, lessons learned and conclusion in sections 6, 7 and 8, respectively.

2 Task Description

Similar to the first edition, the task consists of labeling each token/word in the input test data with one out of 8 labels: *lang1, lang2, fw, mixed, unk, ambiguous, other* and *named entities (ne)*. The labels *fw* and *unk* were added in this edition of the shared task and are derived from tokens that used to be labeled as *other*. The *lang1, lang2* labels correspond to the two languages in the language pair, for example with SPA-ENG, *lang1* would be ENG and *lang2* would be SPA. The *fw* label is used to tag tokens that belong to a language other than the two languages in the language pair. The *mixed* label is used to tag words composed of code-switched morphemes, such as the word uber*eando* ('driving for Uber') in SPA-ENG. The *unk* label is used to tag tokens that are gibberish or unintelligible. The *ambiguous* label is used to tag words that could be labeled as either language in the language pair and the context surrounding the word is not enough to determine a specific language, for example the word *a* is a determiner in English and a preposition in Spanish and it can be hard to tell which language it belongs to without the surrounding context. The *other* label is used to tag usernames, emoticons, symbols, punctuation marks, and other similar tokens that do not represent words. Lastly, the *ne* label is used to tag named entities, which are proper nouns and must be identified correctly in order to properly conduct an analysis of CS data. This is due to the fact that named entities are usually kept the same even as languages switch. Named entities are problematic even for human annotators and require a lot of work, including defining absolute and correct guidelines for annotation.

In Table 1 we show examples of code-switched tweets that are found in our data. We have posted the annotation guidelines for SPA-ENG, but it can be generalized to the MSA-DA language pair as well. This is possible because we want to have a universal set of annotation labels that can be used to correctly annotate new data with the least amount of error possible. We keep improving the guidelines to accommodate findings from the previous shared task as well as new relevant research.

3 Related Work

The earliest work on CS data within the NLP community dates back to research done by Joshi (1982) on an approach to parsing CS data. Following work has been described in the First Shared Task on Language Identification in Code-Switched Data held at EMNLP 2014 (Solorio et al., 2014). Since the first edition of the task, new research has come to light involving CS data.

There has been work on language identification of different language pairs in CS text, such as improvements on dialect identification in Arabic (Al-Badrashiny et al., 2015) and detection of intra-word CS in Dutch and dialect varieties (Nguyen and Cornips, 2016). There has also been work on POS tagging and parsing such as parsing of bilingual code-switched text (Vilares et al., 2015a), POS tagging of Hindi-English CS social media text (Sequiera et al., 2015; Jamatia et al., 2015) and shallow parsing of Hindi-English CS social media text (Sharma et al., 2016). Another area where there has been some new research work is in sentiment analysis, such as emotion detection in Chinese-English code-switched texts (Lee and Wang, 2015) and sentiment analysis on Spanish-English Twitter posts (Vilares et al., 2015b).

(Kosoff, 2014) carried out a sociolinguistic investigation focused on the use of code-switching in the complex speech community of Egyptian Twitter users. It studies the combinations of Modern Standard Arabic(MSA), Egyptian Colloquial Arabic, English, and Arabizi; whether it is a Modern

Standard Arabic or Egyptian Colloquial Arabic. The research goal was to describe the code switching phenomena situation found in this Egyptian twitter community.

We also had contributions of new CS corpora, such as a collection of Arabic-Moroccan Darija social media CS data (Samih and Maier, 2016), a collection of Turkish-German CS tweets (Özlem Çetinoğlu, 2016), a large collection of Modern Standard Arabic and Egyptian Dialectal Arabic CS data (Diab et al., 2016) and a collection of sentiment annotated Spanish-English tweets (Vilares et al., 2016). Other work includes improving word alignment and MT models using CS data (Huang and Yates, 2014), improving OCR in historical documents that contain code-switched text (Garrette et al., 2015), the definition of an objective measure of corpus level complexity of code-switched texts (Gambäck and Das, 2016) and (Begum et al., 2016) presented an annotation scheme for annotating the pragmatic functions of CS in Hindi-English code-switched tweets. There is still more research to be done involving CS data, and we hope this second edition of the shared task will help motivate further research.

4   Data Sets

The data for the shared task was collected from Twitter. We decided to use Twitter because it has a large user base from a multitude of countries and this provides a good space to find code-switched data. Twitter also provides an API which makes it easier to crawl and collect data. However, there are limitations to the amount of data that can be collected and restrictions to how we can share data.

Language Pair	Training	Development	Test
MSA-DA	8,862	1,117	1,262 (1,258)
SPA-ENG	8,733	1,857	18,237 (10,716)

Table 2: Data set statistics for SPA-ENG and MSA-DA.

In Table 2 we show the statistics for the data sets used in the shared task. These statistics were taken at the moment the data was released, but they can change with time due to tweets becoming unavailable. To account for this limitation, we used the maximum amount of tweets that all participants had in common after submission of the test data, which

we show in parenthesis.

4.1   SPA-ENG

For SPA-ENG, we used the training and test corpora from the EMNLP 2014 shared task as this year's training corpus and development corpus, respectively. However, the previous shared task did not have the same labels we are using this year. We had in-lab annotators follow a simple mapping process: they went through all the tokens previously labeled as *other* that are not usernames, emoticons or symbols and either changed them to *fw*, *unk* or kept them as *other*. The annotators used the annotation guidelines posted on the shared task website to make the decisions required for the mapping.

We made improvements to the quality of the data with the help of our in-lab annotators. We performed quality checks for label inconsistencies by manually looking at the labels of word types that had more than one label and changing them to the correct one if needed. We also verified and fixed the tokenization of the data to remove single whitespaces that appeared as tokens and to correctly tokenize emoticons and other symbols.

Building the new test corpus consisted of first finding code-switched data and secondly annotating the data. Finding code-switched tweets is not an easy task, so we followed a series of steps to help us locate a good amount of code-switched tweets. First, similar to the previous task, we selected geographical areas where there is a strong presence of bilingual speakers, specifically Miami and New York. Secondly, we performed a search within these areas for popular Spanish language radio stations with active Twitter accounts. Then, we selected the Twitter accounts of radio stations that code-switched in their tweets and collected them. From here, we looked for code-switched tweets within the accounts of users that are followed by and that follow the radio stations and collected them as well. Finally, we examined the accounts of users that interact with these users and check for code-switched tweets. In total, we obtained tweets from 21 users and a total of 61,943 tweets.

The annotation process consisted of three steps: in-lab pre-annotation, crowd-sourcing and in-lab quality check. Our in-lab pre-annotation was performed by training an SVM with the training corpus from the previous shared task and then annotating our test data with the language label. We then used a pattern matching algorithm with regular expressions to label tokens with *other*. Following that, we ranked our word types by token frequency score and selected the top thousand most frequent words and manually verified the labels and fixed them where necessary. We then propagated this to the entire data set and separated the affected tokens and considered them as annotated. Next, we took the rest of the unannotated data set and used CrowdFlower to annotate it. We used a subset of the training corpus (one that contained roughly equally distributed tokens for each label) as our gold data for quality control within the crowd-sourcing task. After the first round of annotation was completed, we took tokens with a confidence score under 0.75 and resubmitted them to CrowdFlower in an attempt to improve the quality of the tags. Finally, we manually went through the most frequent tokens that had more than one label assigned and verified them to get rid of inconsistencies and further improve the quality. This whole process of annotation cost us roughly $1,100, which comes out to about $0.02 per tweet. In order to have the best possible quality in the data, we first selected the top 35K tweets ranked by overall tweet confidence, which was taken to be the lowest confidence among the tokens for that tweet. From here we selected all the code-switched tweets and 10k monolingual tweets. This became the official test data set for the shared task. We later decided to remove tweets that contain URLs in them for consistency with the training and development corpora as they did not contain URLs. This is the subset of test data that we end up using to rank the participating systems.

In Table 3 we show the statistics of the data set used to evaluate the participating systems. This includes only the tweets that all the participants managed to crawl from Twitter, and it is not the complete data set.

4.2 MSA-DA

For the MSA-DA language pair, the Egyptian dialect is used as the Arabic dialect, EGY. We combined the Train, Test-1, and Test-2 corpora that we used in the EMNLP 2014 shared task to create the new training and development corpora. The data

Monolingual Tweets	Code-Switched Tweets
4,626	6,090
Label	**Tokens**
ambiguous	4
lang1	16,944
lang2	77,047
mixed	4
ne	2,092
fw	19
other	25,311
unk	25
Total	**121,446**

Table 3: Test Data statistics for SPA-ENG.

was crawled and collected from Twitter. We perform a number of quality checks on the old data to overcome any issues that the participants may face. One of these checks is that all the old tweets are re-crawled from Twitter to reduce the percentage of missing tweets. The missing tweets and the tweets that contained white spaces were removed. This step was performed as a validation step. After the validation step, we accepted and published 9,979 Tweets (8,862 tweets for the training set, and 1,117 tweets for the development set).

Building a new test corpus required crawling new data and annotating the crawled data. As we did in the previous shared task, we used the Tweepy library to harvest the timeline of 26 Egyptian Public Figures. We have some filtration criteria that we applied on the new test set. Since we are using the tweets that we introduced in the EMNLP 2014 CS shared task, we set the crawling script to harvest only the tweets that were created in 2014, to maintain consistency in topics with the training/dev data sets. Also, the tweets that contain URLs and re-tweets were excluded. The total number of harvested tweets after applying the filtration criteria was 12,028 tweets. This number of tweets was bigger than what we needed for the test set. So, we chose only 1,262 tweets. However, before choosing the 1,262 tweets, we wanted to consider the public figure whose tweets contain more code-switching points. So, we input all the tweets into the Automatic Identification of Dialectal Arabic (AIDA2) tool (Al-Badrashiny et al., 2015) to perform token level language identification for the EGY and MSA tokens in context. According to AIDA2s output we chose a certain percentage of tweets from the Public Figure whose CS percentage in his/her tweets is more than 35%. We used the improved version of the Arabic Tweets Token Assigner which is made available through the shared task website [3] to avoid the misalignment issues and guarantee consistency.

Two Egyptian native speakers were asked to perform the annotation. They were trained to get involved with the project's concepts and related linguistic issues to increase their productivity and accuracy. Our Annotation team used two types of CS tag-sets: a) a rich version which is Arabic dialects oriented and it is used in our lab; and, b) a reduced CS tag-set which is consistent. The two tag-sets are mappable to each other (we mapped our tag set to the six tags). In our annotation, we used *lang1* to represent MSA, and *lang2* for Egyptian words, *ambiguous* when the context cant help decide if a word is MSA or DA, and foreign word (*fw*) for non-Arabic word even it is in Arabic script or Latin script. To manage the annotation quality, the annotations were checked when initially performed and then checked again at the end of the task. The Inter-Annotator Agreement (IAA) was measured by using 10% of the total number of data to ensure the performance and agreement among annotators. A specialist linguist carried out adjudication and revisions of accuracy measurements. We approached a stable Inter Annotator Agreement (IAA) of over 90% pairwise agreement.

Monolingual Tweets	Code-Switched Tweets
1,044	214
Label	**Tokens**
ambiguous	117
lang1	5,804
lang2	9,630
mixed	1
ne	2,363
fw	0
other	2,743
unk	0
Total	**20,658**

Table 4: Test Data statistics for MSA-DA.

Table 4 shows the statistics of the MSA-DA test set used to evaluate the participating systems. It contains only the tweets that all the participants managed to crawl from Twitter, and it's not the complete

data set.

5 Survey of Shared Task Systems

This year we received submissions from nine different teams, which is two more teams than the previous shared task. All teams participated in the SPA-ENG task, while four teams also participated in the MSA-DA task. There was a wide variety of system architectures ranging from simple rule based systems all the way to more complex machine learning implementations. Most of the systems submitted did not change anything in the implementation to tackle one language pair or the other, which implies that the participants were highly interested in building language independent systems that could be easily scaled to multiple language pairs.

In Table 5 we show a summary of the the the architectures of the systems submitted by the participants. All teams, with the exception of (Chanda et al., 2016), used some sort of machine learning algorithm in their systems. The algorithm of choice by most participants was the Conditional Random Fields (CRF). This is no surprise since CRFs fit the problem nicely due to the sequence labeling nature of the task as it was evidenced in the high performance by CRFs achieved in the previous shared task.

A new addition this year is the use of deep learning algorithms by two of the participants. Deep learning is now much more prevalent in NLP than it was two years ago when the previous shared task was held. (Jaech et al., 2016) used a convolutional neural network (CNN) to obtain word vectors which are then fed as a sequence to a bidirectional long short term memory recurrent neural network (LSTM) to map the sequence to a label. The system submitted by (Samih et al., 2016) used the output of a pair of LSTMs along with a CRF and post-processing to obtain the final label mapping. These systems are perhaps more complex than traditional machine learning algorithms, but the trade off for performance is evident in the results.

Most of the participants included some sort of external resource in their system. Among them we can find large monolingual corpora, language specific dictionaries, Part-of-Speech taggers, word embeddings and Named Entity Recognizers. Other fea-

---

[3] http://care4lang1.seas.gwu.edu/cs2/call.html

System	Traditional Machine Learning	Deep Learning	Rules	External Resources	LM	Case	Affixes	Context
(Al-Badrashiny and Diab, 2016)	CRF	-	-	SPLIT, Gigaword	✓	-	-	-
(Xia, 2016)	CRF	-	-	fastText	-	✓	✓	±1
(Jaech et al., 2016)	-	CNN, LSTM	-	-	-	-	-	-
(Shirvani et al., 2016)	Logistic Regression	-	-	GNU Aspell, NER, POS tagger	-	-	✓	-
(Chanda et al., 2016)	-	-	✓	NER, Dictionaries	-	-	-	±1
(Samih et al., 2016)	CRF	LSTM	-	Gigaword, word2vec	-	✓	✓	±1
(Shrestha, 2016)	CRF	-	-	-	-	✓	✓	-
(Sikdar and Gambck, 2016)	CRF	-	-	Babelnet, Babelfy	-	✓	✓	±2

Table 5: Summary of the architectures of the systems submitted.

tures used in some of the systems were language models, word case information (Title, Uppercase, Lowercase), affixes and surrounding context.

6 Results

Same as the previous shared task, we used the following metrics to evaluate the submitted systems: Accuracy, Precision, Recall and F-measure. We use regular F-measure to rank the systems at the tweet level and the weighted average F-measure to rank the systems at token level to account for the imbalanced distribution of the labels.

To evaluate the systems, we first took the subset of tweets that all participants had in common to provide a fair comparison among them. We designed a simple lexicon-based baseline system by taking only the lexicon for *lang1, lang2* from the training corpus. We labeled symbols, emoticons, usernames, punctuation marks and URLs as other. If we find an unseen token or have a tie, we assign the majority class label. We compare the results of all participants to this baseline.

To calculate the performance of the systems at the tweet level, we use the predicted token level information to determine if a tweet is code-switched or monolingual. If the tweet has at least one token from each language (*lang1, lang2*), then it is labeled a code-switched. Otherwise, the tweet is labeled as monolingual. Table 6 shows the tweet level results for all submitted systems in both language pairs,

ranked by the average weighted f-measure. We can see that the best performing systems in SPA-ENG perform better than the best performing systems in MSA-DA, which indicates that this is a more difficult task for the MSA-DA language pair as both languages are closely related, as opposed to SPA-ENG.

In Table 7 we show the token level results for all submitted systems. We report the F-measure for each class and the weighted average F-measure, Avg-F, which we used to rank the systems. From the results, we can see that the least difficult class to predict is the *other* class, where most systems obtained an F-measure over 97%. We can also discern that for the classes with a minority amount of tokens (*ambiguous, mixed, fw, unk*) were the hardest to predict, with most systems obtaining an F-measure of 0%. This is to be expected as we only had a small number of samples in our training and test data and in the case of the MSA-DA data set, there were no samples for *fw* or *unk*. Precisely because of the small amount of samples for these classes, the results do not affect in a significant way the weighed averaged F-measure score used to rank the systems. However, it is still important to correctly predict these classes in order to make a more thorough analysis of CS data.

For SPA-ENG, all the systems beat the baseline at the tweet level evaluation by at least 16%. The best performing system here was (Shirvani et al., 2016) with an Avg-F-measure of 91.3%, which is

Test Set	System	Monolingual F-1	Code-switched F-1	Weighted F-1
SPA-ENG	Baseline	0.54	0.69	0.607
	(Al-Badrashiny and Diab, 2016)*†	0.83	0.69	0.77
	(Chanda et al., 2016)$^\delta$	0.83	0.75	0.79
	(Xia, 2016)	0.86	0.79	0.83
	(Shrestha, 2016)	0.90	0.86	0.88
	(Sikdar and Gambck, 2016)	0.91	0.87	0.89
	IIIT Hyderabad$^\top$	0.91	0.88	0.898
	(Jaech et al., 2016)	0.91	0.88	0.898
	(Samih et al., 2016)*	0.92	0.88	0.90
	(Shirvani et al., 2016)	0.93	0.9	**0.913**
MSA-DA	Baseline	0.47	0.31	0.44
	(Shrestha, 2016)	0.72	0.34	0.66
	(Al-Badrashiny and Diab, 2016)-1*	0.75	0.43	0.69
	(Jaech et al., 2016)	0.83	0.25	0.73
	(Al-Badrashiny and Diab, 2016)-2*	0.83	0.37	0.75
	(Samih et al., 2016)*	0.89	0.50	**0.83**

Table 6: Tweet level performance results. We ranked the systems using the weighted average F-measure, Weighted-F1. A '†' denotes a late submission. A '*' denotes systems submitted by co-organizers of the shared task. A 'δ' denotes the participant submission is missing a small number of tokens from one tweet. A $^\top$ denotes the participant did not submit a system description.

1.3% higher than the second best system (Samih et al., 2016). At the token level, all but one system outperformed the baseline. The best performing system was also (Shirvani et al., 2016) with an Avg-F-measure of 97.3%, which is 0.4% higher than the second best performing system (IIIT Hyderabad).[4]

For MSA-DA, all the submitted systems outperform the baseline at the tweet level by at least 20%. At tweet level, (Samih et al., 2016) achieved 83%, which the highest Avg-F-measure. The second highest Avg-F-measure was achieved by (Al-Badrashiny and Diab, 2016)-2. Their Avg-F-measure was 75%. At the token level, all systems beat the baseline by at least 7%. Also, (Samih et al., 2016) succeed in achieving the highest Avg-F-measure which is 87.6%. citegwu:16-2 and (Al-Badrashiny and Diab, 2016)-1 achieve the second and the third best performing systems, with Avg-F-measures of 85.1%, 82.8%, respectively.

It is not easy to determine overall winners because not all participants submitted a system for both language-pairs. However, for the SPA-ENG data set the system by (Shirvani et al., 2016) was the best performing at both the tweet and token level evaluations. On the other hand, the system by (Samih et al., 2016) was the best performing at both tweet and token level for the MSA-DA data set.

---

[4]The participants did not submit a system description.

7   Lessons Learned

This year we had to deal with the same issues we encountered with Twitter, including data loss and sharing restrictions. However, we decided to cope with these issues as we found it harder to identify other sources of data where we could easily search and find samples of code-switched text.

In the process of annotation, we believe that pre-annotating the data using our previous data as training helps speed up the process of in-lab annotations and thus reduces the amount of data that has to be annotated through crowd-sourcing. We took several measures to ensure we obtained high quality data from crowd-sourcing, but it still proves to be a challenge and we obtain a fair amount of noise. The problem is exacerbated in the MSA-DA set due to the fact that there is inherently considerable amount of data overlap due to homographs between the two varieties of the language. Also, a big part of the errors made by crowd-sourcing annotators involve named entities, probably because the annotators do not take the context into account in an effort to be fast and collect money quickly.

For a future shared task, we will consider giving the crowd-sourcing annotators less choices in order to reduce error, along with providing a simpler annotation guideline with a greater amount of examples.

Test Set	System	lang1	lang2	NE	other	ambiguous	mixed	fw	unk	Avg-F	Avg-A
SPA-ENG	(Chanda et al., 2016)	0.478	0.689	0.153	0.466	0.0	0.0	0.01	0.003	0.603	0.536
	Baseline	0.595	0.852	0.0	0.979	0.0	0.0	0.0	0.0	0.828	0.811
	(Al-Badrashiny and Diab, 2016)*[†]	0.828	0.959	0.256	0.982	0.0	0.0	0.0	0.0	0.933	0.938
	(Xia, 2016)	0.873	0.965	0.379	0.993	0.0	0.0	0.0	0.0	0.947	0.949
	(Shrestha, 2016)	0.919	0.978	0.481	0.994	0.0	0.0	0.0	0.0	0.964	0.965
	(Sikdar and Gambck, 2016)	0.928	0.979	0.510	0.996	0.0	0.0	0.0	0.045	0.967	0.965
	(Jaech et al., 2016)	0.929	0.982	0.480	0.994	0.0	0.0	0.0	0.0	0.968	0.969
	(Samih et al., 2016)*	0.930	0.980	0.551	0.995	0.0	0.0	0.0	0.034	0.968	0.967
	IIIT Hyderabad[⊤]	0.931	0.979	0.645	0.991	0.0	0.0	0.0	0.013	0.969	0.966
	(Shirvani et al., 2016)	0.938	0.984	0.603	0.996	0.0	0.0	0.0	0.029	**0.973**	0.973
MSA-DA	Baseline	0.534	0.421	0.0	0.883	0.0	0.0	-	-	0.463	0.513
	(Jaech et al., 2016)	0.603	0.603	0.468	0.712	0.0	0.0	-	-	0.594	0.599
	(Shrestha, 2016)	0.699	0.722	0.745	0.975	0.0	0.0	-	-	0.747	0.747
	(Al-Badrashiny and Diab, 2016)-2*	0.767	0.833	0.828	0.986	0.0	0.0	-	-	0.828	0.826
	(Al-Badrashiny and Diab, 2016)-1*	0.802	0.860	0.827	0.988	0.0	0.0	-	-	0.851	0.852
	(Samih et al., 2016)*	0.854	0.904	0.77	0.957	0.0	0.0	-	-	**0.876**	0.879

Table 7: Token level performance results. We ranked the systems using the weighted average F-measure, Avg-F. A '-' indicates that there were no tokens labeled under this class in the test data set. A '[†]' denotes a late submission. A '*' denotes systems submitted by co-organizers of the shared task. A '[δ]' denotes the participant submission is missing a small number of tokens from one tweet. A [⊤] denotes the participant did not submit a system description.

Another thing we have in mind is to further improve our code-switched tweet evaluation by taking into account the predicted positions of the code-switch points instead of just labeling the tweets as CS or monolingual.

8 Conclusion

We had a very successful second shared task on language identification on code-switched data. We received submissions from 9 different teams, up from 7 teams in the previous task. Overall, this year's systems achieved a higher level of performance when compared to previous shared task. This is a good indicator of a higher understanding and interest in the problem. We also see that the results of the previous shared task influenced the decisions the participants made when designing their systems, as evidenced by the majority of the systems relying on a CRF for sequence labeling. In contrast to the previous shared task, we received submissions that used deep learning algorithms and techniques, which shows that the participants are thinking of different ways to take on the problem. On the other end, we had one rule-based system that didn't perform as well as the others and perhaps is an indicator that machine learning is definitely the baseline architecture to use for language identification in CS data.

In contrast to the previous shared task, the results are more consistent between token/tweet level performance, with the same teams ranking first at both levels of the same language pair. This is an indication that there were less errors made, leading to less confusion of the CS points. Also different from the previous task, this year we only looked at two different language pairs, but we maintain that these two pairs are a good representation of CS occurrences.

We have shown that there is great interest in researching language identification on code-switched data and we have provided a competitive shared task that will help push forward the development of systems and corpora with the goal of improving our understanding of code-switching.

Acknowledgments

We would like to thank our in-lab annotators for their help in generating new test data for the shared task. We also want to thank all the participants for their contributions and interest in the problem. This work was partially supported by grants 1462143 and 1462142 from the National Science Foundation.

References

Mohamed Al-Badrashiny and Mona Diab. 2016. A system for the code-switching workshop shared task 2016. In *Proceedings of The Second Workshop on Computational Approaches to Code Switching*.

Mohamed Al-Badrashiny, Heba Elfardy, and Mona Diab. 2015. Aida2: A hybrid approach for token and sentence level dialect identification in arabic. *CoNLL 2015*, page 42.

Rafiya Begum, Kalika Bali, Monojit Choudhury, Koustav Rudra, and Niloy Ganguly. 2016. Functions of code-switching in tweets: An annotation framework and some initial experiments. In Nicoletta Calzolari (Conference Chair), Khalid Choukri, Thierry Declerck, Sara Goggi, Marko Grobelnik, Bente Maegaard, Joseph Mariani, Helene Mazo, Asuncion Moreno, Jan Odijk, and Stelios Piperidis, editors, *Proceedings of the Tenth International Conference on Language Resources and Evaluation (LREC 2016)*, Paris, France, may. European Language Resources Association (ELRA).

Arunavha Chanda, Dipankar Das, and Chandan Mazumdar. 2016. Anonymous submission for emnlp 2016 code-switching workshop shared task: System description. In *Proceedings of The Second Workshop on Computational Approaches to Code Switching*.

Mona Diab, Mahmoud Ghoneim, Abdelati Hawwari, Fahad AlGhamdi, Nada AlMarwani, and Mohamed Al-Badrashiny. 2016. Creating a large multi-layered representational repository of linguistic code switched arabic data. In Nicoletta Calzolari (Conference Chair), Khalid Choukri, Thierry Declerck, Sara Goggi, Marko Grobelnik, Bente Maegaard, Joseph Mariani, Helene Mazo, Asuncion Moreno, Jan Odijk, and Stelios Piperidis, editors, *Proceedings of the Tenth International Conference on Language Resources and Evaluation (LREC 2016)*, Paris, France, may. European Language Resources Association (ELRA).

Björn Gambäck and Amitava Das. 2016. Comparing the level of code-switching in corpora. In Nicoletta Calzolari (Conference Chair), Khalid Choukri, Thierry Declerck, Sara Goggi, Marko Grobelnik, Bente Maegaard, Joseph Mariani, Helene Mazo, Asuncion Moreno, Jan Odijk, and Stelios Piperidis, editors, *Proceedings of the Tenth International Conference on Language Resources and Evaluation (LREC 2016)*, Paris, France, may. European Language Resources Association (ELRA).

Dan Garrette, Hannah Alpert-Abrams, Taylor Berg-Kirkpatrick, and Dan Klein. 2015. Unsupervised code-switching for multilingual historical document transcription. In *Proceedings of the 2015 Conference of the North American Chapter of the Association for Computational Linguistics: Human Language Technologies*, pages 1036–1041.

Fei Huang and Alexander Yates. 2014. Improving word alignment using linguistic code switching data. In *EACL*, pages 1–9.

Aaron Jaech, George Mulcaire, Mari Ostendorf, and Noah A. Smith. 2016. A neural model for language identification in code-switched tweets. In *Proceedings of The Second Workshop on Computational Approaches to Code Switching*.

Anupam Jamatia, Björn Gambäck, and Amitava Das. 2015. Part-of-speech tagging for code-mixed english-hindi twitter and facebook chat messages. In *Proceedings of Recent Advances in Natural Language Processing Hissar, Bulgaria, Sep 79 2015*, page 239248.

Aravind K Joshi. 1982. Processing of sentences with intra-sentential code-switching. In *Proceedings of the 9th conference on Computational linguistics-Volume 1*, pages 145–150. Academia Praha.

Zoë Kosoff. 2014. Code-switching in egyptian arabic: A sociolinguistic analysis of twitter. *Al-Arabiyya: Journal of the American Association of Teachers of Arabic*, 47(1):83–99.

Sophia Yat Mei Lee and Zhongqing Wang. 2015. Emotion in code-switching texts: Corpus construction and analysis. *ACL-IJCNLP 2015*, page 91.

Dong Nguyen and Leonie Cornips. 2016. Automatic detection of intra-word code-switching. *ACL 2016*, page 82.

Özlem Çetinoğlu. 2016. A turkish-german code-switching corpus. In Nicoletta Calzolari (Conference Chair), Khalid Choukri, Thierry Declerck, Sara Goggi, Marko Grobelnik, Bente Maegaard, Joseph Mariani, Helene Mazo, Asuncion Moreno, Jan Odijk, and Stelios Piperidis, editors, *Proceedings of the Tenth International Conference on Language Resources and Evaluation (LREC 2016)*, Paris, France, may. European Language Resources Association (ELRA).

Younes Samih and Wolfgang Maier. 2016. An arabic-moroccan darija code-switched corpus. In Nicoletta Calzolari (Conference Chair), Khalid Choukri, Thierry Declerck, Sara Goggi, Marko Grobelnik, Bente Maegaard, Joseph Mariani, Helene Mazo, Asuncion Moreno, Jan Odijk, and Stelios Piperidis, editors, *Proceedings of the Tenth International Conference on Language Resources and Evaluation (LREC 2016)*, Paris, France, may. European Language Resources Association (ELRA).

Younes Samih, Suraj Maharjan, Mohammed Attia, and Thamar Solorio. 2016. Emnlp code-switching 2016 hhu-uh-g team system. In *Proceedings of The Second Workshop on Computational Approaches to Code Switching*.

Royal Sequiera, Monojit Choudhury, and Kalika Bali. 2015. Pos tagging of hindi-english code mixed text from social media: Some machine learning experiments. In *ICON 2015 Proceedings*.

Arnav Sharma, Sakshi Gupta, Raveesh Motlani, Piyush Bansal, Manish Shrivastava, Radhika Mamidi, and Dipti M. Sharma. 2016. Shallow parsing pipeline - hindi-english code-mixed social media text. In *Proceedings of the 2016 Conference of the North American Chapter of the Association for Computational Linguistics: Human Language Technologies*, pages 1340–1345, San Diego, California, June. Association for Computational Linguistics.

Rouzbeh Shirvani, Mario Piergallini, Gauri Shankam Gautam, and Mohamed Chouikha. 2016. System submission for language identification in spanish-english codeswitching. In *Proceedings of The Second Workshop on Computational Approaches to Code Switching*.

Prajwol Shrestha. 2016. Codeswitching detection via lexical features in conditional random fields. In *Proceedings of The Second Workshop on Computational Approaches to Code Switching*.

Utpal Sikdar and Bjrn Gambck. 2016. Language identification in code-switched text using conditional random fields and babelnet. In *Proceedings of The Second Workshop on Computational Approaches to Code Switching*.

Thamar Solorio, Elizabeth Blair, Suraj Maharjan, Steven Bethard, Mona Diab, Mahmoud Ghoneim, Abdelati Hawwari, Fahad AlGhamdi, Julia Hirschberg, Alison Chang, and Pascale Fung. 2014. Overview for the First Shared Task on Language Identification in Code-Switched Data. In *Proceedings of The First Workshop on Computational Approaches to Code Switching, held in conjunction with EMNLP 2014.*, pages 62–72.

David Vilares, Miguel A Alonso, and Carlos Gómez-Rodríguez. 2015a. One model, two languages: training bilingual parsers with harmonized treebanks. *arXiv preprint arXiv:1507.08449*.

David Vilares, Miguel A Alonso, and Carlos Gómez-Rodriguez. 2015b. Sentiment analysis on monolingual, multilingual and code-switching twitter corpora. In *6th Workshop On Computational Approaches To Subjectivity, Sentiment And Social Media Analysis WASSA 2015*, page 2.

David Vilares, Miguel A. Alonso, and Carlos Gómez-Rodríguez. 2016. En-es-cs: An english-spanish code-switching twitter corpus for multilingual sentiment analysis. In Nicoletta Calzolari (Conference Chair), Khalid Choukri, Thierry Declerck, Sara Goggi, Marko Grobelnik, Bente Maegaard, Joseph Mariani, Helene Mazo, Asuncion Moreno, Jan Odijk, and Stelios Piperidis, editors, *Proceedings of the Tenth International Conference on Language Resources and Evaluation (LREC 2016)*, Paris, France, may. European Language Resources Association (ELRA).

Meng Xuan Xia. 2016. Codeswitching language identification using subword information enriched word vectors. In *Proceedings of The Second Workshop on Computational Approaches to Code Switching*.

Multilingual Code-switching Identification via LSTM Recurrent Neural Networks

Younes Samih
Dept. of Computational Linguistics
Heinrich Heine University,
Düsseldorf, Germany
samih@phil.hhu.de

Suraj Maharjan
Dept. of Computer Science
University of Houston
Houston, TX, 77004
smaharjan2@uh.edu

Mohammed Attia
Google Inc.
New York City
NY, 10011
attia@google.com

Laura Kallmeyer
Dept. of Computational Linguistics
Heinrich Heine University,
Düsseldorf, Germany
kallmeyer@phil.hhu.de

Thamar Solorio
Dept. of Computer Science
University of Houston
Houston, TX, 77004
solorio@cs.uh.edu

Abstract

This paper describes the HHU-UH-G system submitted to the EMNLP 2016 Second Workshop on Computational Approaches to Code Switching. Our system ranked first place for Arabic (MSA-Egyptian) with an F1-score of 0.83 and second place for Spanish-English with an F1-score of 0.90. The HHU-UH-G system introduces a novel unified neural network architecture for language identification in code-switched tweets for both Spanish-English and MSA-Egyptian dialect. The system makes use of word and character level representations to identify code-switching. For the MSA-Egyptian dialect the system does not rely on any kind of language-specific knowledge or linguistic resources such as, Part Of Speech (POS) taggers, morphological analyzers, gazetteers or word lists to obtain state-of-the-art performance.

1 Introduction

Code-switching can be defined as the act of alternating between elements of two or more languages or language varieties within the same utterance. The main language is sometimes referred to as the 'host language', and the embedded language as the 'guest language' (Yeh et al., 2013). Code-switching is a wide-spread linguistic phenomenon in modern informal user-generated data, whether spoken or written. With the advent of social media, such as Facebook posts, Twitter tweets, SMS messages, user comments on the articles, blogs, etc., this phenomenon is becoming more pervasive. Code-switching does not only occur across sentences (inter-sentential) but also within the same sentence (intra-sentential), adding a substantial complexity dimension to the automatic processing of natural languages (Das and Gambäck, 2014). This phenomenon is particularly dominant in multilingual societies (Milroy and Muysken, 1995), migrant communities (Papalexakis et al., 2014), and in other environments due to social changes through education and globalization (Milroy and Muysken, 1995). There are also some social, pragmatic and linguistic motivations for code-switching, such as the the intent to express group solidarity, establish authority (Chang and Lin, 2014), lend credibility, or make up for lexical gaps.

It is not necessary for code-switching to occur only between two different languages like Spanish-English (Solorio and Liu, 2008), Mandarin-Taiwanese (Yu et al.,) and Turkish-German (Özlem Çetinoglu, 2016), but it can also happen between three languages, e.g. Bengali, English and Hindi (Barman et al., 2014), and in some extreme cases between six languages: English, French, German, Italian, Romansh and Swiss German (Volk and Clematide, 2014). Moreover, this phenomenon can occur between two different dialects of the same language as between Modern Standard Arabic (MSA) and Egyptian Dialect (Elfardy and Diab, 2012), or MSA and Moroccan Arabic (Samih and Maier,

Proceedings of the Second Workshop on Computational Approaches to Code Switching, pages 50–59,
Austin, TX, November 1, 2016. ©2016 Association for Computational Linguistics

2016a; Samih and Maier, 2016b). The current shared task is limited to two scenarios: a) code-switching between two distinct languages: Spanish-English, b) and two language varieties: MSA-Egyptian Dialect.

With the massive increase in code-switched writings in user-generated content, it has become imperative to develop tools and methods to handle and process this type of data. Identification of languages used in the sentence is the first step in doing any kind of text analysis. For example, most data found in social media produced by bilingual people is a mixture of two languages. In order to process or translate this data to some other language, the first step will be to detect text chunks and identify which language each chunk belongs to. The other categories like named entities, mixed, ambiguous and other are also important for further language processing.

2 Related Works

Code-switching has attracted considerable attention in theoretical linguistics and sociolinguistics over several decades. However, until recently there has not been much work on the computational processing of code-switched data. The first computational treatment of this linguistic phenomenon can be found in (Joshi, 1982). He introduces a grammar-based system for parsing and generating code-switched data. More recently, the detection of code-switching has gained traction, starting with the work of (Solorio and Liu, 2008), and culminating in the first shared task at the "First Workshop on Computational Approaches to Code Switching" (Solorio et al., 2014). Moreover, there have been efforts in creating and annotating code-switching resources (Özlem Çetinoglu, 2016; Elfardy and Diab, 2012; Maharjan et al., 2015; Lignos and Marcus, 2013). Maharjan et al. (2015) used a user-centric approach to collect code-switched tweets for Nepali-English and Spanish-English language pairs. They used two methods, namely a dictionary based approach and CRF GE and obtained an F1 score of 86% and 87% for Spanish-English and Nepali-English respectively at word level language identification task. Lignos and Marcus (2013) collected a large number of monolingual Spanish and English tweets and used ratio list method to tag each token with by its dom-

inant language. Their system obtained an accuracy of 96.9% at word-level language identification task.

The task of detecting code-switching points is generally cast as a sequence labeling problem. Its difficulty depends largely on the language pair being processed.

Several projects have treated code-switching between MSA and Egyptian Arabic. For example, Elfardy et al. (2013) present a system for the detection of code-switching between MSA and Egyptian Arabic which selects a tag based on the sequence with a maximum marginal probability, considering 5-grams. A later version of the system is named AIDA2 (Al-Badrashiny et al., 2015) and it is a more complex hybrid system that incorporates different classifiers and components such as language models, a named entity recognizer, and a morphological analyzer. The classification strategy is built as a cascade voting system, whereby a conditional Random Field (CRF) classifier tags each word based on the decisions from four other underlying classifiers.

The participants of the "First Workshop on Computational Approaches to Code Switching" had applied a wide range of machine learning and sequence learning algorithms with some using additional online resources like English dictionary, Hindi-Nepali wiki, dbpedia, online dumps, LexNorm, etc. to tackle the problem of language detection in code-switched tweets on Nepali-English, Spanish-English, Mandarin-English and MSA Dialects (Solorio et al., 2014). For MSA-Dialects, two CRF-based systems, a system using language-independent extended Markov models, and a system using a CRF autoencoder have been presented; the latter proved to be the most successful.

The majority of the systems dealing with word-level language identification in code-switching rely on linguistic resources (such as named entity gazetteers and word lists) and linguistic information (such as POS tags and morphological analysis), and they use machine learning methods that have been typically used with sequence labeling problems, such as support vector machine (SVM), conditional random fields (CRF) and n-gram language models. Very few, however, have recently turned to recurrent neural networks (RNN) and word embedding with remarkable success. (Chang and Lin, 2014) used a RNN architecture and combined it with pre-trained word2vector skip-gram word embeddings, a log bilinear model that allows words with similar contexts to have similar embeddings. The word2vec embeddings were trained on a large Twitter corpus of random samples without filtering by language, assuming that different languages tend to share different contexts, allowing embeddings to provide good separation between languages. They showed that their system outperforms the best SVM-based systems reported in the EMNLP'14 Code-Switching Workshop.

Vu and Schultz (2014) proposed to adapt the recurrent neural network language model to different code-switching behaviors and even use them to generate artificial code-switching text data. Adel et al. (2013) investigated the application of RNN language models and factored language models to the task of identifying code-switching in speech, and reported a significant improvement compared to the traditional n-gram language model.

Our work is similar to that of Chang and Lin (2014) in that we use RNNs and word embeddings. The difference is that we use long-short-term memory (LSTM) with the added advantage of the memory cells that efficiently capture long-distance dependencies. We also combine word-level with character-level representation to obtain morphology-like information on words.

3   Model

In this section, we will provide a brief description of LSTM, and introduce the different components of our code-switching detection model. The architecture of our system, shown in Figure 1, bears resemblance to the models introduced by Huang et al. (2015), Ma and Hovy (2016), and Collobert et al. (2011).

3.1   Long Short-term Memory

A recurrent neural network (RNN) belongs to a family of neural networks suited for modeling sequential data. Given an input sequence $x = (x_1, ..., x_n)$, an RNN computes the output vector y_t of each word x_t by iterating the following equations from $t = 1$ to n:

$$h_t = f(W_{xh}x_t + W_{hh}h_{t-1} + b_h)$$
$$y_t = W_{hy}h_t + b_y$$

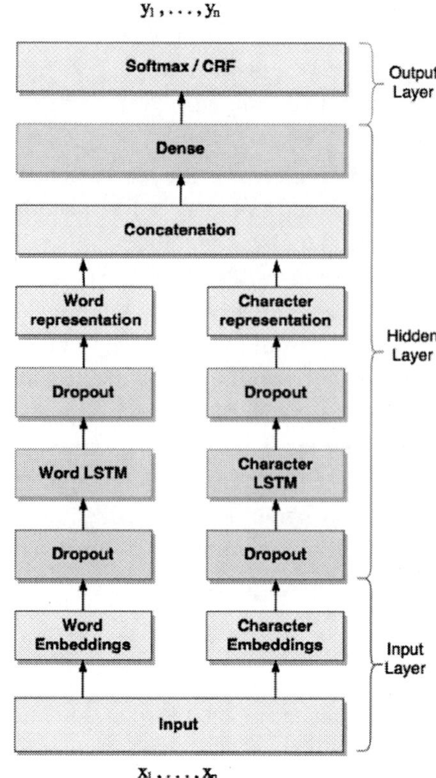

Figure 1: System Architecture.

where h_t is the hidden states vector, W denotes weight matrix, b denotes bias vector and f is the activation function of the hidden layer. Theoretically RNN can learn long distance dependencies, still in practice they fail due the vanishing/exploding gradient (Bengio et al., 1994). To solve this problem , Hochreiter and Schmidhuber (1997) introduced the long short-term memory RNN (LSTM). The idea consists in augmenting the RNN with memory cells to overcome difficulties with training and efficiently cope with long distance dependencies. The output of the LSTM hidden layer h_t given input x_t is computed via the following intermediate calculations: (Graves, 2013):

$$i_t = \sigma(W_{xi}x_t + W_{hi}h_{t-1} + W_{ci}c_{t-1} + b_i)$$
$$f_t = \sigma(W_{xf}x_t + W_{hf}h_{t-1} + W_{cf}c_{t-1} + b_f)$$
$$c_t = f_t c_{t-1} + i_t \tanh(W_{xc}x_t + W_{hc}h_{t-1} + b_c)$$
$$o_t = \sigma(W_{xo}x_t + W_{ho}h_{t-1} + W_{co}c_t + b_o)$$
$$h_t = o_t \tanh(c_t)$$

where σ is the logistic sigmoid function, and i, f, o and c are respectively the input gate, forget gate, output gate and cell activation vectors. More interpretation about this architecture can be found in (Lipton et al., 2015). Figure 2 illustrates a single LSTM memory cell (Graves and Schmidhuber, 2005)

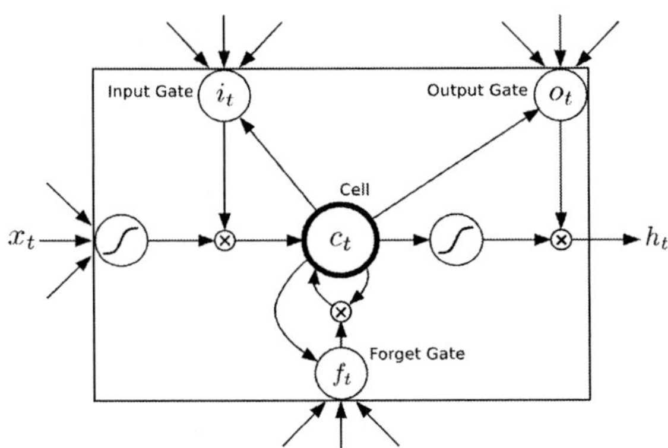

Figure 2: A Long Short-Term Memory Cell.

3.2 Word- and Character-level Embeddings

Character embeddings A very important element of the recent success of many NLP applications, is the use of character-level representations in deep neural networks. This has shown to be effective for numerous NLP tasks (Collobert et al., 2011; dos Santos et al., 2015) as it can capture word morphology and reduce out-of-vocabulary. This approach has also been especially useful for handling languages with rich morphology and large character sets (Kim et al., 2016). We also find this important for our code-switching detection model particularly for the Spanish-English data as the two languages have different orthographic sequences that are learned during the training phase.

Word pre-trained embeddings Another crucial component of our model is the use of pre-trained vectors. The basic assumption is that words from different languages (or language varieties) may appear in different contexts, so word embeddings learned from a large multilingual corpus, should provide an accurate separation between the languages at hand. Following Collobert et al. (2011), we use pre-trained word embeddings for Arabic, Spanish and English to initialize our look-up table.

Words with no pre-trained embeddings are randomly initialized with uniformly sampled embeddings. To use these embeddings in our model, we simply replace the one hot encoding word representation with its corresponding 300-dimensional vector. For more details about the data we use to train our word embeddings for Arabic and Spanish-English, see Section 4.

3.3 Conditional Random Fields (CRF)

When using LSTM RNN for sequence classification, the resulting probability distribution of each step is supposed to be independent from each other. Still we assume that code-switching tags are highly related to each other. To exploit these kind of labeling constraints, we resort to Conditional Random Fields (CRF) (Lafferty et al., 2001). CRF, a sequence labeling algorithm, predicts labels for a whole sequence rather than for the parts in isolation as shown in Equation 1. Here, s_1 to s_m represent the labels of tokens x_1 to x_m respectively, where m is the number of tokens in a given sequence. After we have this probability value for every possible combination of labels, the actual sequence of labels for this set of tokens will be the one with the highest probability.

$$p(s_1...s_m|x_1...x_m) \tag{1}$$

$$p(\vec{s}|\vec{x};\vec{w}) = \frac{exp(\vec{w}.\vec{\Phi}(\vec{x},\vec{s}))}{\sum_{\vec{s'}\epsilon S^m} exp(\vec{w}.\vec{\Phi}(\vec{x},\vec{s'}))} \tag{2}$$

Equation 2 shows the formula for calculating the probability value from Equation 1. Here, S is the set of labels. In our case S =*{lang1, lang2, ambiguous, ne, mixed, other, fw, unk }*. $\vec{w}$ is the weight vector for weighting the feature vector $\vec{\Phi}$.

3.3.1 Feature Templates

The feature templates extract feature values based on the current position of the token, current token's label and previous token's label and the entire tweet. These functions normally output binary values (0 or 1). These feature functions can be represented mathematically as $\Phi(\vec{x}, j, s_{j-1}, s_j)$. We use the following feature templates.

Morphological Features: In order to capture the information contained in the morphology of tokens, we used features like, all upper case, title case, begins with punctuation, @, is digit, is alphanumeric, contains apostrophe, ends with a vowel, consonant vowel ratio, has accented characters, prefixes and suffixes of the current token and of its previous or next token.

Character n-gram Features: character bigrams and trigrams.

Word Features: This feature uses token in its lowercase (hash-tag is removed from the token). Also, it tries to capture the context surrounding the token using the previous and next two tokens as features.

Shape Features: Collins (2002) defined a mapping from each character to its type. The type function blinds all characters but preserves the case information. The digits are replaced by # and all other punctuation characters are copied as they are. For example: "London" is transformed to "Xxxxxx", "PG-500' is transformed to "XX-###'. Another variation of the same function maps each character to its type but the repeated characters and not repeated in the mapping. So "London" is transformed to "Xx*". We use both of these variations in our system. These features are designed to capture the *named entity*.

Word Character Representations: The final representations from the char-word LSTM model before feeding to softmax layers for each token are used as features to the CRF.

3.4 LSTM-CRF for Code-switching Detection

Our neural network architecture consists of the following three layers:

- Input layer: comprises both character and word embeddings.

- Hidden layer: two LSTMs map both words and character representations to hidden sequences.

- Output layer: a Softmax or a CRF computes the probability distribution over all labels.

At the input layer a look-up table is randomly initialized mapping each word in the input to d-dimensional vectors for sequences of characters and sequences of words. At the hidden layer, the output from the character and word embeddings is used as the input to two LSTM layers to obtain fixed-dimensional representations for characters and words. At the output layer, a softmax or a CRF is applied over the hidden representation of the two

LSTMs to obtain the probability distribution over all labels. Training is performed using stochastic gradient descent with momentum, optimizing the cross entropy objective function.

3.5 Optimization

Due to the relatively small size the training data set and development data set in both Arabic and Spanish-English, overfitting poses a considerable challenge for our code-switching detection system. To make sure that our model learns significant representations, we resort to dropout (Hinton et al., 2012) to mitigate overfitting. The basic idea of dropout consists in randomly omitting a certain percentage of the neurons in each hidden layer for each presentation of the samples during training. This encourages each neuron to depend less on other neurons to detect code-switching patterns. We apply dropout masks to both embedding layers before inputting to the two LSTMs and to their output vectors as shown in Fig. 1. In our experiments we find that dropout decreases overfitting and improves the overall performance of the system.

4 Dataset

The shared task organizers made available the tagged dataset for Spanish-English and Arabic (MSA-Egyptian) code-switched language pairs. The Spanish-English dataset consists of 8,733 tweets (139,539 tokens) as training set, 1,587 tweets (33,276 tokens) as development set and 10,716 tweets (121,446 tokens) as final test set. Similarly, the Arabic (MSA-Egyptian) dataset consists of 8,862 tweets (185,928 tokens) as training set, 1,117 tweets (20,688 tokens) as development set and 1,262 tweets (20,713 tokens) as final test set.

For Arabic we trained different word embeddings using word2vec (Mikolov et al., 2013) from a corpus of total size of 383,261,475 words, consisting of dialectal texts of Facebook posts (8,241,244), Twitter tweets (2,813,016), user comments on the news (95,241,480), and MSA texts of news articles of 276,965,735 words. Likewise, for Spanish-English, we combined English gigaword corpus (Graff et al., 2003) and Spanish gigaword corpus (Graff, 2006) before we trained different word embeddings on the final corpus.

Labels	CRF (feats)	CRF (emb)	CRF (feats+ emb)	word LSTM	char LSTM	char-word LSTM
ambiguous	0.00	0.02	0.00	0.00	0.00	0.00
fw	0.00	0.00	0.00	0.00	0.00	0.00
lang1	0.97	0.97	0.97	0.93	0.94	0.96
lang2	0.96	0.95	0.96	0.91	0.89	0.93
mixed	0.00	0.00	0.00	0.00	0.00	0.00
ne	0.52	0.51	0.57	0.34	0.13	0.32
other	1.00	1.00	1.00	0.85	1.00	1.00
unk	0.04	0.08	0.10	0.00	0.00	0.04
Accuracy	0.961	0.960	**0.963**	0.896	0.923	0.954

Table 1: F1 score results on Spanish-English development dataset. (feats = hand-crafted features, emb = representations for each token) The last three columns use softmax.

Labels	CRF (feats)	CRF (emb)	CRF (feats+ emb)	word LSTM	char LSTM	char-word LSTM
ambiguous	0.00	0.00	0.00	0.00	0.00	0.00
lang1	0.80	0.88	0.88	0.86	0.57	0.88
lang2	0.83	0.91	0.91	0.92	0.23	0.92
mixed	0.00	0.00	0.00	0.00	0.00	0.00
ne	0.83	0.84	0.86	0.84	0.66	0.84
other	0.97	0.97	0.97	0.92	0.97	0.97
Accuracy	0.829	0.894	0.896	0.896	0.530	**0.900**

Table 2: F1 score results on MSA-Egyptian development dataset. (feats = hand-crafted features, emb = representations for each token) The last three columns use softmax.

Data preprocessing: We transformed Arabic scripts to SafeBuckwalter (Roth et al., 2008), a character-to-character mapping that replaces Arabic UTF alphabet with Latin characters to reduce size and streamline processing. Also in order to reduce data sparsity, we converted all Persian numbers (e.g. ٢ ٠١) to Arabic numbers (e.g. 1, 2), Arabic punctuation (e.g. '،' and '؛') to Latin punctuation (e.g. ',' and ';'), removed kashida (elongation character) and vowel marks, and separated punctuation marks from words.

5 Experiments and Results

We explored different combinations of hand-crafted features (Section 3.3.1), word LSTM and char-word LSTM models with CRF and softmax classifier to identify the best system. Table 1 and 2 show the results for different settings for Spanish-English and MSA-Egyptian on the development dataset respectively. For the Spanish-English dataset, we find that combining the character and word representations learned with a char-word LSTM system with hand-crafted features and then using CRF as a sequence classifier gives the highest overall accuracy

Scores	Es-En	MSA
Monolingual F1	0.92	0.890
Code-switched F1	0.88	0.500
Weighted F1	0.90	0.830

Table 3: Tweet level results the test dataset.

Label	Recall	Precision	F-score
ambiguous	0.000	0.000	0.000
fw	0.000	0.000	0.000
lang1	0.922	0.939	0.930
lang2	0.978	0.982	0.980
mixed	0.000	0.000	0.000
ne	0.639	0.484	0.551
other	0.992	0.998	0.995
unk	0.120	0.019	0.034
Accuracy			0.967

Table 4: Token level results on Spanish-English test dataset.

of 0.963. Also, we notice that the addition of character and word representations improves the F1-score for *named entity* and *unknown* tokens. For the MSA-Egyptian dataset, we find that a char-word LSTM model with softmax classifier is better than the CRF as this setting gives us the highest overall accuracy of 0.90. Moreover, the addition of character and word representations to hand-crafted features improves the F1 score for *named entity*. Based on these results, our final system for Spanish-English uses CRF with hand-crafted features and character and word representations learned with a char-word LSTM model and the MSA-Egyptian uses char-word LSTM model with softmax as classifier. We do not use any kind of hand-crafted features for the MSA-Egyptian dataset.

Our final system outperformed all other participants' systems for the MSA-Egyptian dialects in terms of tweet level and token level performance.

Label	Recall	Precision	F-score
ambiguous	0.000	0.000	0.000
fw	0.000	0.000	0.000
lang1	0.877	0.832	0.854
lang2	0.913	0.896	0.904
mixed	0.000	0.000	0.000
ne	0.729	0.829	0.777
other	0.938	0.975	0.957
unk	0.000	0.000	0.000
Accuracy			0.879

Table 5: Token level results on MSA-DA test dataset.

For the Spanish-English dataset, our system ranks second in terms of tweet level performance and third in terms of token level accuracy. Table 3, 4 and 5 show the final results for tweet and token level performance for the Spanish-English and MSA-Egyptian datasets. For the MSA dataset, the difference between our system and the second highest scoring system is 8% and 2.7% in terms of tweet level weighted F1 score and token level accuracy. Similarly for the Spanish-English dataset, the difference between our system and the highest scoring system is 1.3% and 0.6% in terms of tweet level weighted F1 score and token level accuracy. Our system consistently ranks first for language identification for the MSA-Egyptian dataset (5% and 4% above the second highest system for *lang1* and *lang2* respectively). For the Spanish-English dataset, our system ranks third (0.8% below the highest scoring system) and third (0.4% below the highest scoring system) for *lang1* and *lang2* respectively. However, our system has consistently shown weaker performance in identifying *nes*. Nonetheless, the overall results show that our system outperforms other systems with relatively high margin for the MSA-Egyptian dataset and lags behind other systems with relatively low margin for the Spanish-English dataset.

6 Analysis

6.1 What is being captured in char-word representations?

In order to investigate what the char-word LSTM model is learning, we feed the tweets from the Spanish-English and MSA-Egyptian development datasets to the system and take the vectors formed by concatenation of character representation and word representation before feeding them into softmax layer. We then project them into 2D space by reducing the dimension of the vectors to 2 using Principle Component Analysis (PCA). We see, in Figure 3, that the trained neural network has learned to cluster the tokens according to their label type. Moreover, the position of tokens in 2D space also revels that *ambiguous* and *mixed* tokens are in between *lang1* and *lang2* clusters.

Figure 3(a) for Spanish-English shows that the char-word LSTM model has learned to separate the

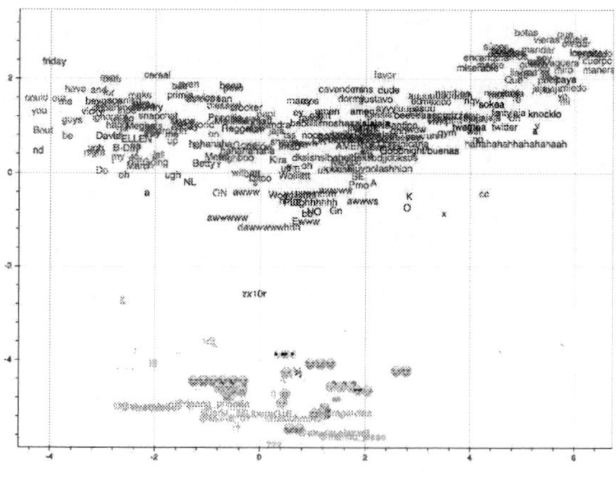

(a) Spanish-English

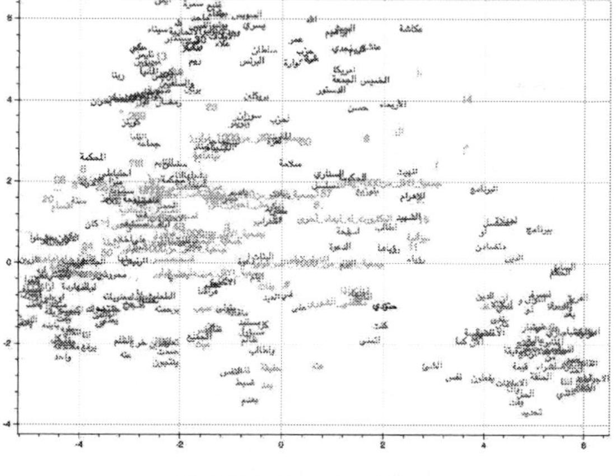

(b) MSA-Egyptian Dialects

Figure 3: Projection of char-word LSTM representation into 2D using PCA. The tokens belonging to different categories are mapped as *ambiguous*: purple, *ne*: blue, *mixed*: black, *other*: orange, *lang1*: red, *lang2*: green

other tokens from rest of the tokens. These tokens are well separated and are situated at the bottom of the figure. Moreover, the *unknown* token are closer to the *other* tokens. The *nes* as spread between *lang1* and *lang2* clusters. Named entities like *ELLEN, beyounce, friday, March, Betty* are closer to *lang1* cluster whereas, other named entities like *Mexico, Santino, gustavo, Norte* are closer to *lang2* cluster. Not only the named entities, the *mixed, ambiguous* tokens also exhibit the similar phenomena.

Similarly, Figure 3(b) for MSA-Egyptian generally shows successful separation of tokens, with *lang1* in red on the right, *lang2* in green on the left

Most likely	Score	Most unlikely	Score
$unk \Rightarrow unk$	1.789	$lang1 \Rightarrow mixed$	-0.172
$ne \Rightarrow ne$	1.224	$mixed \Rightarrow lang1$	-0.196
$fw \Rightarrow fw$	1.180	$amb \Rightarrow other$	-0.244
$lang1 \Rightarrow lang1$	1.153	$ne \Rightarrow mixed$	-0.246
$lang2 \Rightarrow lang2$	1.099	$mixed \Rightarrow other$	-0.254
$other \Rightarrow other$	0.827	$fw \Rightarrow lang1$	-0.282
$lang1 \Rightarrow ne$	0.316	$ne \Rightarrow lang2$	-0.334
$other \Rightarrow lang1$	0.222	$unk \Rightarrow ne$	-0.383
$lang2 \Rightarrow mixed$	0.216	$lang2 \Rightarrow lang1$	-0.980
$lang1 \Rightarrow other$	0.191	$lang1 \Rightarrow lang2$	-0.993

Table 6: Most likely and unlikely transitions learned by CRF model for the Spanish-English dataset.

and *ne* in blue on the top. The *other* token occupies the space between the clusters for *lang1*, *lang2* and *ne* with more inclination toward *lang1*. We also notice that *other* in Arabic contains a large amount of hashtags, due to their particular annotation scheme.

6.2 CRF Model

Table 6 shows the most likely and unlikely transitions learned by the CRF model for the Spanish-English dataset. It is interesting to see that the transition from *lang1* to *lang1* and from *lang2* to *lang2* are much likely than *lang1* to *lang2* or *lang2* to *lang1*. This suggests that people especially in Twitter do not normally switch from one language to another while tweeting. Even, if they switch, there are very few code-switch points in the tweets. However, people tweeting in Spanish have more tendency to use mixed tokens than people tweeting in English. We also dumped the top features for the task and found that *word.hasaps* is the top feature to identify token as English. Moreover, features like *word.startpunt*, *word.lower:number* are top features to identify tokens as *other*. The features like *char bigram, trigram, words, suffix and prefix* are the top features to distinguish between English and Spanish tokens.

6.3 Error Analysis for Arabic

When we conducted an error analysis on the output of the Arabic development set for our system, we found the following mistagging types:

- Punctuation marks, user names starting with '@' and emoticons are not tagged as *other*.

- Bad segmentation in the text affects the decision, e.g. عمروموسي EamormuwsaY "Amr Musa".

- Abbreviations: أ 'A' "Mr." and م 'm' "eng." are not consistently treated across the dataset.

- There are cases of true ambiguity, e.g. كريم 'kariym', which can be an adjective "generous" or a person's name "Kareem".

- Clitic attachment can obscure tokens, e.g. وطنطاوي waTanoTAwiy "and-Tantawy".

- Spelling errors can increase data sparsity, e.g. اسكندرية Asokanoriy~ap "Alexandria".

Based on this error analysis we developed a post-processor to handle deterministic annotation decision. The post-processor applies the tag *other* in the following cases:

- Non-alphabetic characters, e.g. punctuation marks and emoticons.

- Numbers already receiving *ne* tag, e.g. ٢٥ يناير "25 January".

- Strings with Latin script.

- Words starting with a @ character that usually represents user names.

6.4 Error Analysis for Spanish-English

From Table 1, it is clear that the most difficult categories are *ambiguous* and *mixed*. These are rare tokens and hence the system could not learn to distinguish them. During analyzing the mistakes on the development set, we found that the annotation of frequent tokens like *jaja, haha* with their spelling variations were inconsistent. Hence, even though the system was correctly predicting the labels, they were marked as incorrect. In addition, we also found that some *lang2* tokens like *que, amor, etc* were wrongly annotated as *lang1*.

In most cases, the system predicted either *lang1* or *lang2* for names of series, games, actor, day, apps (*friday, skype, sheyla, beyounce, walking dead, endless love, flappy bird, dollar tree*). We noticed that all these tokens were in lowercase. Similarly, the system mis-predicted all uppercase tokens as *ne*. For eg. *RT, DM, JK, GO, BOY* were annotated as *lang1* but, the system predicted them as *ne*. Moreover, we found that the tokens like *lol, lmao, yolo, jk* were incorrectly annotated as *ne*.

The system predicted the interjections like *aww, uhh, muah, eeeahh, ughh* as either *lang1* or *lang2* but they were annotated as *unk*.

In order to improve the performance for *ne*, we tagged each token with Ark-Tweet NLP tagger (Owoputi et al., 2013). We then changed the label for the tokens tagged as proper nouns with confidence score greater than 0.98 to *ne*. This improved the F1-score for *ne* from 0.53 to 0.57.

7 Conclusion

In this paper we present our system for identifying and classifying code-switched data for Spanish-English and MSA-Egyptian. The system uses a neural network architecture that relies on word-level and character-level representations, and the output is fine-tuned (only in the Spanish-English data) with a CRF classifier for capturing sequence and contextual information. Our system is language independent in the sense that we have not used any language-specific knowledge or linguistic resources such as, POS taggers, morphological analyzers, gazetteers or word lists, and the main architecture is applied to both language sets. Our system considerably outperforms other systems participating in the shared task for Arabic, and is ranked second place for the Spanish-English at tweet-level performance.

Acknowledgments

We would like to thank Wolfgang Maier for enlightening discussions and the three anonymous reviewers for helpful comments and suggestions. This work was partially funded by Deutsche Forschungsgemeinschaft (DFG).

References

Heike Adel, Ngoc Thang Vu, and Tanja Schultz. 2013. Combination of recurrent neural networks and factored language models for code-switching language modeling. In *Proceedings of the 51st Annual Meeting of the Association for Computational Linguistics*, pages 206–211, Sofia, Bulgaria.

Mohamed Al-Badrashiny, Heba Elfardy, and Mona Diab. 2015. AIDA2: A hybrid approach for token and sentence level dialect identification in arabic. In *Proc. CoNLL*.

Utsab Barman, Amitava Das, Joachim Wagner, and Jennifer Foster. 2014. Code mixing: A challenge for language identification in the language of social media. In *Proceedings of The First Workshop on Computational Approaches to Code Switching*, pages 13–23, Doha, Qatar.

Yoshua Bengio, Patrice Simard, and Paolo Frasconi. 1994. Learning long-term dependencies with gradient descent is difficult. *IEEE transactions on neural networks*, 5(2):157–166.

Joseph Chee Chang and Chu-Cheng Lin. 2014. Recurrent-neural-network for language detection on twitter code-switching corpus. *arXiv:1412.4314v2*.

Michael Collins. 2002. Ranking algorithms for named-entity extraction: Boosting and the voted perceptron. In *Proceedings of the 40th Annual Meeting on Association for Computational Linguistics*, pages 489–496. Association for Computational Linguistics.

R. Collobert, J. Weston, L. Bottou, M. Karlen, K. Kavukcuoglu, and P. Kuksa. 2011. Natural language processing (almost) from scratch. *Journal of Machine Learning Research*, 12:2493–2537.

Amitava Das and Björn Gambäck. 2014. Identifying languages at the word level in code-mixed indian social media text. In *In Proceedings of the 11th International Conference on Natural Language Processing*, pages 169–178, Goa, India.

Cicero dos Santos, Victor Guimaraes, RJ Niterói, and Rio de Janeiro. 2015. Boosting named entity recognition with neural character embeddings. In *Proceedings of NEWS 2015 The Fifth Named Entities Workshop*, page 25.

Heba Elfardy and Mona Diab. 2012. Simplified guidelines for the creation of large scale dialectal Arabic annotations. In *Proc. LREC*.

Heba Elfardy, Mohamed Al-Badrashiny, and Mona Diab. 2013. Code switch point detection in Arabic. In *Proc. NLDB*.

David Graff, Junbo Kong, Ke Chen, and Kazuaki Maeda. 2003. English gigaword. *Linguistic Data Consortium, Philadelphia*.

Dave Graff. 2006. Ldc2006t12: Spanish gigaword corpus. *Philadelphia: LDC*.

Alex Graves and Jürgen Schmidhuber. 2005. Framewise phoneme classification with bidirectional lstm and other neural network architectures. *Neural Networks*, 18(5):602–610.

Alex Graves. 2013. Generating sequences with recurrent neural networks. *arXiv preprint arXiv:1308.0850*.

Geoffrey E Hinton, Nitish Srivastava, Alex Krizhevsky, Ilya Sutskever, and Ruslan R Salakhutdinov. 2012.

Improving neural networks by preventing co-adaptation of feature detectors. *arXiv preprint arXiv:1207.0580*.

Sepp Hochreiter and Jürgen Schmidhuber. 1997. Long short-term memory. *Neural computation*, 9(8):1735–1780.

Zhiheng Huang, Wei Xu, and Kai Yu. 2015. Bidirectional LSTM-CRF models for sequence tagging. *CoRR*, abs/1508.01991.

Aravind K Joshi. 1982. Processing of sentences with intra-sentential code-switching. In *Proc. COLING*.

Yoon Kim, Yacine Jernite, David Sontag, and Alexander M Rush. 2016. Character-aware neural language models. In *Thirtieth AAAI Conference on Artificial Intelligence*.

John D. Lafferty, Andrew McCallum, and Fernando C. N. Pereira. 2001. Conditional random fields: Probabilistic models for segmenting and labeling sequence data. In *Proc. ICML*.

Constantine Lignos and Mitch Marcus. 2013. Toward web-scale analysis of codeswitching. In *87th Annual Meeting of the Linguistic Society of America*.

Zachary C Lipton, David C Kale, Charles Elkan, and Randall Wetzell. 2015. A critical review of recurrent neural networks for sequence learning. *CoRR*, abs/1506.00019.

Xuezhe Ma and Eduard Hovy. 2016. End-to-end sequence labeling via bi-directional lstm-cnns-crf. In *Proceedings of the 54th Annual Meeting of the Association for Computational Linguistics (Volume 1: Long Papers)*, pages 1064–1074, Berlin, Germany, August. Association for Computational Linguistics.

Suraj Maharjan, Elizabeth Blair, Steven Bethard, and Thamar Solorio. 2015. Developing language-tagged corpora for code-switching tweets. In *Proc. LAW IX at NAACL*.

Tomas Mikolov, Kai Chen, Greg Corrado, and Jeffrey Dean. 2013. Efficient estimation of word representations in vector space. *CoRR*, abs/1301.3781.

Lesley Milroy and Pieter Muysken. 1995. *One Speaker, Two Languages: Cross-Disciplinary Perspectives on Code-Switching*. Cambridge Univ. Press.

Olutobi Owoputi, Brendan O'Connor, Chris Dyer, Kevin Gimpel, Nathan Schneider, and Noah A Smith. 2013. Improved part-of-speech tagging for online conversational text with word clusters. Association for Computational Linguistics.

Evangelos E. Papalexakis, Dong Nguyen, and A. Seza Doğruöz. 2014. Predicting code-switching in multilingual communication for immigrant communities. In *Proceedings of The First Workshop on Computational Approaches to Code Switching*, pages 42–50, Doha, Qatar.

Ryan Roth, Owen Rambow, Nizar Habash, Mona Diab, and Cynthia Rudin. 2008. Arabic morphological tagging, diacritization, and lemmatization using lexeme models and feature ranking. *Proceedings of the Conference of American Association for Computational Linguistics (ACL08)*.

Younes Samih and Wolfgang Maier. 2016a. An Arabic-Moroccan Darija code-switched corpus. In *Proc. LREC*.

Younes Samih and Wolfgang Maier. 2016b. Detecting code-switching in moroccan arabic. In *Proceedings of SocialNLP @ IJCAI-2016*, New York.

Thamar Solorio and Yang Liu. 2008. Learning to predict code-switching points. In *Proc. EMNLP*, pages 973–981.

Thamar Solorio, Elizabeth Blair, Suraj Maharjan, Steven Bethard, Mona Diab, Mahmoud Ghoneim, Abdelati Hawwari, Fahad AlGhamdi, Julia Hirschberg, Alison Chang, and Pascale Fung. 2014. Overview for the first shared task on language identification in code-switched data. In *Proc. CS Workshop at EMNLP*.

Martin Volk and Simon Clematide. 2014. Detecting code-switching in a multilingual alpine heritage corpus. In *Proceedings of The First Workshop on Computational Approaches to Code Switching*, pages 24–33, Doha, Qatar.

Ngoc Thang Vu and Tanja Schultz. 2014. Exploration of the impact of maximum entropy in recurrent neural network language models for code-switching speech. In *Proceedings of The First Workshop on Computational Approaches to Code Switching*, pages 34–41, Doha, Qatar.

Ching-Feng Yeh, Aaron Heidel, Hong-Yi Lee, and Lin-Shan Lee. 2013. Recognition of highly imbalanced code-mixed bilingual speech with frame-level language detection based on blurred posteriorgram. *IEEE*, 2013.

Liang-Chih Yu, Wei-Cheng He, Wei-Nan Chien, and Yuen-Hsien Tseng. Identification of code-switched sentences and words using language modeling approaches. *Mathematical Problems in Engineering*, 978.

Özlem Çetinoglu. 2016. A turkish-german code-switching corpus. In *Proceedings of the Tenth International Conference on Language Resources and Evaluation (LREC 2016)*, Portorož, Slovenia.

A Neural Model for Language Identification in Code-Switched Tweets

Aaron Jaech[1] **George Mulcaire**[2] **Shobhit Hathi**[2] **Mari Ostendorf**[1] **Noah A. Smith**[2]

[1]Electrical Engineering [2]Computer Science & Engineering
University of Washington, Seattle, WA 98195, USA
ajaech@uw.edu, gmulc@uw.edu, shathi@uw.edu
ostendor@uw.edu, nasmith@cs.washington.edu

Abstract

Language identification systems suffer when working with short texts or in domains with unconventional spelling, such as Twitter or other social media. These challenges are explored in a shared task for Language Identification in Code-Switched Data (LICS 2016). We apply a hierarchical neural model to this task, learning character and contextualized word-level representations to make word-level language predictions. This approach performs well on both the 2014 and 2016 versions of the shared task.

1 Introduction

Language identification (language ID) remains a difficult problem, particulary in social media text where informal styles, closely related language pairs, and code-switching are common. Progress on language ID is needed especially since downstream tasks, like translation or semantic parsing, depend on it.

Continuous representations for language data, which have produced new states of the art for language modeling (Mikolov et al., 2010), machine translation (Bahdanau et al., 2015), and other tasks, can be useful for language ID. For the Language Identification in Code-Switched Data shared task (LICS 2016), we submitted a hierarchical character-word model closely following Jaech et al. (2016b), focusing on word-level language ID. Our discussion of the model closely follows that paper.

This model, which we call C2V2L ("character to vector to language") is hierarchical in the sense that it explicitly builds a continuous representation for each word from its character sequence, capturing orthographic and morphology-related patterns,

and then combines those word-level representations to use context from the full word sequence before making predictions for each word. The use of character representations is well motivated for code-switching tasks, since the presence of multiple languages means that one is more likely to encounter a previously unseen word.

Our model does not require special handling of casing or punctuation, nor do we need to remove the URLs, usernames, or hashtags, and it is trained end-to-end using standard procedures.

2 Model

Our model has two main components, though they are trained together, end-to-end. The first, "char2vec," applies a convolutional neural network (CNN) to a whitespace-delimited word's Unicode character sequence, providing a word vector. The second is a bidirectional LSTM recurrent neural network (RNN) that maps a sequence of such word vectors to a language label.

2.1 Char2vec

The first layer of char2vec embeds characters. An embedding is learned for each Unicode code point that appears at least twice in the training data, including punctuation, emoji, and other symbols. If C is the set of characters then we let the size of the character embedding layer be $d = \lceil \log_2 |C| \rceil$. (If each dimension of the character embedding vector holds just one bit of information then d bits should be enough to uniquely encode each character.) The character embedding matrix is $\mathbf{Q} \in \mathbb{R}^{d \times |C|}$. Words are given to the model as a sequence of characters. When each character in a word of length l is replaced by its embedding vector we get a matrix $\mathbf{C} \in \mathbb{R}^{d \times (l+2)}$. There are $l + 2$ columns in C be-

Proceedings of the Second Workshop on Computational Approaches to Code Switching, pages 60–64,
Austin, TX, November 1, 2016. ©2016 Association for Computational Linguistics

cause padding characters are added to the left and right of each word.

The char2vec architecture uses two sets of filter banks. The first set is comprised of matrices $\mathbf{H}_{a_i} \in \mathbb{R}^{d \times 3}$ where i ranges from 1 to n_1. The matrix $\mathbf{C}$ is narrowly convolved with each $\mathbf{H}_{a_i}$, a bias term b_a is added and an ReLU non-linearity, $\mathrm{ReLU}(x) = \max(0, x)$, is applied to produce an output $\mathbf{T}_1 = \mathrm{ReLU}(\mathrm{conv}(\mathbf{C}, \mathbf{H}_a) + \mathbf{b}_a)$. $\mathbf{T}_1$ is of size $n_1 \times l$ with one row for each of the filters and one column for each of the characters in the input word. Since each $\mathbf{H}_{a_i}$ is a filter with a width of three characters, the columns of $\mathbf{T}_1$ each hold a representation of a character tri-gram. During training, we apply dropout on $\mathbf{T}_1$ to regularize the model. The matrix $\mathbf{T}_1$ is then convolved with a second set of filters $\mathbf{H}_{b_i} \in \mathbb{R}^{n_1 \times w}$ where b_i ranges from 1 to $3n_2$ and n_2 controls the number of filters of each of the possible widths, $w = 3, 4$, or 5. Another convolution and ReLU non-linearity is applied to get $\mathbf{T}_2 = \mathrm{ReLU}(\mathrm{conv}(\mathbf{T}_1, \mathbf{H}_b) + \mathbf{b}_b)$. Max-pooling across time is used to create a fix-sized vector $\mathbf{y}$ from $\mathbf{T}_2$. The dimension of $\mathbf{y}$ is $3n_2$, corresponding to the number of filters used.

Similar to Kim et al. (2016) who use a highway network after the max-pooling layer, we apply a residual network layer. The residual network uses a matrix $\mathbf{W} \in \mathbb{R}^{3n_2 \times 3n_2}$ and bias vector $\mathbf{b}_3$ to create the vector $\mathbf{z} = \mathbf{y} + f_R(\mathbf{y})$ where $f_R(\mathbf{y}) = \mathrm{ReLU}(\mathbf{W}\mathbf{y} + \mathbf{b}_3)$. The resulting vector $\mathbf{z}$ is used as a word embedding vector in the word-level LSTM portion of the model.

There are three differences between our version of the model and the one described by Kim et al. (2016). First, we use two layers of convolution instead of just one, inspired by Ling et al. (2015a) which uses a 2-layer LSTM for character modeling. Second, we use the ReLU function as a nonlinearity as opposed to the tanh function. ReLU has been highly successful in computer vision in conjunction with convolutional layers (Jarrett et al., 2009). Finally, we use a residual network layer instead of a highway network layer after the max-pooling step, to reduce the model size.

2.2 Sentence-level Context

The sequence of word embedding vectors is processed by a bi-LSTM, which outputs a sequence of

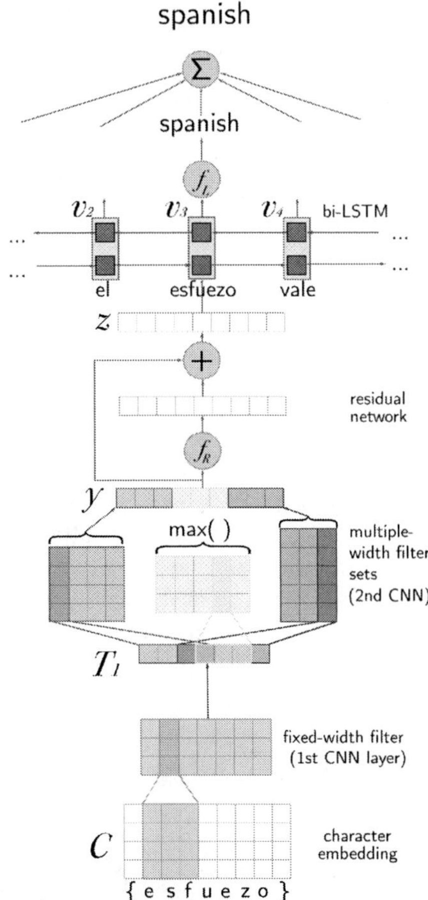

Figure 1: C2V2L model architecture. The model takes the word "esfuezo," a misspelling of the Spanish word "esfuerzo," and maps it to a word vector via the two CNN layers and the residual layer. The word vector is then combined with others via the LSTM, and a prediction made for each word.

vectors, $[\mathbf{v}_1, \mathbf{v}_2, \mathbf{v}_3 \dots \mathbf{v}_T]$ where T is the number of words in the tweet. All LSTM gates are used as defined by Sak et al. (2014). Dropout is used as a regularizer on the inputs to the LSTM (Pham et al., 2014). The output vectors $\mathbf{v}_i$ are transformed into probability distributions over the set of languages by applying an affine transformation followed by a softmax:

$$\mathbf{p}_i = f_L(\mathbf{v}_i) = \frac{\exp(\mathbf{A}\mathbf{v}_i + b)}{\sum_{t=1}^{T} \exp(\mathbf{A}\mathbf{v}_t + b)}$$

The final affine transformation can be interpreted as a language embedding, where each language is represented by a vector of the same dimensionality as the LSTM outputs. The goal of the LSTM then is (roughly) to maximize the dot product of each word's representation with the language embedding(s) for that token. The loss is the cross-entropy between each word's prediction and the corresponding gold label for that word.

3 Implementation Details

3.1 Preprocessing

The data contains many long and repetitive character sequences such as "hahahaha..." or "arghhhhh...". To deal with these, we restricted any sequence of repeating characters to at most five repetitions where the repeating pattern can be from one to four characters. There are many tweets that string together large numbers of usernames or hashtags without spaces between them. These create extra long "words" that cause our implementation to use more memory and do extra computation during training. We therefore enforce the constraint that there must be a space before any URL, username, or hashtag. To deal with the few remaining extra-long character sequences, we force word breaks in non-space character sequences every 40 bytes. This primarily affects languages that are not space-delimited like Chinese. We do not perform any special handling of casing or punctuation nor do we need to remove the URLs, usernames, or hashtags as has been done in previous work (Zubiaga et al., 2014).

3.2 Training and Tuning

Training is done using minibatches of size 25 and a learning rate of 0.001 using Adam (Kingma and Ba, 2015), and continued for 50,000 minibatches.

There are only four hyperparameters to tune for each model: the number of filters in the first convolutional layer, the number of filters in the second convolutional layer, the size of the word-level LSTM vector, and the dropout rate.

To tune hyperparameters, we trained 10 models with random parameter settings on 80% of the data from the Spanish-English training set, and chose the settings from the model that performed best on the remaining 20%. We then retrained on the full training set with these settings (respectively, 59, 108, 23, and 25%). Our final model architecture has roughly

177K parameters.

4 Experiments

Because C2V2L produces language predictions for every word, the architecture is well suited to analysis of code-switched text, in which different words may belong to different languages. We used the Spanish-English dataset from the EMNLP 2014 shared task on Language Identification in Code-Switched Data (Solorio et al., 2014), and the Spanish-English and Arabic-MSA datasets from the EMNLP 2016 version of the shared task. Each dataset is a collection of monolingual and code-switched tweets in two main languages: English and Spanish, or Modern Standard Arabic (MSA) and Arabic dialects.

4.1 LICS 2014

The LICS 2014 dataset (Zubiaga et al., 2014) comes from a language ID shared task that focused on tweets that code-switch between two languages. While several language pairs were included in the shared task, we evaluated only on Spanish-English in these experiments. There are approximately 110,000 labeled examples in the training data and 34,000 in the test set. The data is unbalanced, with over twice as many examples in English (74,000) as in Spanish (35,000). A further 30,000 are labeled "other" for punctuation, emoji, and unintelligible words. There are also a small number of examples labeled "NE" for named entities (2.16%), "mixed" for words that include both English and Spanish (0.03%), and "ambiguous" for words that could be interpreted as either language in context (0.22%). "NE" and "other" are predicted as if they were separate languages, but the 'ambiguous' label is ignored.

C2V2L performed well at this task, scoring 95.1 F_1 for English (which would have achieved second place in the 2014 shared task, out of eight entries), 94.1 for Spanish (second place), 36.2 for named entities (fourth place) and 94.2 for Other (third place).[1] While our code-switching results are not quite state-of-the-art, they show that our model learns accurate word-level predictions.

---

[1]Full results for the 2014 shared task can be found at `http://emnlp2014.org/workshops/CodeSwitch/results.php`.

Lang. pair (L1-L2)	L1	L2	NE	other
Spanish-English (ours)	0.931	0.977	0.454	0.910
Spanish-English (best)	0.931	0.977	0.537	0.994
Arabic-MSA (ours)	0.603	0.603	0.468	0.712
Arabic-MSA (best)	0.854	0.904	0.828	0.988

Table 1: F1 scores for the LICS 2016 shared task. The best result from any system in each category is provided for comparison.

4.2 LICS 2016

The LICS 2016 shared task uses a similar format. Here, the training and development sets for each language pair correspond to the training and test sets from LICS 2014, and new data was added to create a new test set. However, labels were updated to correct errors and add two new categories: "fw" (foreign word) for examples that belong to a language other than the main two, and "unk" for examples that cannot be classified. We ignore "unk" and "fw."

We submitted labels for both available language pairs: Spanish-English and Arabic-MSA (distinguishing Modern Standard Arabic from Arabic dialects). Partial results,[2] showing only the four largest categories, are given in Table 1.

Our results for Spanish-English are competitive with the best submitted systems. We ranked first or tied for first in F_1 for the primary categories, English and Spanish, out of nine submitted systems. On Arabic-MSA, we came in last among five systems. This is likely due in part to the fact that we tuned only on Spanish-English data and did not make any adjustments when training the Arabic-MSA model. A model that is tuned to the specific language pair, and perhaps handled the 'other' category with regular expressions in preprocessing, would likely perform better.

5 Related Work

Language ID has a long history both in the speech domain (House and Neuburg, 1977) and for text (Cavnar and Trenkle, 1994). Previous work on the text domain mostly uses word or character n-gram features combined with linear classifiers (Hurtado et al., 2014; Gamallo et al., 2014). Chang and Lin (2014) outperformed the top results for

English-Spanish and English-Nepali in the EMNLP 2014 Language Identitication in Code-Switched Data (Solorio et al., 2014), using an RNN with skip-gram word embeddings and character n-gram features. Word-level language ID has also been studied by Mandal et al. (2015) in the context of question answering and by King and Abney (2013). Both used primarily character n-gram features.

Several other studies have investigated the use of character sequence models in language processing. These techniques were first applied only to create word embeddings (dos Santos and Zadrozny, 2015; dos Santos and Guimaraes, 2015) and then later extended to have the word embeddings feed directly into a word-level RNN. Applications include part-of-speech (POS) tagging (Ling et al., 2015b), language modeling (Ling et al., 2015a), dependency parsing (Ballesteros et al., 2015), translation (Ling et al., 2015b), and slot filling text analysis (Jaech et al., 2016a). A more extensive discussion of related work on language ID and character sequence models can be found in Jaech et al. (2016b).

6 Conclusion

We present C2V2L, a hierarchical neural model for language ID that preforms competitively on challenging word-level language ID tasks. Without feature engineering, we achieved the best performance in two common categories and good results in two others. Future work could include adapting C2V2L for other sequence labeling tasks, having shown that the current architecture already performs well.

Acknowledgments

We thank the anonymous reviewers for helpful feedback. Part of this material is based upon work supported by a subcontract with Raytheon BBN Technologies Corp. under DARPA Prime Contract No. HR0011-15-C-0013. This work was also supported by a gift to the University of Washington by Google. Views expressed are those of the authors and do not reflect the official policy or position of the Department of Defense of the U.S. government.

References

Dzmitry Bahdanau, Kyunghyun Cho, and Yoshua Bengio. 2015. Neural machine translation by jointly

---

[2]Full results can be found at `http://care4lang1.seas.gwu.edu/cs2/results.html`

learning to align and translate. In *Proc. Int. Conf. Learning Representations (ICLR)*.

Miguel Ballesteros, Chris Dyer, and Noah Smith. 2015. Improved transition-based parsing by modeling characters instead of words with LSTMs. In *Proc. Conf. Empirical Methods Natural Language Process. (EMNLP)*.

William B. Cavnar and John M. Trenkle. 1994. N-gram-based text categorization. In *In Proc. of SDAIR-94, 3rd Annual Symposium on Document Analysis and Information Retrieval*, pages 161–175.

Joseph Chee Chang and Chu-Cheng Lin. 2014. Recurrent-neural-network for language detection on Twitter code-switching corpus. *CoRR*, abs/1412.4314.

Cicero dos Santos and Victor Guimaraes. 2015. Boosting named entity recognition with neural character embeddings. In *Proc. ACL Named Entities Workshop*.

Cicero dos Santos and Bianca Zadrozny. 2015. Learning character-level representations for part-of-speech tagging. In *Proc. Int. Conf. Machine Learning (ICML)*.

Pablo Gamallo, Marcos Garcia, and Susana Sotelo. 2014. Comparing ranking-based and naive Bayes approaches to language detection on tweets. In *TweetLID@ SEPLN*.

Arthur S House and Edward P Neuburg. 1977. Toward automatic identification of the language of an utterance. *The Journal of the Acoustical Society of America*, 62(3):708–713.

Lluís F Hurtado, Ferran Pla, and Mayte Giménez. 2014. ELiRF-UPV en TweetLID: Identificación del idioma en Twitter. In *TweetLID@ SEPLN*.

Aaron Jaech, Larry Heck, and Mari Ostendorf. 2016a. Domain adaptation of recurrent neural networks for natural language understanding. In *Proc. Conf. Int. Speech Communication Assoc. (INTERSPEECH)*.

Aaron Jaech, George Mulcaire, Shobhit Hathi, Mari Ostendorf, and Noah A. Smith. 2016b. Hierarchical character-word models for language identification. In *Proc. Int. Workshop on Natural Language Processing for Social Media (SocialNLP)*.

Kevin Jarrett, Koray Kavukcuoglu, Marc'Aurelio Ranzato, and Yann Lecun. 2009. What is the best multistage architecture for object recognition? In *2009 IEEE 12th International Conference on Computer Vision*. IEEE.

Yoon Kim, Yacine Jernite, David Sontag, and Alexander Rush. 2016. Character-aware neural language models. In *Proc. AAAI*.

Ben King and Steven Abney. 2013. Labeling the languages of words in mixed-language documents using weakly supervised methods. In *Proc. Conf. North American Chapter Assoc. for Computational Linguistics: Human Language Technologies (NAACL-HLT)*.

Diederik Kingma and Jimmy Ba. 2015. Adam: A method for stochastic optimization. In *Proc. Int. Conf. Learning Representations (ICLR)*.

Wang Ling, Tiago Luís, Luís Marujo, Ramón Fernandez Astudillo, Silvio Amir, Chris Dyer, Alan W Black, and Isabel Trancoso. 2015a. Finding function in form: Compositional character models for open vocabulary word representation. In *Proc. Conf. Empirical Methods Natural Language Process. (EMNLP)*.

Wang Ling, Isabel Trancoso, Chris Dyer, and Alan Black. 2015b. Character-based neural machine translation. *arXiv preprint arXiv:1511.04586v1*.

Soumik Mandal, Somnath Banerjee, Sudip Kumar Naskar, Paolo Rosso, and Sivaji Bandyopadhyay. 2015. Adaptive voting in multiple classifier systems for word level language identification. In *the Working Notes in Forum for Information Retrieval Evaluation (FIRE)*.

Tomas Mikolov, Martin Karafiát, Lukas Burget, Jan Cernockỳ, and Sanjeev Khudanpur. 2010. Recurrent neural network based language model. In *Proc. Conf. Int. Speech Communication Assoc. (INTERSPEECH)*.

V. Pham, T. Bluche, C. Kermorvant, and J. Louradour. 2014. Dropout improves recurrent neural networks for handwriting recognition. In *Proc. Int. Conf. on Frontiers in Handwriting Recognition (ICFHR)*.

Hasim Sak, Andrew W Senior, and Françoise Beaufays. 2014. Long short-term memory recurrent neural network architectures for large scale acoustic modeling. In *Proc. Conf. Int. Speech Communication Assoc. (INTERSPEECH)*.

Thamar Solorio, Elizabeth Blair, Suraj Maharjan, Steven Bethard, Mona Diab, Mahmoud Ghoneim, Abdelati Hawwari, Fahad AlGhamdi, Julia Hirschberg, Alison Chang, et al. 2014. Overview for the first shared task on language identification in code-switched data. In *Proc. Int. Workshop on Computational Approaches to Linguistic Code Switching (CALCS)*.

Arkaitz Zubiaga, Inaki San Vicente, Pablo Gamallo, José Ramom Pichel Campos, Iñaki Alegría Loinaz, Nora Aranberri, Aitzol Ezeiza, and Víctor Fresno-Fernández. 2014. Overview of TweetLID: Tweet language identification at SEPLN 2014. In *TweetLID@ SEPLN*.

SAWT: Sequence Annotation Web Tool

Younes Samih and **Wolfgang Maier** and **Laura Kallmeyer**
Heinrich Heine University
Department of Computational Linguistics
Universitätsstr. 1, 40225 Düsseldorf, Germany
{samih,maierwo,kallmeyer}@phil.hhu.de

Abstract

We present SAWT, a web-based tool for the annotation of token sequences with an arbitrary set of labels. The key property of the tool is simplicity and ease of use for both annotators and administrators. SAWT runs in any modern browser, including browsers on mobile devices, and only has minimal server-side requirements.

1 Introduction

Code-switching (Bullock and Toribio, 2009) occurs when speakers switch between different languages or language variants within the same context. In the Arab world, for instance, it is a common phenomenon. Both Modern Standard Arabic (MSA) and Dialectal Arabic (DA) variants co-exist, MSA and DA being used for formal and informal communication, respectively (Ferguson, 1959). Particularly recently, the computational treatment of code-switching has received attention (Solorio et al., 2014).

Within a project concerned with the processing of code-switched data of an under-resourced Arabic dialect, Moroccan *Darija*, a large code-switched corpus had to be annotated token-wise with the extended label set from the EMNLP 2014 Shared Task on Code-Switching (Solorio et al., 2014; Samih and Maier, 2016). The label set contains three labels that mark MSA and DA tokens, as well as tokens in another language (English, French, Spanish, Berber). Furthermore, it contains labels for tokens which mix two languages (e.g., for French words to

which Arabic morphology is applied), for ambiguous words, for Named Entities, and for remaining material (such as punctuation).

The annotation software tool had to fulfill the following requirements.

- It should excel at sequence annotation and not do anything else, i.e., "featuritis" should be avoided, furthermore it should be as simple as possible to use for the annotators, allowing for a high annotation speed;

- It should not be bound to a particular label set, since within the project, not only code-switching annotation, but also the annotation of Part-of-Speech was envisaged;

- It should allow for post-editing of tokenization during the annotation;

- It should be web-based, due to the annotators being at different physical locations;

- On client side, it should be platform-independent and run in modern browsers including browsers on mobile devices, using modern technologies such as Bootstrap[1] which provide a responsive design, without requiring a local installation of software;

- On server side, there should be safe storage; furthermore, the administration overhead should be kept minimal and there should only be minimal software requirements for the server side.

---

[1] http://getbootstrap.com

Proceedings of the Second Workshop on Computational Approaches to Code Switching, pages 65–70,
Austin, TX, November 1, 2016. ©2016 Association for Computational Linguistics

Even though several annotation interfaces for similar tasks have been presented, such as COLANN (Benajiba and Diab, 2010), COLABA (Diab et al., 2010), and DIWAN (Al-Shargi and Rambow, 2015), they were either not available or did not match our needs.

We therefore built SAWT. SAWT has been successfully used to create a code-switched corpus of 223k tokens with three annotators (Samih and Maier, 2016). It is currently used for Part-of-Speech annotation of Moroccan Arabic dialect data. The remainder of the article is structured as follows. In section 2 we present the different aspects of SWAT, namely, its data storage model, its server side structure and its client side structure. In section 3, we review related work, and in section 4, we conclude the article.

2   SAWT

SAWT is a web application. Its client side is machine and platform independent and runs in any modern browser. On the server side, only a PHP-enabled web server (ideally Apache HTTP server) and a MySQL database instance are needed.

We now describe our strategy for data storage, as well as the server side and the client side of SAWT.

2.1   Data storage

Data storage relies on a MySQL database. One table in the database is used to store the annotator accounts. At present, there is no separate admin role, all users are annotators and cannot see or modify what the other annotators are doing.

The annotation of a text with a label set by a given user requires two MySQL tables. One table contains the actual text which is to be annotated by the user, and the other table receives the annotation; this table pair is associated with the user account which is stored in the user table mentioned above. In the first table, we store one document per row. We use the first column for a unique ID; the text is put in the second column. It is white-space tokenized at the moment it is loaded into the annotation interface (see below). In the second table, we store the annotation. Again, the document ID is put into the first column. The labels are stored in the remaining columns (one column per label).

2.2   Server side and administration

The complete code of SAWT will be distributed on github. The distribution will contain the complete web application code, as well as two Python scripts to be used for configuration.

The first script configures the SAWT installation and the database. It takes a configuration file as parameter (the distribution will contain a configuration file template), in which the following parameters must be specified:

- *List of tags*: A space-separated list of tags to be used in the annotation. From this list, the PHP code for the model and the view are generated which handle the final form in the interface. The generated code is then copied to the correct locations within the complete web application code.

- *Server information*: MySQL server IP, port and user account information.

- *Predictor*: The interface can show suggestions for each token, provided that a suitable sequence labeling software with a pre-trained model runs on the web server. If suggestions are desired, then in the configuration file, the corresponding path and parameters for the software must be given. If the parameter is left blank, no suggestions are shown.

- *Search box activation*: A boolean parameter indicating if a search box is desired. In the search box, the annotator can look up his previous annotations for a certain token.

- *Utility links*: The top border of the user interface consists of a link bar, the links for which can be freely configured. In our project, e.g., they are used for linking to the list of Universal POS tags (Petrov et al., 2012), to a list of Arabic function words, to an Arabic Morphological Analyzer (MADAMIRA) (Pasha et al., 2014), and to an Arabic screen keyboard, as can be seen in figures 2 and 3.

Once the configuration script has been run, the web application code must be copied to a suitable place within a web server installation.

In order to upload a text which is to be annotated by a certain user, the second script must be used. It takes the following command line parameters.

- *Input data*: The name of the file containing the data to be annotated. The text must be pre-tokenized (one space between each token), and there must be one document per line.

- *Server information*: MySQL server IP, port, and user account information.

- *Annotator information*: Annotator user name. If the annotator account does not exist in the respective database table, it is created, and a password must be specified.

Of course, this script can be used any number of times. At runtime, it will connect to the database and create two tables for the annotation (as mentioned above, one for the data itself and one for the annotation). It will insert the data in the first one, and insert the user account in the user account table, if necessary.

In general, for security reasons, two different servers should be used for front-end (web application) and back-end (database), but in principle, nothing stands in the way of installing everything on a single machine or even locally.

2.3 Client side and annotator interface

The client side interface is written with several technologies. As a basis, we have used a MVC PHP framework, namely CodeIgniter version 3.0.[2] Furthermore, in order to achieve a responsive mobile-ready design, we have employed to the Bootstrap framework, HTML 5, and JQuery.[3]

When accessing the URL where SAWT is located, the annotator is queried its user name and password. After logging in, the annotation interface is shown. On top of the page, a link bar makes available several tools which are useful for the annotation, to be freely configured during installation (see above). If configured (see above), a search box is shown, in which the annotator can look up his previous annotations of a token. In a top line above the text, the ID of the

document is shown, the number of tokens to be annotated, and the annotation progress, i.e., the number of tokens which have already been annotated (in previous documents). Also it is shown if the current document itself has already been annotated. Finally, there are buttons to navigate within the documents (first, previous, next, last).

For the annotation, the interface pulls the first document to be annotated from the database, applies white-space tokenization, and renders it for presentation to the user. The material to be annotated is presented with one document per page and token per line. Each line has four columns, the first one showing the absolute token ID within the complete corpus, the second one showing the token to be annotated, the third one showing a prediction of a possible tag (if configured), and the fourth one showing the possible labels. There is an edit facility, in which the annotator can correct an erroneous tokenization of the document. If an edit is performed, the modified document is white-space tokenized again and reloaded in the interface.

For label selection, we offer check-boxes. Even though radio buttons would seem to be the more natural choice, check-boxes allow us to assign several tags to a single token. This is, e.g., essential for Part-of-Speech annotation in Arabic: Due to a rich morphology, a single word can incorporate several POS functions (Habash, 2010). When the user has finished the annotation of a document, a button must be clicked. This button first triggers a validation function which checks the annotation for completeness. If there are tokens which have not been annotated, a colored alert bar is shown. Otherwise, a form is submitted which saves the annotation in the database; then the next document is loaded and rendered for annotation. We have implemented the policy that an annotator cannot change the annotation of a document once it is submitted. However, a minimal change in the code could allow a post-editing of the annotation.

We have tested the interface extensively in Google Chrome (on both PC and Android) and Mozilla Firefox.

As an example, figure 2 shows a screenshot of the annotator interface configured for Part-of-Speech annotation with the Google Universal Part-of-Speech tag set (Petrov et al., 2012). Figure 3

---

[2]http://codeigniter.net
[3]http://jquery.com

Figure 1: Screenshot of SAWT: Annotation on Android device

shows a screenshot of code-switching annotation done in the context of our earlier work (Samih and Maier, 2016). Finally, figure 1 shows a screenshot of the POS annotation interface used on the Asus Nexus 7 2013 tablet running Google Chrome on Android 6.

3 Related Work

As mentioned above, we are not aware of a software which would have fulfilled our needs exactly. Previously released annotation software can be grouped into several categories.

Systems such as GATE (Cunningham et al., 2002), CLaRK (Simov et al., 2003) and MMAX2 (Müller and Strube, 2006) are desktop-based software. They offer a large range of functions, and are in general oriented towards more complex annotation tasks, such as syntactic treebank annotation.

In the context of Arabic dialect annotation, several systems have been created. COLANN_GUI (Benajiba and Diab, 2010), which unfortunately was not available to us, is a web application that specialized on dialect annotation. DIWAN (Al-Shargi and Rambow, 2015) is a desktop application for dialect annotation which can be used online.

The systems that came closest to our needs were WebANNO (Yimam et al., 2013) and BRAT (Stenetorp et al., 2012). Both are web-based and built with modern technologies. They allow for a multi-layered annotation, including a token-wise annotation. However, we decided against them due to fact that we just needed the token-wise annotation and we wanted the simplest annotator interface possible. For just sequence annotation, our annotator interface allows for a very high speed, since only one click per token is required.

4 Conclusion

We have presented SAWT, a web-based tool for sequence annotation. The main priorities of the tool are ease of use on the client side and a low requirements for the server side.

SAWT is under active development. We are currently simplifying the installation process on server side and plan to offer an admin role in the front-end. Furthermore, we want to provide a way of obtaining the annotation in a standardized format (TEI) directly from the database.

Acknowledgments

We would like to thank Ikram Zeraa and Miloud Samih for enlightening discussions and the three anonymous reviewers for helpful comments and suggestions. The authors were partially funded by Deutsche Forschungsgemeinschaft (DFG).

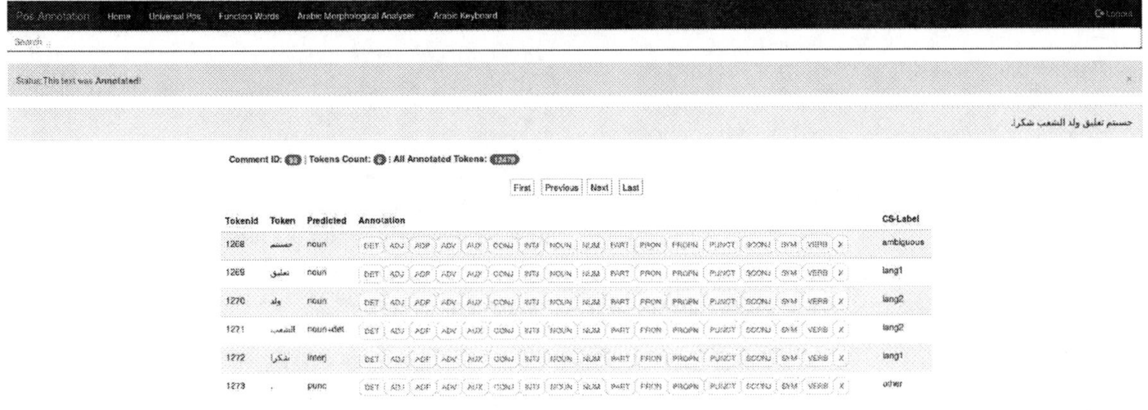

Figure 2: Screenshot of SAWT: Annotation with Universal Part Of Speech tags

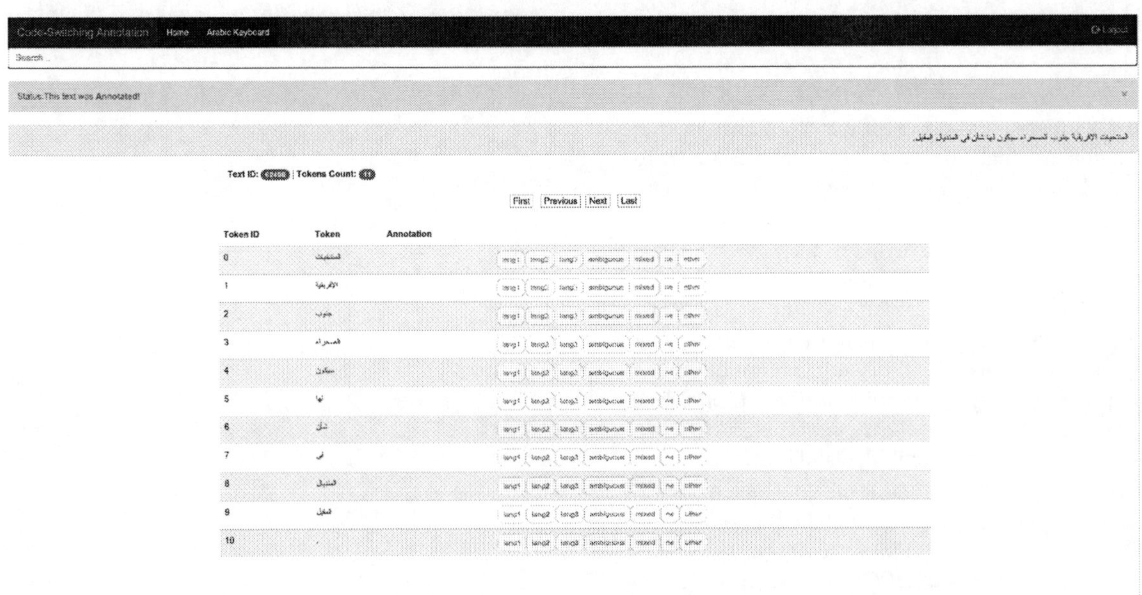

Figure 3: Screenshot of SAWT: Annotation with code-switching labels

References

Faisal Al-Shargi and Owen Rambow. 2015. Diwan: A dialectal word annotation tool for Arabic. In *Proceedings of the Second Workshop on Arabic Natural Language Processing*, pages 49–58, Beijing, China. Association for Computational Linguistics.

Yassine Benajiba and Mona Diab. 2010. A web application for dialectal Arabic text annotation. In *Proceedings of the LREC Workshop for Language Resources (LRs) and Human Language Technologies (HLT) for Semitic Languages: Status, Updates, and Prospects*, Valletta, Malta. ELRA.

Barbara E. Bullock and Almeida Jacqueline Toribio. 2009. *The Cambridge handbook of linguistic code-switching*. Cambridge University Press.

Hamish Cunningham, Diana Maynard, Kalina Bontcheva, and Valentin Tablan. 2002. Gate: an architecture for development of robust hlt applications. In *Proceedings of the 40th annual meeting on association for computational linguistics*, pages 168–175. Association for Computational Linguistics.

Mona Diab, Nizar Habash, Owen Rambow, Mohamed Altantawy, and Yassine Benajiba. 2010. COLABA: Arabic dialect annotation and processing. *Proceedings of the LREC Workshop for Language Resources (LRs) and Human Language Technologies (HLT) for Semitic Languages: Status, Updates, and Prospects*, pages 66–74.

Charles Ferguson. 1959. Diglossia. *Word*, 15:325–340.

Nizar Y. Habash. 2010. Introduction to Arabic natural language processing. *Synthesis Lectures on Human Language Technologies*, 3(1):1–187.

Christoph Müller and Michael Strube. 2006. Multi-level annotation of linguistic data with mmax2. *Corpus technology and language pedagogy: New resources, new tools, new methods*, 3:197–214.

Arfath Pasha, Mohamed Al-Badrashiny, Mona Diab, Ahmed El Kholy, Ramy Eskander, Nizar Habash, Manoj Pooleery, Owen Rambow, and Ryan Roth. 2014. Madamira: A fast, comprehensive tool for morphological analysis and disambiguation of arabic. In *Proceedings of the Ninth International Conference on Language Resources and Evaluation (LREC'14)*, pages 1094–1101, Reykjavik, Iceland.

Slav Petrov, Dipanjan Das, and Ryan McDonald. 2012. A universal part-of-speech tagset. In *Proceedings of the Eight International Conference on Language Resources and Evaluation (LREC)*, Istanbul, Turkey.

Younes Samih and Wolfgang Maier. 2016. An arabic-moroccan darija code-switched corpus. In *Proceedings of the Tenth International Conference on Language Resources and Evaluation (LREC 2016)*, Portoroz, Slovenia.

Kiril Simov, Alexander Simov, Milen Kouylekov, Krasimira Ivanova, Ilko Grigorov, and Hristo Ganev. 2003. Development of corpora within the CLaRK system: The BulTreeBank project experience. In *Proceedings of the tenth conference on European chapter of the Association for Computational Linguistics-Volume 2*, pages 243–246. Association for Computational Linguistics.

Thamar Solorio, Elizabeth Blair, Suraj Maharjan, Steven Bethard, Mona Diab, Mahmoud Ghoneim, Abdelati Hawwari, Fahad AlGhamdi, Julia Hirschberg, Alison Chang, and Pascale Fung. 2014. Overview for the first shared task on language identification in code-switched data. In *Proceedings of the First Workshop on Computational Approaches to Code Switching*, pages 62–72, Doha, Qatar.

Pontus Stenetorp, Sampo Pyysalo, Goran Topić, Tomoko Ohta, Sophia Ananiadou, and Jun'ichi Tsujii. 2012. brat: a web-based tool for nlp-assisted text annotation. In *Proceedings of the Demonstrations at the 13th Conference of the European Chapter of the Association for Computational Linguistics*, pages 102–107, Avignon, France, April. Association for Computational Linguistics.

Seid Muhie Yimam, Iryna Gurevych, Richard Eckart de Castilho, and Chris Biemann. 2013. Webanno: A flexible, web-based and visually supported system for distributed annotations. In *Proceedings of the 51st Annual Meeting of the Association for Computational Linguistics: System Demonstrations*, pages 1–6, Sofia, Bulgaria, August. Association for Computational Linguistics.

Accurate Pinyin-English Codeswitched Language Identification

Meng Xuan Xia and **Jackie Chi Kit Cheung**
McGill University
3480 University, Rm. 318
Montreal, Quebec H3A 0E9, Canada
`meng.xia@mail.mcgill.ca, jcheung@cs.mcgill.ca`

Abstract

Pinyin is the most widely used romanization scheme for Mandarin Chinese. We consider the task of language identification in Pinyin-English codeswitched texts, a task that is significant because of its application to codeswitched text input. We create a codeswitched corpus by extracting and automatically labeling existing Mandarin-English codeswitched corpora. On language identification, we find that SVM produces the best result when using word-level segmentation, achieving 99.3% F1 on a Weibo dataset, while a linear-chain CRF produces the best result at the letter level, achieving 98.2% F1. We then pass the output of our models to a system that converts Pinyin back to Chinese characters to simulate codeswitched text input. Our method achieves the same level of performance as an oracle system that has perfect knowledge of token-level language identity. This result demonstrates that Pinyin identification is not the bottleneck towards developing a Chinese-English codeswitched Input Method Editor, and future work should focus on the Pinyin-to-Chinese character conversion step.

1 Introduction

As more people are connected to the Internet around the world, an increasing number of multilingual texts can be found, especially in informal, online platforms such as Twitter and Weibo[1](Ling et al., 2013). In this paper, we focus on short Mandarin-English mixed texts, in particular those that involve intra-sentential *codeswitching*, in which the two languages are interleaved within a single utterance or sentence. Example 1 shows one such case, including the original codeswitched text (CS), and its Mandarin (MAN) and English (EN) translations:

(1) CS: 这个thermal exchanger的thermal
conductivity太低.
MAN: 这个换热器的热传导系数太低.
EN: The thermal conductivity of this thermal
exchanger is too low.

A natural first step in processing codeswitched text is to identify which parts of the text are expressed in which language, as having an accurate codeswitched language identification system seems to be a crucial building block for further processing such as POS tagging. Recently, Solorio et al. (2014) organized the first shared task towards this goal. The task is to identify the languages in codeswitched social media data in several language pairs, including Mandarin-English (MAN-EN). Since Chinese characters are assigned a different Unicode encoding range than Latin-script languages like English, identifying MAN-EN codeswitched data is relatively straightforward. In fact, the baseline system in the shared task, which simply stores the vocabularies of the two languages seen during training, already achieves 90% F1 on identifying Mandarin segments. Most of the remaining errors are due to misclassifying English segments and named entities, which constitute a separate class in the shared task.

We focus in this paper on performing language identification between Pinyin and English,

---

[1]Weibo is a micro-blogging service similar to Twitter that is widely used in China.

71

Proceedings of the Second Workshop on Computational Approaches to Code Switching, pages 71–79,
Austin, TX, November 1, 2016. ©2016 Association for Computational Linguistics

where Pinyin is the most widely used romanization schemes for Mandarin. It is the official standard in the People's Republic of China and in Singapore. It is also the most widely used method for Mandarin speaking users to input Chinese characters using Latin-script keyboards. Example 2 shows the same codeswitched sentence, in which the Chinese characters have been converted to Pinyin:

(2) *Zhege* Thermal Exchanger *de* Thermal Conductivity *taidi.*

Distinguishing Pinyin from English or other languages written with the Roman alphabet is an important problem with strong practical motivations. Learners of both English and Chinese could benefit from a system that allows them to input codeswitched text (Chung, 2002). More generally, accurate Pinyin-English codeswitched language identification could allow users to input Mandarin-English codeswitched text more easily. A Chinese Input Method Editor (IME) system that detects Pinyin and converts it into the appropriate Chinese characters would save users from having to repeatedly toggle between the two languages when typing on a standard Latin-script keyboard.

Since Pinyin is written with the same character set as English[2], character encoding is no longer a reliable indicator of language. For example, *she, long,* and *bang* are Pinyin syllables that are also English words. *Tisane* is a English word, and is also a concatenation of three valid Pinyin syllables: *ti, sa,* and *ne.* Thus, contextual information will be needed to resolve the identity of the language.

Our contributions are as follows. First, we construct two datasets of Pinyin-English codeswitched data by converting the Chinese characters in Mandarin-English codeswitched data sets to Pinyin, and propose a new task to distinguish Pinyin from English in this codeswitched text. Then, we compare several approaches to solving this task. We consider the level of performance when training the model at the level of words versus individual letters[3] in order to see whether having word

---

[2]We consider the version of Pinyin without tone diacritics, which is very common in Chinese IMEs.

[3]We chose the term letter rather than character to avoid confusion with the use of character as in Chinese characters.

boundaries would affect performance. Two standard classification methods, SVMs and linear-chain CRFs are compared for both settings. We find that SVM produces better results on the word-level setting, achieving 99.3% F1 on a Weibo dataset. CRF produces better results on the letter-level setting, achieving 98.2% F1 on the same dataset. Lastly, we pass the output of our models to a system that converts Pinyin back to Chinese characters as an extrinsic evaluation. The result shows that word-level models produce better conversion performance. Our automatic conversion method achieves the same level of performance as an oracle system with perfect knowledge of token-level language identity. This result demonstrates that Pinyin identification is not the bottleneck towards developing a Chinese-English codeswitched IME, and that future work should focus on the Pinyin-to-Chinese character conversion step.

2 Related Work

Several models for MAN-EN codeswitched language identification were developed as part of the *First Shared Task on Language Identification in Codeswitched Data* (Chittaranjan et al., 2014; King et al., 2014). The most common technique was to employ supervised machine learning algorithms (e.g., extended Markov Models and Conditional Random Field) to train a classifier.

Codeswitched language identification has been previously studied with other language pairs, (Carter et al., 2013; Nguyen and Dogruoz, 2014; Vyas et al., 2014; Das and Gambäck, 2013; Voss et al., 2014). However, very few articles discuss codeswitched Pinyin-English input specifically. There has been research on improving the error tolerance of Pinyin-based IME. Chen and Lee (2000) propose a statistical segmentation and a trigram-based language model to convert Pinyin sequences into Chinese character sequences in a manner that is robust to single-character Pinyin misspellings. They also propose a paradigm called *modeless Pinyin* that tries to eliminate the necessity of toggling on and off the Pinyin input method. While their modeless Pinyin works on Pinyin generating a single Chinese character or a single English word, our experiments in this paper attempt to generate *an entire sequence* of Chinese characters and English words.

Research in improving the codeswitched text input experience also exists for other languages that use a non-alphabetic writing system, such as Japanese. Ikegami and Tsuruta (2015) propose a modeless Japanese input method that automatically switches the input mode using models with n-gram based binary classification and dictionary.

3 Task and Dataset

3.1 Task Definition

Given a Pinyin-English codeswitched input as shown in Example 2, the main task is to identify the segments of the input that are in Pinyin as *pinyin*, segments that are in English as *non-pinyin*, punctuation and whitespaces as *other* as shown in Example 3. The *other* label is used to tag tokens that do not represent actual words in both languages.

(3) Input:

Zhege␣Thermal␣Exchanger␣de␣Thermal␣Conductivity␣taidi.

Output:

Zhege␣**Thermal␣Exchanger**␣*de*␣**Thermal ␣Conductivity**␣*taidi.*

Segments in bold, italic and underlined are labeled as *non-pinyin*, *pinyin* and *others*, respectively.

Separating *other* label from *non-pinyin* prevents such tokens identifiable using a simple dictionary method from artificially inflating the performance of the models during evaluation.

We do not follow the annotation scheme of the shared task in putting named entities into their own class (Solorio et al., 2014). In the Pinyin-English case, named entities clearly belong to either the *pinyin* class or the *non-pinyin* class, and Pinyin named entities would eventually need to be converted to Chinese characters in any case. Furthermore, named entity annotations are not available in the Weibo corpus that we construct.

3.2 Corpus Construction

We created two Pinyin-English codeswitched corpora automatically, by converting Mandarin-English codeswitched data. Our Mandarin-English corpora are obtained via two sources.

ENMLP We used the training data provided by the First Workshop on Computational Approaches to Code Switching of EMNLP 2014 (Solorio et al., 2014). The workshop provides a codeswitched Mandarin-English training data that contains 1000 tweets crawled from Twitter. The Chinese part of the data is in traditional Chinese.

WEIBO We downloaded 102995 Weibo entries using Cnpameng (Liang et al., 2014), a freely available Weibo crawler. Most of the entries are written in Simplified Chinese. Only a small proportion of the entries (about 1%) contain Mandarin-English codeswitched content. We removed entries that are not codeswitched and sampled 3000 of the remaining entries. In this corpus, most tokens are Chinese, with only one or two English words embedded. Chinese characters account for about 95% of the tokens.

Preprocessing and labeling The Mandarin-English codeswitching corpora are not directly usable in our experiments; we need to first convert the Chinese characters to Pinyin. We used *jieba*[4], a library for segmenting a Chinese sentence into a list of Chinese words. For each word, we used *pypinyin*[5], a Python library that converts Chinese words, both Traditional Chinese and Simplified Chinese, into Pinyin. We then label each Pinyin sequence as *pinyin*, white spaces and punctuation as *other*, and English words as *non-pinyin*, as described above.

The Mandarin-English codeswitched data we collected all contain short sentences[6]. This was by design, as we are interested in intra-sentential codeswitching. We expect that inter-sentential

---

[4]https://github.com/fxsjy/jieba
[5]https://github.com/mozillazg/python-pinyin
[6]Twitter and Weibo impose 140 max characters per microblog

Segmentation	Label	Count	Percentage
word-based	pinyin	2704	52.4%
	non-pinyin	716	13.8%
	others	1736	33.8%
letter-based	pinyin	12619	69.8%
	non-pinyin	3659	20.3%
	others	1777	9.9%

Table 1: Frequency count of labels on EMNLP corpus

Segmentation	Label	Count	Percentage
word-based	pinyin	16883	61.3%
	non-pinyin	1506	5.5%
	others	8970	33.2%
letter-based	pinyin	84305	84.6%
	non-pinyin	6294	6.3%
	others	9105	9.1%

Table 2: Frequency count of labels on WEIBO corpus

codeswitching would not require frequent Pinyin IME mode toggling, and labeling them for their language would also be easier.

The frequency counts of each label in the EMNLP corpus and the WEIBO corpus are shown in Tables 1 and 2, respectively.

4 Models

We propose two classes of models to solve the task: Word-Based Models and Letter-Based Models. They differ in how the input is segmented. We compared these two segmentation schemes with the goal to test whether automatic Pinyin word segmentation is needed to accurately identify Pinyin and English tokens.

Word-Based Models (WBM) The input is segmented into one of (1) a Pinyin sequence representing Chinese words[7], (2) an English word, or (3) other (space and punctuation). Each chunk is labeled as one of *pinyin*, *non-pinyin* or *other*. The Pinyin sequences representing Chinese words are indirectly segmented according to the word segmentation of

---

[7]Note that a Chinese word can be either a single Chinese character or a concatenation of multiple Chinese characters.

the corresponding Mandarin characters. Example 3 illustrates the WBM.

Letter-Based Models (LBM) The input is segmented into individual letters. Each letter is labeled as one of *pinyin*, *non-pinyin* or *other*.

For each of the schemes above, we experimented with two discriminative supervised machine learning algorithms: Support Vector Machines (SVMs) and linear-chain Conditional Random Fields (CRFs). We chose to experiment with SVMs and CRFs in order to see whether a standard classification approach suffices or if a sequence model is needed. These methods have also been shown to perform well in previous work on language identification tasks (King and Abney, 2013; Chittaranjan et al., 2014; Lin et al., 2014; Bar and Dershowitz, 2014; Goutte et al., 2014).

4.1 Feature Extraction

We selected features to pass into our models by drawing upon recent work in codeswitched language identification (Chittaranjan et al., 2014; Lin et al., 2014; Nguyen and Dogruoz, 2014). We explored a number of different options for features, and the final set was chosen based on performance on a held-out development set, as follows.

Word-Based Models (WBM) The following features were chosen for each segment s:

- Identity of s, converted to lower case
- Whether s is a legal sequence of Pinyin
- Whether s is upper-cased
- Whether s is capitalized
- Whether s is a number
- The token occurring prior to s in the sequence
- The token occurring after to s in the sequence

Letter-Based Models (LBM) The following features were chosen for each segment t:

- Identity of t, converted to lower case
- Whether t is upper-cased
- Whether t is a number
- The token occurring prior to t in the sequence
- The token occurring after to t in the sequence

We initially experimented with several other features, but found that they did not improve performance on the development set, so we did not include them in the final system. In the WBM setting, we tried adding Part-Of-Speech (POS) tags as features, but found that existing POS taggers do not handle codeswitched data well. For both WBM and LBM, we tried to add a boolean feature to indicate whether the segment is at the start or end of the input but this turned out to be unhelpful.

4.2 Baseline Dictionary-Based Method

We compared these methods against a baseline, which labels a concatenation of valid Pinyin syllables[8] as *pinyin*, whitespaces and punctuation as *others* and the rest as *non-pinyin*.

5 Experiment 1: Language Identification

We tested our models on the two codeswitching corpora that we created. We split each corpus into training (80%) and testing (20%) subsets. We also created a held-out development set by randomly sampling 100 entries from EMNLP corpus, and used it to select the feature sets described in Section 4.1. We kept the same set of features for the WEIBO corpus, without performing any additional tuning.

We trained the CRF model using CRF-suite (Okazaki, 2007) and the SVM model using Scikit-learn (Pedregosa et al., 2011). The models were tested using commonly defined evaluation measures — Precision, Recall and F1 (Powers, 2011) at the word level for WBMs and at the letter level for LBMs.

5.1 Results

As shown in Table 3, all the WBM machine learning algorithms performed better than the baseline. The average P, R and F1 for each model were calculated without taking into account the values from the *other* label. This prevents the *other* class, which

______

[8]We used the list of 411 valid symbols available at
`https://github.com/someus/Pinyin2Hanzi/`
`blob/master/Pinyin2Hanzi/util.py#L127`

can largely be predicted by whether the segment is a whitespace or punctuation character, from artificially inflating results. The SVM-WBM model performed the best with an F1 of 0.980 on EMNLP corpus and 0.993 on WEIBO corpus. In LBM settings, only CRF outperformed the baseline with an F1 of 0.962 on the EMNLP corpus and 0.982 on the WEIBO corpus.

Note that the baseline F1 for the *other* class is not at 1.0 because baseline method's dictionary of punctuation and whitespace characters were constructed from the training set, and does not exhaustively cover all possible characters of this class.

Since there is, to our knowledge, no previous study on Pinyin-English codeswitched text input, we cannot perform direct comparison against existing work. In terms of similar tasks involving codeswitched text, the top-performing MAN-EN language identification system achieved an F1 of 0.892 (Chittaranjan et al., 2014), but the annotation scheme includes a category for named entities. Ikegami and Tsuruta (2015) achieved an F1 of 0.97 on codeswitched Japanese-English text input using an n-gram-based approach.

In the WEIBO corpus, the F1 performances of the models are very high, at up to 0.982 and 0.993. This could be because each entry in the Weibo corpus contains only one or two occurrences of single English words embedded into a sequence of Pinyin. The non-pinyin words are often proper nouns (these tokens are often capitalized), English words or acronyms that do not have a translation in Chinese. In this context, it is less common to see English words that are also valid Pinyin.

While SVM performs the best with WBM, it does not perform as well with LBM. The lower performance of SVM-LBM is caused by the limited access to contextual information (only the letter directly before and after each token). By contrast, CRF-LBM can naturally take into account the sequence ordering information. This result shows that a sequence model like CRF is needed for LBM.

Model	label	P	R	F1
baseline	non-pinyin	0.762	0.875	0.815
	pinyin	0.962	0.950	0.956
	other	0.986	0.945	0.965
	avg / total	0.920	0.934	0.926
SVM-WBM	non-pinyin	0.967	0.944	0.956
	pinyin	0.980	0.992	0.986
	other	0.990	0.980	0.985
	avg / total	**0.977**	**0.982**	**0.980**
CRF-WBM	non-pinyin	0.948	0.919	0.934
	pinyin	0.981	0.989	0.985
	other	0.974	0.974	0.974
	avg / total	0.974	0.974	0.974

(a) WBM performance on EMNLP corpus

Model	label	P	R	F1
baseline	non-pinyin	0.865	0.880	0.872
	pinyin	0.965	0.965	0.965
	other	0.986	0.948	0.967
	avg / total	0.943	0.946	0.944
SVM-LBM	non-pinyin	0.785	0.612	0.688
	pinyin	0.893	0.953	0.922
	other	0.995	0.968	0.982
	avg / total	0.869	0.877	0.870
CRF-LBM	non-pinyin	0.930	0.902	0.916
	pinyin	0.969	0.982	0.975
	other	0.995	0.959	0.977
	avg / total	**0.960**	**0.964**	**0.962**

(b) LBM performance on EMNLP corpus

Model	label	P	R	F1
baseline	non-pinyin	0.510	0.905	0.652
	pinyin	0.990	0.948	0.969
	other	0.991	0.941	0.965
	avg / total	0.951	0.945	0.943
SVM-WBM	non-pinyin	0.973	0.948	0.960
	pinyin	0.995	0.996	0.996
	other	0.992	0.995	0.994
	avg / total	**0.993**	**0.992**	**0.993**
CRF-WBM	non-pinyin	0.963	0.913	0.937
	pinyin	0.992	0.995	0.994
	other	0.989	0.992	0.991
	avg / total	0.990	0.988	0.989

(c) WBM performance on WEIBO corpus

Model	label	P	R	F1
Baseline	non-pinyin	0.632	0.920	0.749
	pinyin	0.993	0.966	0.979
	other	0.990	0.935	0.962
	avg / total	0.968	0.963	0.963
SVM-LBM	non-pinyin	0.932	0.565	0.703
	pinyin	0.967	0.997	0.982
	other	1.000	0.987	0.993
	avg / total	0.965	0.967	0.963
CRF-LBM	non-pinyin	0.929	0.820	0.871
	pinyin	0.986	0.995	0.990
	other	0.997	0.988	0.992
	avg / total	**0.982**	**0.983**	**0.982**

(d) LBM performance on WEIBO corpus

Table 3: The performance of the models in terms of precision (P), recall (R), and F1, for each of the three classes. The avg/total row represents the average of the pinyin and non-pinyin classes, weighted by their frequencies in the dataset. We excluded the *other* category from the avg, because that class mostly consists of whitespace and punctuation.

5.2 Discussion and error analysis

We consider here the causes of the remaining errors. First, some errors are due to segments that are both legal English words and legal Pinyin sequences, as discussed in Section 4.2. For example, *you (有)*, a word that occurs both in Mandarin and English with high frequency, is difficult for our models. Having additional POS information available to the models would be helpful, as 有 is a verb in Mandarin, while *you* is a pronoun in English.

Another source of errors is the presence of mixed Pinyin, Chinese characters and English *within individual words*. These errors are often found in user names (i.e., Twitter handlers). For example:

(4) @*eggchen* 呼叫nico我完全不到你耶

The twitter handle *eggchen*, labeled as *non-pinyin* in the gold standard, is a concatenation of English word *egg* and raw Pinyin *chen*. With CRF-LBM, since the word boundary information was not available, CRF-LBM wrongly labels *chen* as *pinyin*, separated from *eggchen*.

Finally, the LBMs sometimes fail to correctly predict codeswitching boundaries. Taking an example in the dataset: "desledge" was an input sequence where "de" has gold standard label pinyin and "sledge" has gold standard label non-pinyin. In the CRF-WBM, the word boundary information is given, so the model is able to predict the labels correctly. The CRF-LEMB model predicted that the entire sequence "deseldge" is "non-pinyin".

6 Experiment 2: Converting Pinyin to Chinese characters

Next, we experimented with converting the Pinyin-English codeswitched inputs back to the original Mandarin-English sentences in an end-to-end, extrinsic evaluation. Pinyin is the most widely used method for Mandarin users to input Chinese characters using Latin-script keyboards. Improvements in the language identification step transfer over to the next step of Chinese characters generation.

Converting Pinyin to Chinese characters is not an easy task, as there are many possible Chinese characters for each Pinyin syllable. Modern Pinyin Input Methods use statistical methods to rank the possible character candidates in descending probability and predict the top-ranked candidate as the output (Chen and Lee, 2000; Zheng et al., 2011).

Task Given a Pinyin-English codeswitched input and the corresponding labels produced by our codeswitched language identification models, produce Mandarin-English codeswitched output by converting the parts labelled as Pinyin to Chinese characters.

Method We use a representative approach that models the conversion from Pinyin to Chinese characters as a Hidden Markov model (HMM), in which Chinese characters are the hidden states and Pinyin syllables are the observations. The model is trained from *SogouT* corpus (Liu et al., 2012), and the Viterbi algorithm is used to generate the final output.

We used a Python implementation of this model[9] to convert *pinyin* segments to Chinese characters while leaving *others* and *non-pinyin* segments unchanged.

We use the Pinyin-English codeswitched input, paired with language identification labels from Baseline, SVM-WBM, or CRF-LBM to generate Mandarin-English codeswitched output. We then evaluated these outputs against the gold standard by measuring precision, recall, and F1 on the Chinese characters. We also compare against an oracle topline, which has perfect knowledge of the segmentation of the input into Pinyin vs non-Pinyin. For the CRF-LBM, we used the Smith–Waterman algorithm (Smith and Waterman, 1981) to align the output produced by the CRF-LBM method with the gold-standard words.

6.1 Results

Model	P	R	F1
Oracle	*0.576*	*0.576*	*0.576*
Baseline	0.511	0.576	0.541
SVM-WBM	**0.571**	**0.562**	**0.566**
CRF-LBM	0.405	0.407	0.406

Table 4: Performance of generated Mandarin-English codeswitched sentences – EMNLP Corpus

Model	P	R	F1
Oracle	*0.590*	*0.590*	*0.590*
Baseline	0.564	0.590	0.578
SVM-WBM	**0.589**	**0.590**	**0.590**
CRF-LBM	0.491	0.511	0.500

Table 5: Performance of generated Mandarin-English codeswitched sentences – WEIBO Corpus

As shown in Tables 4 and 5, with SVM-WBM, the F1 of the generated Mandarin-English codeswitched outputs are better than the baseline in both corpora for all labels, and achieves a level of performance close to the oracle method. This result shows that our contribution to accurate language identification in transliteration codeswitching pairs is able to improve the performance of Pinyin IME in codeswitching context. Furthermore, the result demonstrates

---

[9]*Pinyin2Hanzi*: `https://github.com/someus/Pinyin2Hanzi`.

that Pinyin identification is not the bottleneck towards developing a Chinese-English codeswitched IME, at least if word boundary information is given. Future work should focus on the Pinyin-to-Chinese character conversion step.

The higher performance of the WBM models compared to the LBM models suggests that having correct word boundaries is crucial for identifying Pinyin-English codeswitched input at higher accuracies.

Note that F1 measure of both the oracle, Baseline and SVM-WBM models are better in WEIBO corpus in comparison to EMNLP corpus. This is backed by their higher F1-measure in the language identification step.

6.2   Error analysis

There is much room for improvement in the results. Despite CRF-LBM achieving higher than Baseline F1-measure in the language identification steps, the Mandarin-English generation accuracy of CRF-LBM is lower than baseline. The sources of this lower accuracy are the following:

Presence of mixed raw pinyin.   As described in Section 5.2, CRF-LBM labels the majority of raw pinyin as "pinyin". Consequently, it made the mistake of converting them to Chinese characters where they should not be.

Failure to properly predict codeswitching word boundary.   An example was given previously in Section 5.2. Each failure in predicting codeswitching word boundary produces two errors, one for the first word and one for the second. This double penalty explains why despite of CRF-LBM having higher F1 than baseline in experiment 1, it is doing worse than baseline in experiment 2.

7   Conclusion

Having an accurate codeswitched language identification system serves as a crucial building block for further processing such as POS tagging. Our results on Pinyin-English codeswitched language identification experiments provide novel contributions to language identifications on transliteration pairs. We find that SVM performs the best at the word level while CRF performs the best at the letter level.

In the second experiment, we developed an automatic method that converts Pinyin-English codeswitched text to Mandarin-English text as an extrinsic evaluation of our models. We showed that word-level models produce better conversion performance. One of our automatic word-level methods achieves the same level of performance as an oracle system that has perfect knowledge of token-level language identity. This result demonstrates that Pinyin identification is not the bottleneck towards developing a Chinese-English codeswitched IME, and future work should focus on the Pinyin-to-Chinese character conversion step.

Our approach could also be considered for other languages with non-Latin-based writing systems and a corresponding romanization scheme, such as Japanese and Romaji (Krueger and Neeson, 2000).

References

Kfir Bar and Nachum Dershowitz. 2014. The Tel Aviv University System for the Code-Switching Workshop Shared Task. *EMNLP 2014*, page 139.

Simon Carter, Wouter Weerkamp, and Manos Tsagkias. 2013. Microblog language identification: Overcoming the limitations of short, unedited and idiomatic text. *Language Resources and Evaluation*, 47(1):195–215.

Zheng Chen and Kai-Fu Lee. 2000. A new statistical approach to Chinese Pinyin input. In *Proceedings of the 38th annual meeting on association for computational linguistics*, pages 241–247. Association for Computational Linguistics.

Gokul Chittaranjan, Yogarshi Vyas, and Kalika Bali Monojit Choudhury. 2014. Word-level language identification using CRF: Code-switching shared task report of MSR India system. In *Proceedings of The First Workshop on Computational Approaches to Code Switching*, pages 73–79.

Kevin KH Chung. 2002. Effective use of Hanyu Pinyin and English translations as extra stimulus prompts on learning of Chinese characters. *Educational Psychology*, 22(2):149–164.

Amitava Das and Björn Gambäck. 2013. Code-Mixing in Social Media Text. The Last Language Identification Frontier? *Traitement Automatique des Langues (TAL): Special Issue on Social Networks and NLP, TAL*, 54(3):41–64.

Cyril Goutte, Serge Léger, and Marine Carpuat. 2014. The NRC system for discriminating similar languages. In *Proceedings of the First Workshop on Applying NLP Tools to Similar Languages, Varieties and Dialects*, pages 139–145.

Yukino Ikegami and Setsuo Tsuruta. 2015. Hybrid method for modeless Japanese input using N-gram based binary classification and dictionary. *Multimedia Tools and Applications*, 74(11):3933–3946.

Ben King and Steven P Abney. 2013. Labeling the Languages of Words in Mixed-Language Documents using Weakly Supervised Methods.

Levi King, Sandra Kübler, and Wallace Hooper. 2014. Word-level language identification in The Chymistry of Isaac Newton. *Digital Scholarship in the Humanities*, page fqu032.

Mark Henry Krueger and Kevin Daniel Neeson. 2000. Japanese text input method using a limited roman character set, August 1. US Patent 6,098,086.

Bin Liang, Yiqun Liu, Min Zhang, Shaoping Ma, Liyun Ru, and Kuo Zhang. 2014. Searching for people to follow in social networks. *Expert Systems with Applications*, 41(16):7455–7465.

Chu-Cheng Lin, Waleed Ammar, Lori Levin, and Chris Dyer. 2014. The CMU submission for the shared task on language identification in code-switched data. In *Proceedings of the First Workshop on Computational Approaches to Code Switching*, pages 80–86.

Wang Ling, Guang Xiang, Chris Dyer, Alan W Black, and Isabel Trancoso. 2013. Microblogs as Parallel Corpora. *ACL (1)*, pages 176–186.

Yiqun Liu, Fei Chen, Weize Kong, Huijia Yu, Min Zhang, Shaoping Ma, and Liyun Ru. 2012. Identifying web spam with the wisdom of the crowds. *ACM Transactions on the Web (TWEB)*, 6(1):2.

Dong Nguyen and A Seza Dogruoz. 2014. Word level language identification in online multilingual communication. In *Proceedings of the 2013 Conference on Empirical Methods in Natural Language Processing*.

Naoaki Okazaki. 2007. CRFsuite: a fast implementation of Conditional Random Fields (CRFs).

F. Pedregosa, G. Varoquaux, A. Gramfort, V. Michel, B. Thirion, O. Grisel, M. Blondel, P. Prettenhofer, R. Weiss, V. Dubourg, J. Vanderplas, A. Passos, D. Cournapeau, M. Brucher, M. Perrot, and E. Duchesnay. 2011. Scikit-learn: Machine Learning in Python. *Journal of Machine Learning Research*, 12:2825–2830.

David Martin Powers. 2011. Evaluation: from precision, recall and F-measure to ROC, informedness, markedness and correlation.

Temple F Smith and Michael S Waterman. 1981. Identification of common molecular subsequences. *Journal of molecular biology*, 147(1):195–197.

Thamar Solorio, Elizabeth Blair, Suraj Maharjan, Steven Bethard, Mona Diab, Mahmoud Ghoneim, Abdelati Hawwari, Fahad AlGhamdi, Julia Hirschberg, Alison Chang, et al. 2014. Overview for the first shared task on language identification in code-switched data. *EMNLP 2014*, page 62.

Clare R Voss, Stephen Tratz, Jamal Laoudi, and Douglas M Briesch. 2014. Finding Romanized Arabic Dialect in Code-Mixed Tweets. In *LREC*, pages 2249–2253.

Yogarshi Vyas, Spandana Gella, Jatin Sharma, Kalika Bali, and Monojit Choudhury. 2014. POS Tagging of English-Hindi Code-Mixed Social Media Content. In *EMNLP*, volume 14, pages 974–979.

Yabin Zheng, Chen Li, and Maosong Sun. 2011. Chime: An efficient error-tolerant chinese pinyin input method. In *IJCAI*, volume 11, pages 2551–2556.

Unraveling the English-Bengali Code-Mixing Phenomenon

Arunavha Chanda
a.chanda@columbia.edu
Columbia University

Dipankar Das
dipankar.dipnil2005@gmail.com
Jadavpur University

Chandan Mazumdar
chandanm@cse.jdvu.ac.in
Jadavpur University

Abstract

Code-mixing is a prevalent phenomenon in modern day communication. Though several systems enjoy success in identifying a single language, identifying languages of words in code-mixed texts is a herculean task, more so in a social media context. This paper explores the English-Bengali code-mixing phenomenon and presents algorithms capable of identifying the language of every word to a reasonable accuracy in specific cases and the general case. We create and test a predictor-corrector model, develop a new code-mixed corpus from Facebook chat (made available for future research) and test and compare the efficiency of various machine learning algorithms (J48, IBk, Random Forest). The paper also seeks to remove the ambiguities in the token identification process.

1 Introduction

Code-mixing is a phenomenon in linguistics which is exhibited by multi-lingual people. Essentially, an utterance in which the speaker makes use of the grammar and lexicon of more than one language is said to have undergone code-mixing or code-switching (Appel and Muysken, 2005). Though some linguists draw a distinction between the terms "code-mixing" and "code-switching", we shall refer to both phenomena as "code-mixing" in general and draw distinctions regarding the context of switching when required (Muysken, 2000).

With English as the primary language on the internet, one would intuitively expect English to be the major language of use in social media as well. However, it comes as a bit of a surprise that around half of the messages on Twitter are in non-English languages (Schroeder, 2010). For multilingual people, we notice a tendency to communicate in all/several of the languages that they know. This arises from the fact that some multilingual speakers feel a higher level of comfort in their native language than in English. Apart from this, some conversational topics are more fluid in a particular language and some expressions convey the message properly only in one's native language.

In social media, code-mixing between languages such as English and Spanish (both of which employ a Roman script) is much simpler to analyze (apart from potential spelling mistakes) since the words used in normal Spanish and used in social media are spelled and used in almost entirely the same way and using the same script. However, when we consider languages that employ different scripts, most people do not have patience to switch between scripts while writing. Thus, people convert words from their language into the Roman script when mixing with English. In our analysis, we consider one such language, which is extremely fertile when it comes to code-mixing with English: Bengali. We wish to explore some procedures to identify languages in social media and internet search contexts in code-mixed English-Bengali texts.

The rest of the sections are as follows. Section 2 introduces the background of English-Bengali code-mixed data, especially in social media. Section 3 discusses the related work in the field of exploration. Section 4 speaks of the difficulties and hurdles in

80

Proceedings of the Second Workshop on Computational Approaches to Code Switching, pages 80–89,
Austin, TX, November 1, 2016. ©2016 Association for Computational Linguistics

this language identification task. In Section 5, we talk about the nature of code-switching instances that we have found in our corpora. Section 6 lists the techniques and tools we use in our experiments and Section 7 shares the details, results and observations from those experiments. In Section 8, we have a general discussion of our observations and we close in Section 9 with conclusions and future goals.

2 Background of English-Bengali Code-Mixing in Social Media

India is a linguistic area with one of the longest histories of contact, influence, use, teaching and learning of English-in-diaspora in the world (Kachru and Nelson, 2006). English is the *de facto lingua franca* in India and also an official language of the country (Guha, 2011). Thus, a huge number of Indians active on the internet are able in English communication to some degree. India also enjoys huge diversity in language. Apart from Hindi, it has several regional languages that are the primary tongue of people native to the region. Thus, a very vibrant trilingualism exists in large parts of the nation- This is seen more strongly in regions where the regional language is very widely spoken, like Bengali, which had an estimated 207 million speakers worldwide in 2007 (Microsoft Encarta, 2007). As a result, these languages are very likely to have a strong influence not only on daily speech, but also on internet and social media activities.

A significant feature of Indian multilingualism is that it is complementary. People speak in different languages in different scenarios. For example, an upper-middle class Bengali student would speak in Bengali at home, communicate in public in Hindi and in college in English. This is an integral part of the Indian composite culture (Sharma, 2001).

Due to this usage of multiple languages, code-mixing becomes inevitable and naturally spills over to social media and internet as well. In case of Bengali, since the language is very strongly tied to the daily lives of people, people have a very strong tendency to use it in written text as well. Bengali not only has a different script, but a vastly different alphabet as well. This heralds several new problems, which we discuss in the next section.

3 Related Work

Language identification and patterns in code-mixed data by itself is a field that has been explored for a very long time. Early linguistic research includes the work done in Spanish-English verbal communication by John Lipski, where he identifies the levels of linguistic competence in bilingual people as one of the root causes of code-switching (Lipski, 1978). Aravind Joshi presents a similar argument as well, in the case of Marathi-English code-switching (Joshi, 1982).

While that certainly is a big factor, there are other factors as well that we have spoken of earlier. The varying levels of diversity at the national, regional and local levels also influence different varieties of code-switching and between different languages as well (Singh and Gorla, 2007).

The Bengali-English code-switching phenomenon has historically been explored very little. A few groups have recently begun exploring the possibilities of language identification in these code-mixed situations. However, there are a few fundamental differences between their works and our work.

In other research works, some ambiguity is left with regard to the words that are present in both English and Bengali either by removing them (Das and Gambäck, 2013) or by classifying them as mixed (Depending on suffixes or word-level mixing) (Barman et al., 2014). However, such ambiguity needs to be removed, if we are required to utilize such type of data for further analysis or use them for building models of sentiment and/or predictive analysis, since people generally use mixed or ambiguous words in some single language context as well, which is why they code-mix in the first place.

In both of the other research works mentioned, the groups composed their own corpus from a Facebook group and the posts and comments by members (Das and Gambäck, 2013; Barman et al., 2014). Both of the groups also use N-gram pruning and dictionary checks.

Das and Gambäck (2013) also utilize SVM, while Barman et al (2014) use a word-length feature along with capitalization checks. We discuss relative accuracy in section 8.

4 Difficulties and Challenges in Language Identification

We shall introduce some of the problems and hurdles we faced during the system development and discuss them here.

4.1 Scarcity of uniform transliteration rules

During conversion of scripts, different people use different rules to decide the spellings of words. Suppose for instance, the Bengali word for "less", which contains the letters: "k"+"short a"+"m"+"short a". The short "a" vowel is a silent vowel in Bengali and indicates the lingering consonant sound at the end. In this case, this word would be transcribed in the IPA (International Phonetic Alphabet) as: IPA:[kɔm].

Due to letterwise transliteration, this word would be spelled in a dictionary conversion as "kama" owing to it's construction in Bengali language and the presence of silent/transformed "a" vowels.

However, interestingly, people tend to think of pronunciation rather than construction when converting the script, and the most socially acceptable spelling of this word is "kom". Such instances dominate a large portion of Bengali writing in social media.

Apart from this, there exist several occurrences of spelling variations. The word for "good" in Bengali is pronounced IPA:[b^halo]. Since the [v] sound doesn't exist in Bengali, some assign the [b^h] sound to the letter "V" and spell good as "valo" rather than the standard spelling, "bhalo". This type of spelling variation exists in innumerable other words, but all versions are easily recognized by readers.

4.2 English slang terms

There is also the problem of modern English chat terms and colloquial terms like "lol" for "laughing out loud" and "gr8" for "great".

4.3 Bengali word forms

Bengali morphology relies heavily on "sandhi" and root transformation. For example, the word for "song" in Bengali is "*gaan*" and "singing" is "*gaowa*". However, "sang" would be "*geyechhilam*"/ "*geyechhilo*"/ "*geyechhilen*"/ "*geyechhile*" based on the subject and the honorific used. But,

none of these match with the basic words "gaan" or "gaowa". This is very common in morphology and causes serious problems, since these are not noted in a dictionary. This would make us lose a huge number of words that come in sentences, because several words in such sentences are not in raw form, but transformed.

4.4 Ambiguous words

Generally, in many other studies, we have many words which could be both English and Bengali owing to their spelling. For instance, "hole" exists in English (IPA:[hoʊl]) and in Bengali (IPA:[hole] meaning "if {something} happens"). Individually, there is no way of knowing whether the word written in the English "hole" or the Bengali "hole", since they are spelled similarly. However, since we deal with sentences, we take into consideration the language that the surrounding words are in to get a sense of the context of the sentence. The English "hole" is likelier to be surrounded by more English words while the Bengali "hole" is likelier to be surrounded by more Bengali words. Thus, we have this context information that helps us.

4.5 Lack of Tagged Datasets

Being a less explored language, there is a dearth of English-Bengali code-mixed tagged datasets. For this reason, we use one corpus from the FIRE 2013 conference (hosted by the Information Retrieval Society of India), that consists of phrases such as search terms, and one corpus that we have built and tagged from social media messages exchanged on Facebook by college students and adults from West Bengal, India.

4.6 Imperfect English dictionary composition in WordNet

In testing for English words, we initially used Word-Net[1] online (Princeton University, 2010). However, we faced some major obstacles with WordNet:

1. A lot of elementary English parts of speech including pronouns, such as "him", "her"; articles like "the"; conjunctions like "and", "because", "for"; prepositions such as "into", "onto", "to" are missing.

---

[1] http://wordnet.princeton.edu

Characteristics	FIRE 2013	Facebook chat
Text units	Phrases	Sentences
Expected source	Search terms	Chat messages
No. of lines	100	81
No. of tokens	539	518

Table 1: Details and statistics on test corpora used.

2. On the other hand, the WordNet repository contains a lot of foreign words and proper nouns, which aren't English words. Since we analyze and separate English from a foreign language, this causes problems, as a word like "Bharat" (native name for India) or "kobe" (Bengali word for "when") should ideally be classified as Bengali, but WordNet makes the system biased towards English.

4.7 Inappropriateness of Bengali dictionary

For checking the Bengali words, we use the Samsad Bengali-English dictionary's digital version (Biswas, 2004). This contains the words in Bengali text as well as a character-wise transliterated versions of the words. However, these English versions once again present to us the problem of "kama" vs "kom" as discussed in Section 4.1.

5 Descriptions of Datasets

The two test corpora we used:

1. **FIRE 2013 corpus**: The FIRE (Forum for Information Retrieval Evaluation) 2013 shared task had an annotated dataset corpus for Development, which we have used as one of our test corpora. It consists of short code-mixed phrases that resemble search queries on the internet (Information Retrieval Society of India, 2013).

2. **Facebook chat corpus**: We have composed our own Facebook chat corpus from the Facebook chats of various people of multiple age ranges, genders, geographic location and topic of discussion.

We also provide the statistics for our test corpora in Table 1.

The Facebook corpus is composed from chat messages, because we felt that a chat was more likely to have code-mixing, since one converses in a more informal setting there, while public posts are less likely to be influenced by code-mixing.

In the composition of our Facebook chat corpus (which has been made publicly available for future research[2]), we wanted to get a variety of styles of texting and mixing. For that reason, we collected text message conversations between Bengali college students, who are acquaintances, college students who were childhood friends, school friends and middle-aged women who are family friends. The annotation was done by an author.

The two corpora vary in their content types. As we see in Table 2, the FIRE 2013 corpus has the Bengali words heavily outweigh the number of English words, whereas in the Facebook chat corpus, we see an extremely level mix of words from both languages.

The "ambiguous words" row notes the number of words (already considered in the Bengali and English counts) that could belong to the other language too (based on our dictionary test). For example, the Bengali word, "more" IPA:[more] in the FIRE 2013 corpus could be the English "more" IPA:[mor] as well. The ambiguous words make up 29.68% of the FIRE 2013 corpus and 41.31% of the Facebook chat corpus. We divide these into two categories:

1. Bengali words that exist in the English dictionary: **Bengali (can be En)** in the table. "more" discussed above is an example of this category.

2. English words that find a match our search in the Bengali dictionary: **English (can be Bn)** in the table. For example, "to" IPA:[tu] in our Facebook chat corpus is an English word. However, a Bengali word, "to" IPA:[θo] also exists.

We notice there are a lot more **Bengali (can be En)** words than **English (can be Bn)** words in the FIRE 2013 corpus, while it is the exact opposite in the Facebook corpus. In fact, an interesting statistic is that out of all the English words in the Facebook chat corpus, 66.93% of the words register a match in the Bengali dictionary, and thus have a much higher likelihood of being wrongly classified. We can attribute this in part to the "Minimum Edit

----

[2]`https://github.com/ArunavhaChanda/Facebook-Code-Mixed-Corpus`

Characteristics	FIRE 2013	Facebook chat
Total words	**539**	**518**
Bengali words	364 (67.53%)	261 (50.39%)
English words	175 (32.47%)	257 (49.61%)
Ambiguous words	**160**	**214**
Bengali (can be En)	115 (71.88%)	42 (19.63%)
English (can be Bn)	45 (28.13%)	172 (80.37%)

Table 2: Details and statistics on test corpora used.

Distance" check in our Bengali search described in section 6.1.1.

6 Techniques and approaches

We have performed several versions of experiments and used different techniques. Our experiments can be divided into two major halves:

- **The first half** consisted of creating our own algorithms and processes that predicted and guessed the language of a word independently, without any machine learning used.

- **The second half** of our experiments were picking and choosing out features for every word and then using various machine learning algorithms on them to classify each word.

6.1 Resources used

6.1.1 Lexicons used

The dictionaries we use are the following:

1. **English dictionary**: We use the Python Enchant library[3] for checking English words and their existence in the dictionary. The good thing about Enchant is that the words included are not only in lemma form, but all kinds of morphological transformations are also included, making checks a lot easier. We also create a slang dictionary of our own containing colloquial English text words such as "LOL" and "gr8". We draw from the works of researchers at the University of Melbourne and University of Texas at Dallas (Han et al., 2012; Liu et al., 2011; Liu et al., 2012). We use this in both halves.

2. **Bengali dictionary**: The Samsada Bengali-English dictionary's digital edition[4] was used for the English transliterations of Bengali words and for a dictionary lookup (Biswas, 2004). What we do here to deal with the transliteration problem, is:

   - If a word in the dictionary ends in "a", we remove the "a" first (to account for the rarely used "short a" in social typing).
   - We then check for a Minimum Edit Distance of 1 character to the test word to indicate a match.

   For instance, when we check for "kom" typed in by someone, and our system is checking against "kama" (which is supposed to be the matching word), we have the "a" stripped from the end and obtain "kam" first. Then, we check for the Minimum Edit Distance between "kom" and "kam" and get 1. Thus, it is declared a match. This also accounts for some of the varied spellings discussed earlier. The Minimum Edit Distance we use incorporates the Levenshtein Distance (Levenshtein, 1966). We use this in both halves.

3. **Bengali suffix list**: We composed a list of common Bengali suffixes to check for transformed words. As discussed earlier, this helps us to deal with Bengali morphology, which is rather different from English morphology. We use this in both halves.

6.1.2 Training corpora used

These were two training corpora we used:

1. **Brown corpus**: We use the Brown corpus provided in the nltk[5] library in Python for a list of English words for creating an English language n-gram profile (Francis and Kučera, 1979). We use this in both halves.

2. **SHRUTI corpus**: We use the SHRUTI Bengali Continuous ASR Speech Corpus[6] to obtain

---

[3]https://pypi.python.org/pypi/pyenchant/

[4]http://dsal.uchicago.edu/dictionaries/biswas-bengali/

[5]http://www.nltk.org

[6]http://cse.iitkgp.ac.in/~pabitra/shruti_corpus.html

Bengali words. We use the same technique of removing "a"s from the ends of words, removing all punctuation, and lowering the case of all the words. Then, we create the n-gram profile for Bengali n-gram profile (Indian Institute of Technology, Kharagpur, 2011). We use this in both halves.

6.2 Algorithms and frameworks used

6.2.1 N-gram text categorization

We have developed an algorithm to using N-gram categorization for individual words. We use the two training corpora and extract every individual word and build language 4-gram profiles with them (since 4-grams give the best results) for Bengali and English. The profile consists of a sorted dictionary of the top 400 most frequently occurring 4-grams. When testing for a word, we find all the 4-grams for that word and then compute the distance of each 4-gram to it's counterpart in both the language profiles. If not found, we just assign it the length of the sorted language profile. We do this for each 4-gram in the word and then find the distances for both languages. The language that it is closer to is assigned as it's n-gram match. We use this in both halves.

6.2.2 WEKA

We use the WEKA (Waikato Environment for Knowledge Analysis) 3 tool for running our Machine Learning Algorithms and finding the success of our future algorithms (Hall et al., 2009). We use this in the second half.

6.2.3 Predictor-corrector algorithm

We will explain this algorithm with an example sentence from the FIRE 2013 corpus, which is entirely in Bengali:

Tormuj   noon   die   khete   kemon   lage
Watermelon   salt   with   to eat   how   taste

Meaning, "How does watermelon taste with salt?"

- Prediction: Our algorithm goes through the sentence identifying the language of each word by checking if it is English first and if not, if it is Bengali. We also perform this the other way around (Bengali, then English) depending on the order we determined. If it is neither, we find the n-gram match. This way, every word

in the sentence gets tagged. In our example sentence, though all words are in Bengali, the words "noon" and "die" are tagged as English, since they are spelled the same way as words in English.

- Correction: In the sentence, the language that has more (predicted) words is declared the default language. After this, for each tagged word, we check if it existed in the non-tagged language's dictionary. If it does, we check the neighborhood (between 2-4 words depending on position in the sentence) of the word, and if the majority/half (depending on the default language) of the words are of the other language, it is corrected to the other language. In our sentence, the default language is Bengali and the words are checked one-by-one. "noon" is a word that can exist in Bengali and is surrounded by 67% Bengali words (2/3). So, it is corrected to Bengali. "die" also can exist in Bengali and is surrounded by 100% Bengali words (4/4 after correcting "noon") and is also corrected to Bengali.

This way, our predictor-corrector method helps achieve better accuracy for ambiguous words. We use this in the first half.

7 Experiments and results

7.1 First half experiments

The following tests were performed in the first half:

1. Regular dictionary search (predictor), in two variants: (i) Check if word is Bengali first, then English. (ii)The reverse. Check for English first and then Bengali.

2. Predictor-corrector method (i) Check Bengali first. (ii) Check English first.

In the first part, whose results are mentioned in table 3, we note that the order in which we checked the language of words played a huge role in our accuracy (We measure accuracy as words correctly classified out of all the words). However, the interesting thing is that this gets reversed for both the corpora. For the Facebook chat corpus, we get a higher accuracy checking English first, while for the FIRE

Tools/Algorithm used	FIRE 2013	Facebook
Predictor (EB)	73.28%	88.22%
Predictor-corrector (EB)	82.56%	88.61%
Predictor (BE)	86.27%	64.86%
Predictor-corrector (BE)	86.09%	75.48%

Table 3: Results of first part. (BE: Bengali, then English; EB: English, then Bengali.)

Process/step	Accuracy
Regular dictionary	72.54%
+ Bengali suffixes	75.51%
+ "a" removals	77.37%
+ n-gram	86.27%

Table 4: Progressive results with features

corpus, we get a higher accuracy checking Bengali first. This knowledge fits in with the statistics we found previously.

From table 2, of the ambiguous words, we noted 71.88% of those in the FIRE corpus were Bengali and 80.37% of those in the Facebook chat corpus were in English. This shows that there is a greater chance of the Bengali words in the FIRE corpus being wrongly classified if we check for them being English first and the reverse for the Facebook chat corpus. However, if we check for words being Bengali first, the FIRE corpus' ambiguous Bengali words have a much higher chance of being correctly classified. This explains the varying effect order of checking has on corpora depending on the composition. Thus, it is not really a viable method unless we know details of word composition.

Another phenomenon we noted was the effect the inclusion of each feature had on the accuracy (Table 4). Before using the n-gram feature in the predictor for the first half experiments, we observed the following:

- Initially, we had only used regular dictionaries (the Samsada dictionary and Python Enchant) on the FIRE 2013 corpus and achieved an accuracy of 72.54% only (Bengali checks first). This was our baseline accuracy.

- After including our Bengali suffix repository, our accuracy increases to 75.51%.

- We include the checks by removing "a" from the ends of words in the Bengali dictionary to increment the accuracy to 77.37%.

- Finally, the accuracy increased with the n-gram feature to 86.27%.

The corrector method is also more useful with the less accurate predictor. This is likely because several of the ambiguous words, which were wrongly classified in the predictor, get accurately classified by the corrector and there are a lot more such words when we check words with the less ambiguous language first (English for FIRE and Bengali for Facebook; since words from the more ambiguous one get wrongly classified more). Thus, the corrector does a good job in such cases, giving accuracy boosts of +9.28% for the FIRE corpus and +10.62% for the Facebook corpus. However, it only marginally improves or reduces the accuracy in the reverse cases (-0.18% for FIRE and +0.39% for Facebook).

7.2 Second half experiments

The second half experiments were performed using WEKA and its machine learning algorithms. We used the following features of words as vectors:

1. Presence in Bengali dictionary (**B** in the table)

2. Presence in English dictionary (**E** in the table)

3. N-gram profile language match (**N** in the table)

4. Percentage of surrounding words that are "predicted" as Bengali: We predict using presence in one dictionary. If the word is in both or neither, we use the n-gram match as the predicted language (**S** in the table). We also use a version of this using majority language in the neighborhood, rather than percentage (**(s)** in the table)

Once we had these, we created arff (Attribute-Relation File Format) files of the words with these features as vectors and then used various algorithms in WEKA to classify the words.

The key results are summarized in table 5

We have listed results using three different classifiers and then with no surrounding data (only dictionaries and n-gram), using binary surrounding data, and using only the N-gram language categorizer.

In terms of classifiers, IBk performs the best, giving us accuracies of 91.65% and 90.54% as seen in the table.

	FIRE 2013				**Facebook chat**			
Classifier+Features	*Precision*	*Recall*	*F-score*	Accuracy	*Precision*	*Recall*	*F-score*	Accuracy
J48; **BENS**	0.895	0.896	0.895	89.61%	0.902	0.902	0.902	90.15%
IBk; **BENS**	**0.918**	**0.917**	**0.915**	**91.65%**	**0.905**	**0.905**	**0.905**	**90.54%**
RF; **BENS**	0.909	0.909	0.907	90.91%	0.893	0.892	0.892	89.19%
J48; **BEN**	0.900	0.887	0.880	88.68%	0.897	0.892	0.892	89.19%
J48; **BEN(s)**	0.909	0.905	0.902	90.54%	0.886	0.884	0.884	88.42%
J48; **N**	0.830	0.790	0.797	79.04%	0.812	0.805	0.804	80.50%

Table 5: Results of second part (Machine Learning). Key: RF=Random Forest

From the sixth row, it is evident that the N-gram categorization is very helpful, but not helpful enough. The fourth row shows us the result from using the dictionaries and breaking ties (word present in both or neither) using the N-gram decision is rather successful, though adding the surrounding data definitely helps the accuracy.

The results of the majority language in the neighborhood as a feature are in the fifth row. Interestingly, this technique caused a drop in accuracy for the Facebook chat corpus, but increased the accuracy for the FIRE 2013 corpus.

We did not use only the dictionaries as sole features, because the classification would have been 2-dimensional and much less useful than the dictionaries with N-gram.

8 Discussion

Comparing to similar tasks (on different corpora) by other groups, our system enjoys a fair amount of success. Compared to Das and Gambäck, our system has enjoyed greater success. They had a best accuracy of 76.37% compared to our 91.65% (Das and Gambäck, 2014). Their system employed SVM implementation, while ours did not. On the other hand, Barman et al achieved 95.98%, which was higher than ours (Barman et al., 2014) . The features used by them have been discussed earlier in section 3. Both these groups used their own corpora composed from similar Facebook groups used by college students. Our corpus has more variety in terms of age group and topics discussed. However, their corpora were larger in size.

One of the major points of discussion that we obtain from our research and experiments is the variation of dominant language in text. In past research, English (the language of the script) is considered the dominant/default language and the mixed language (Bengali, in our case) is considered secondary. However, this is not always the case. The Roman script is not chosen because English is the primary language. It is rather chosen out of convenience.

Hence, we assess the text first at the word level and then at the sentence level. In our corrector method, we assign the language with most words in a sentence as the default language for that sentence and then use our corrector method. It is likelier for a word surrounded by a lot of Bengali words in an English sentence to be Bengali, since code-switching happens mostly in a structured way. Language switch happens for a part of the sentence where the non-dominant language is more suitable. For example (with each 'E' and 'B' representing an English or Bengali word respectively), a code-mixed sentence is much likelier to be EEEEBBBBEEEE or BBBEEEBBBBBEB, than EBEBBBEEBEBE. Considering this, we use the default language information to find the likelihood of a word needing to be corrected.

However, sometimes this correction in context causes a problem. It takes into account that sentences have certain points of code-switching and the switching is not random. This does give us an increase in accuracy for the Facebook chat corpus. However, the FIRE 2013 corpus consists of phrases and search terms and thus have random code-switching points rather than a particular pattern. For example:

She	*toh*	*elo*	*na*	**song**	**lyrics**
He/She	-	come	no		

(Bengali in italics; English in bold). This refers to the lyrics of a song called "*She toh elo na*". The way this sentence begins, one doesn't expect the last two words to be in English. However, since this is not a syntactical sentence, but a search phrase, we have "song lyrics" appear at the end. When our system

R\C	Predictor		Corrector		IBk	
	E	B	E	B	E	B
English	164	11	143	32	139	36
Bengali	132	232	62	302	9	355

Table 6: Confusion matrix, FIRE(EB) {R:Real, C:Classified}

checks for "song", it locates a Bengali word in the dictionary spelled as "cong" IPA:[tʃoŋ]. Since the MED (Minimum Edit Distance) from it is 1, it registers "song" as a potential Bengali word as well. And since it is heavily surrounded by Bengali words, it incorrectly re-tags "song" as a Bengali word. However, the edit check is extremely necessary. A supporting example in our Facebook chat corpus itself exists in the word IPA: [aʃolɛ] (meaning "actually" or "really"). It is spelled in two different ways: "asole" and "ashole". Such variations in spelling exist largely among different people and we need the MED test to verify.

To avoid such errors, in our second half, we do not correct as a post-processing step, but rather choose to include percentage of surrounding Bengali words as a feature in our vector.

Table 6 shows the progressive improvement (and errors) in classification. The number of Bengali words wrongly classified vastly decreases, but the number of English words being wrongly classified slightly increases: a trade-off that seems worth it.

We have also discussed the variations in spelling of Bengali words, and that remains a factor of concern that we have mitigated slightly, but not enough. For instance, people also tend to contract spellings even in Bengali. The word for "good" ("bhalo" [bʰalo]) is also spelled by some people as "valo", which is further contracted to "vlo". There are also acronyms, which can be Bengali or English, and we have no way of identifying them without a repository or a collection of common acronyms in both. Such circumstances are still difficult to deal with and need to be considered in future work.

Ambiguous words being assigned determined languages was one of the major decisions we took early on in our research, since even ambiguous words are written with a certain sentiment and language in mind.

There are problems of using our Bengali suffix list as well. For example, one of the most important suf-

fixes we have here is "te" IPA:[θe], used in "shute" (to sleep), "khete" (to eat), "jete" (to go). One use of this is to make the verb an object verb. For example:

O   khete   gechhe

He/She   to eat   has gone

This sentence means "He has gone to eat". It is necessary to have the suffixes to identify "khete" as a Bengali word and we need to check for the suffix "te" to achieve that. However, for this reason, English words like "cute", "mute" and "forte" are also marked off as existing in the Bengali lexicon. The trade-off is a small one and considering the suffixes helps a lot in identifying Bengali words, it seems justified.

9   Conclusion and Future Work

If we are to carry out sentiment analysis in the future, it will be crucial to identify language and context for every word to understand the sentiment it conveys. Another tool required for sentiment analysis of English-Bengali code-mixed data is a Part-of-Speech tagger for Bengali. The way this will help even in code-mixed context is that once we know the default language of a sentence, it is likely to follow the grammatical/syntactical structure of that language. This helps put all the words in the sentence into context and makes it easier to (a) correct languages, if necessary and (b) helps understand the context of a word and by extension, its sentiment better.

Since Bengali is still a relatively unexplored language in Natural Language Processing, apart from a Part-of-Speech tagger, another hurdle is proper nouns: Names of people, places, landmarks etc are not found in any dictionary. Though the N-gram categorization routine helps a lot in this regard, it would still help to be able to identify these names.

In conclusion, we have given ways to improve language identification in code-mixed English-Bengali data to a large extent. If we are equipped with the POS tagger and the other points mentioned here, we will be at a stage to confidently work on the sentiment analysis of code-mixed data as well.

References

René Appel and Pieter Muysken, 2005. *Code Switching and Code Mixing*. Amsterdam University Press.

Utsab Barman, Amitava Das, Joachim Wagner, and Jennifer Foster. 2014. Code Mixing: A Challenge for Language Identification in the Language of Social Media. In *Proceedings of the First Workshop on Computational Approaches to Code Switching*.

Sailendra Biswas. 2004. *Samsada Bangala abhidhana*. Sahitya Samsad, 7th edition.

Amitava Das and Björn Gambäck. 2013. Code-Mixing in Social Media Text. *Traitement Automatique des Langues*, 54.

Amitava Das and Björn Gambäck. 2014. Identifying Languages at the Word Level in Code-Mixed Indian Social Media Text. In *Proceedings of the 11th International Conference on Natural Language Processing*.

W.N. Francis and H Kučera. 1979. A Standard Corpus of Present-Day Edited American English, for use with Digital Computers (Brown). http://www.helsinki.fi/varieng/CoRD/corpora/BROWN/.

Ramachandra Guha. 2011. *India After Gandhi: The History of the World's Largest Democracy*. Pan Macmillan.

Mark Hall, Eibe Frank, Geoffrey Holmes, Bernhard Pfahringer, Peter Reutemann, and Ian H. Witten. 2009. The WEKA Data Mining Software: An Update. *SIGKDD Explorations*, 11.

Bo Han, Paul Cook, and Timothy Baldwin. 2012. Automatically Constructing a Normalisation Dictionary for Microblogs. In *Proceedings of the 2012 Joint Conference on Empirical Methods in Natural Language Processing and Computational Natural Language Learning*, pages 421–432, Jeju Island, Korea, July. Association for Computational Linguistics.

Indian Institute of Technology, Kharagpur. 2011. SHRUTI Bengali Continuous ASR Speech Corpus. http://cse.iitkgp.ac.in/~pabitra/shruti_corpus.html.

Information Retrieval Society of India. 2013. Datasets for FIRE 2013 Track on Transliterated Search. http://www.isical.ac.in/~fire/2013/.

Aravind K. Joshi. 1982. Processing of sentences with intrasentential code-switching. *COLING-82*, pages 145–150.

Yamuna Kachru and Cecil L. Nelson. 2006. *World Englishes in Asian Contexts*. Hong Kong University Press.

V.I. Levenshtein. 1966. Binary Codes Capable of Correcting Deletions, Insertions and Reversals. *Soviet Physics Doklady*, 10:707–710.

John M. Lipski. 1978. Code-switching and the problem of bilingual competence. *Aspects of bilingualism*, pages 250–264.

Fei Liu, Fuliang Weng, Bingqing Wang, and Yang Liu. 2011. Insertion, Deletion, or Substitution? Normalizing Text Messages without Pre-categorization nor Supervision. In *Proceedings of the 49th Annual Meeting of the Association for Computational Linguistics (ACL 2011)*, pages 71–76.

Fei Liu, Fuliang Weng, and Xiao Jiang. 2012. A Broad-Coverage Normalization System for Social Media Language. In *Proceedings of the 50th Annual Meeting of the Association for Computational Linguistics (ACL 2012)*, pages 1035–1044.

Microsoft Encarta. 2007. Languages Spoken by More Than 10 Million People. http://web.archive.org/web/20071203134724/http://encarta.msn.com/media_701500404/Languages_Spoken_by_More_Than_10_Million_People.html.

Pieter Muysken. 2000. *Bilingual Speech: A Typology of Code-Mixing*. Cambridge University Press.

Princeton University. 2010. About WordNet. http://wordnet.princeton.edu.

Stan Schroeder. 2010. Half of Messages on Twitter Aren't in English [STATS]. http://mashable.com/2010/02/24/half-messages-twitter-english/.

J.C. Sharma. 2001. Multilingualism in India. *Language in India*, 1.

Anil Kumar Singh and Jagadeesh Gorla. 2007. Identification of languages and encodings in a multilingual document. In *Proceedings of ACL-SIGWAC's Web As Corpus3*.

Part-of-speech Tagging of Code-Mixed Social Media Text

Souvick Ghosh
Jadavpur University
Kolkata, WB 700032
India

Satanu Ghosh
MAKAUT
Kolkata, WB 700064
India

Dipankar Das
Jadavpur University
Kolkata, WB 700032
India

Abstract

A common step in the processing of any text is the part-of-speech tagging of the input text. In this paper, we present an approach to tackle code-mixed text from three different languages Bengali, Hindi, and Tamil - apart from English. Our system uses Conditional Random Field, a sequence learning method, which is useful to capture patterns of sequences containing code switching to tag each word with accurate part-of-speech information. We have used various pre-processing and post-processing modules to improve the performance of our system. The results were satisfactory, with a highest of 75.22% accuracy in Bengali-English mixed data. The methodology that we employed in the task can be used for any resource poor language. We adapted standard learning approaches that work well with scarce data. We have also ensured that the system is portable to different platforms and languages and can be deployed for real-time analysis.

1 Introduction

Part-of-Speech (POS) tagging a syntactic analysis usually done after language identification - is one of the key tasks in any language processing applications. It is the process of assigning the appropriate part of speech or lexical category to each word in a sentence. Apart from assigning grammatical categories to words in a text, POS tagging also helps in automatic analysis of any text.

To develop an accurate tagger, it is essential to develop various rules based on the language or large annotated corpus which could be used for discovering the rules and training the model. Accurate annotation of a corpus requires the expertise of linguists which is expensive and time consuming. Also it is not extendable from one language to another. Use of automatic machine learning approaches is inexpensive, fairly accurate and can be extended between languages.

The increasing popularity of social media platforms blogs, micro-posts (e.g. Twitter[1]) and chats (Facebook [2]) - has ensured availability of large amount of code-mixed data. But, texts obtained from various online platforms differ from traditional writings. These texts are predominantly unstructured. Also, many variations can be observed in terms of writing style and vocabulary. Such texts are mostly informal and have multiple languages in a single sentence, or even in a single word. This code-mixed nature of text, coupled with the fact that they are written using Roman script (instead of native script), makes it extremely challenging for linguists and data analysts to process such data. This has given a new dimension to the traditional problems of language identification and POS tagging.

In this paper, we address the problem of part-of-speech tagging in mixed social media data. India is a land of many languages with Hindi and English recognized as the more popular ones. From the Indian perspective, it is generally observed that one of the languages used in social media conversations are either English or Hindi. In this work, all the three mixed scripts contain English as one of the lan-

---

[1]`twitter.com`
[2]`www.facebook.com`

90

Proceedings of the Second Workshop on Computational Approaches to Code Switching, pages 90–97,
Austin, TX, November 1, 2016. ©2016 Association for Computational Linguistics

guages. The Indian languages present are Bengali, Hindi and Tamil.

To tag the words with their corresponding part-of-speech tags, we have used Stanford part-of-speech tagger as our baseline and developed the final system using Conditional Random Field (CRF). We have obtained results for three language pairs, namely Hindi-English (Hi-En), Bengali-English (Bn-En) and Tamil-English (Ta-En). In this paper, we concentrate on building our POS tagger system with minimal external resources. Both our models do not use any language resource in addition to the dataset. While the Stanford POS Tagger uses no additional resource, the CRF model uses only a list of smileys.

The rest of the paper is organized as follows. We present an account of the previous works done in the part-of-speech tagging in Section 2. In Section 3, we discuss the dataset. The system has been described in Section 4. The results and observations have been presented in Section 5 and the conclusion in Section 6.

2 Related Work

Part-of-Speech tagging has been a centre of many researches for the past few decades. Since it started in the middle sixties and early seventies (Greene and Rubin, 1971), a lot of new concepts have been introduced to improve the efficiency of the tagger and to construct the POS taggers for several languages.

Rule based POS tagger was introduced in the nineties (Karlsson et al., 1995) and gave better accuracy than its predecessors. One of the most successful rule based English tagger (Samuelsson and Voutilainen, 1997) had a recall of 99.5% with a precision of around 97%. The rule based taggers consists of complex but accurate constraints which makes them very efficient for disambiguation. Statistical model based tagger (DeRose, 1988; Cutting et al., 1992; Dermatas and Kokkinakis, 1995; Meteer et al., 1991; Merialdo, 1994) are widely used because of the simplicity and the independence of the language models. Most commonly used statistical models are bi-gram, tri-gram and Hidden Markov Model (HMM). The only problem with statistical models is that these kinds of taggers require a large annotated corpus. Machine learning algorithms are statistical in nature but the models are more complicated than simple n-gram. Models for acquiring disambiguation rules and transformation rules from the dataset were constructed in late 80's and early 90's (Hindle, 1989; Brill, 1992; Brill, 1995a; Brill, 1995b). Neural networks have also been used for POS tagging (Nakamura et al., 1990; Schütze, 1993; Ma and Isahara, 1998; Eineborg and Gambäck, 1994). POS taggers were also developed using Support Vector Machine (SVM) (Nakagawa et al., 2001). These taggers were more simple and efficient than the previous taggers. The successor of this tagger was developed by Giménez and Marquez (2004) and the approach they used for POS tagging was considerably faster than its predecessor. A more recent development was the use of Conditional Random Field (CRF) for POS tagging (Sha and Pereira, 2003; Lafferty et al., 2001; Shrivastav et al., 2006). These taggers are better for disambiguation as they find global maximum likelihood estimation.

2.1 POS Taggers for Indian Languages

Recently, a large number of researchers are trying to expand the scope of automatic POS taggers so that they can work on complex non European languages. India is a country with rich linguistics so POS taggers for Indian languages are one of the most explored topics. The first effort was to develop a Hindi POS tagger dated back in the nineties (Bharati et al., 1995). This tagger was based on a morphological analyzer. The analyzer would provide the root word with its morphological features and generalized POS category. Shrivastav et al. (2006) slightly modified this approach by using a decision tree based classifier and achieved an accuracy of 93.45%. Instead of using a full morphological analyzer Shrivastava and Bhattacharyya (2008) used a stemmer to generate suffixes which was in turn used to generate POS tags. Conditional Random Field was also used along with morphological analyzer in a couple of works (Agarwal and Mani, 2006; PVS and Karthik, 2007).

One of the earliest works on Bengali POS tagger was conducted by Seddiqui et al. (2003) and Chowdhury et al. (2004). (Chowdhury et al., 2004) implemented a rule based tagger which hand written rules formulated by expert linguists. In more recent work, Hasan et al. (2007) developed a supervised POS tagger. This method was less effective due to lack of tagged training corpus. In later years, we have seen many works on Bengali POS tagger. One of the most successful taggers was developed by using HMM and Maximum Entropy models (Dandapat and Sarkar, 2006; Dandapat, 2007). They also used a morphological analyzer to compensate for the lack of annotated training corpus. These two models were used to implement a supervised tagger and a semi-supervised tagger. The accuracy achieved was around 88% for both models. Ekbal et al. (2007) carried out further research on the tagger. They annotated a news corpus and created two taggers - one SVM based tagger and another CRF based tagger - which reported an accuracy of 86.84% and 90.3% respectively.

In Tamil, Selvam and Natarajan (2009) proposed a rule based morphological analyzer to annotate the corpora and used it to train the POS tagger. They used the Tamil version of Bible for the tagged corpus and achieved an accuracy of 85.56%. Dhanalakshmi et al. (2009) developed a SVM based tagger using linear programming and a new tagset for Tamil with 32 tags. They used this tagset for building a training corpus and reported an accuracy of 95.63%. Another SVM based POS tagger (Dhanalakshmi et al., 2008) was proposed by them in a different work. They extracted linguistic information using machine learning techniques which was then used to train the tagger. This tagger achieved an accuracy of 95.64%.

Even after decades of research on monolingual POS taggers for Indian languages(mostly Hindi), there are just a few taggers with accuracy over 90%. A new challenge has developed over the past few years in the form of code mixed social media text. This field of research is at a nascent stage. The basic challenges and complexities of social media text are spelling variations and word sense disambiguation. As traditional POS taggers were not efficient for social media text, new taggers targeting social media text were constructed. However, these taggers are mostly monolingual and not suitable for code-mixed text. The first was developed by Gimpel et al. (2011) for tagging English tweets. They developed a new POS tagset and tagged 1827 tweets for training corpus for a CRF tagger with arbitrary local features in log-linear model adaptation. Owoputi et al. (2013) improved the original Twitter POS tagger as they introduced lexical and unsupervised word clustering features. This increased the accuracy from 90% to

93%.

One of the first POS taggers for code-mixed text was developed by Solorio and Liu (2008). They constructed a POS tagger of English-Spanish text by using existing monolingual POS taggers for both the languages. They combined the POS tag information using heuristic procedures and achieved the maximum accuracy of 93.4%. However, this work was not on social media text and hence the difficulties were considerably less. Gella et al. (2013) developed a system to identify word level language and then chunk the individual languages and produce POS tags or every individual chunk. They used a CRF based Hindi POS tagger for Hindi and Twitter POS tagger for English and achieved maximum accuracy of 79%. Vyas et al. (2014) developed a English-Hindi POS tagger for code mixed social media text.

3 Dataset

A recent shared task was conducted by Twelfth International Conference on Natural Language Processing (ICON-2015)[3] , for part-of-speech tagging of transliterated social media text. Organizers released the code mixed train and test set for English-Hindi, English-Bengali and English-Tamil language pairs.

In Table 1, we provide a summary of the dataset in terms of the utterances. The number of utterances have been recorded for both the training and test data. In Table 2, we present a statistics of the number of sentences for each pair of languages in training as well as test data.

Language	Sentences (Training)	Sentences (Test)
Bengali-English	2837	1459
Hindi-English	729	377
Tamil-English	639	279

Table 2: Summary of Dataset (Sentences).

4 System Description

We have followed a supervised approach in this work. We have extracted various features that are pertinent to this task. The various steps involved in POS tagging are listed as follows:

[3]`http://ltrc.iiit.ac.in/icon2015/`
`contests.php`

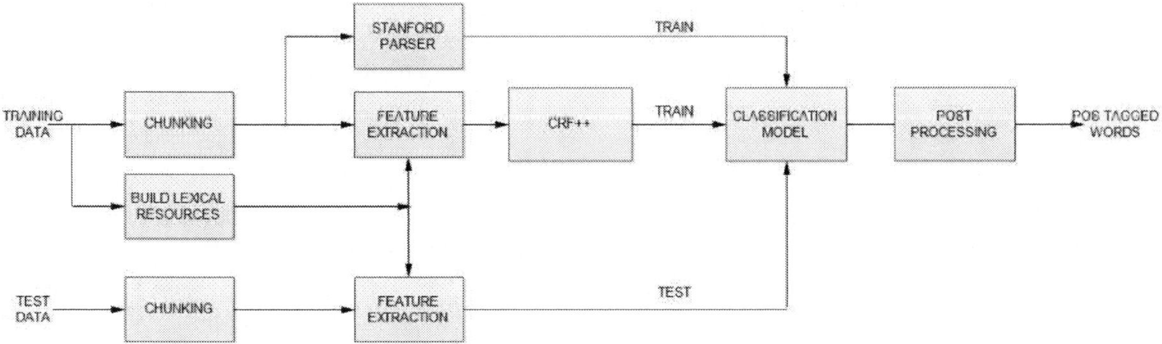

Figure 1: Overview of the System Architecture.

Language Tags	Utterances (Training)	Utterances (Test)
Hindi-English		
English (EN)	6178	8553
Hindi (HI)	5546	411
Others (O)	4231	2248
Total	15955	11212
Bengali-English		
English (EN)	9973	5459
Bengali (BN)	8330	4671
Others (O)	6335	3431
Total	24638	13561
Tamil-English		
English (EN)	1969	819
Tamil (TA)	1716	1155
Others (O)	630	281
Total	4315	2255

Table 1: Summary of Dataset (Utterances).

4.1 Chunking

Each of the three given corpora (Hindi-English, Bengali-English and Tamil-English) contains English as one of the dominant languages. The other dominant language is Bengali, Hindi and Tamil in each of the three texts. The various language tags used in the training data are en (English), hi (Hindi), bn (Bengali), ta (Tamil), ne (Named entities), acro (Acronyms), univ (Universal) and undef (Undefined). For each input file, we have performed chunking on the raw text to segment the words belonging to different language tag. We haves used the language ids to perform chunking. For each of the language tags, we have created a wordlist belonging to that particular language tag. We also maintain a

table containing the file id, word id and position of every word. This table is useful for obtaining the output files from the chunked words.

4.2 Lexicons for Dominant Languages

English, Bengali, Hindi and Tamil were identified as the dominant languages. For each of these four languages, we have created a list of words which belong to any particular POS tag. These lists were constructed from the respective training files. We maintain lists for nouns, verbs and other parts-of-speech for each language. These lists are essential for extracting feature for training our CRF model.

4.3 POS Tagging

We have used two different approaches for POS Tagging of the test data. Both the models use training data for learning and model construction.

4.3.1 POS Tagging Using Stanford POS Tagger

For our baseline, we trained our system using Stanford POS Tagger (Toutanova et al., 2003). Using the training data, we trained the Stanford POS Tagger initially. The architecture (arch property of the tagger) that we used for training was: words(-1,1), unicodeshapes(-1,1), order(2), suffix(4). Four individual models were generated for English, Bengali, Hindi and Tamil. The test data was tagged using these generated models.

4.3.2 POS Tagging Using CRF++

In this work, Conditional Random Field (CRF) has been used to build the framework for word-level language identification classifier. We have used

CRF++ toolkit [4] which is a simple, customizable, and open source implementation of CRF.

The following features were used to train the CRF model:

- Length Of The Current Word

  The length of the current word has been used as one of the features. It is often noted that words belonging to a specific language and part-of-speech are often longer than others (Singh et al., 2008). We have used this feature to exploit word length in determining the part-of-speech of the word.

- Current Word

  For example, if the sentence is *I have been told of the place*, then each word is analyzed at a time. If the word currently being examined for part-of-speech tagging *is been*, then the word *been* is considered as one of the features.

- Previous Two Words

  For example, if the sentence is *I have been told of the place* and current word is *been*, then the previous two words are *I* and *have*.

- Next Two Words

  Using the previous example, if the sentence is *I have been told of the place* and the current word is *been*, then the next two words are *told* and *of*.

- Suffix

  This feature considers of the suffix of every word. If length of a word is more than 3 then suffix of length 3 and 2 are taken. e.g.: *een* and *en* are the suffixes for *been*.

- Prefix

  This feature considers of the prefix of every word. If length of a word more than 3 then prefix of length 3 and 2 are taken. e.g.: *bee* and *be* are the suffixes for *been*.

- If Word Contains Any Symbol

This feature is boolean in nature and represents if the current word contains any symbol. Presence of symbol in a word gives a possible hint about the part-of-speech of the word.

- If Word Contains Any Digit

  Similar to the previous feature, this boolean feature represents if the current word contains any digit. Presence of digit in a word gives a possible hint about the part-of-speech of the word. e.g.: *kheye6ilam, ki6u, ka6e, 6ghanta*

- Is Noun

  This feature represents if the current word is a noun. During the training phase, we build up a list of nouns for every language. This list is used during test phase to evaluate this feature. e.g.: *match, love, khushi, kaam, meye*

- Is Adjective

  This feature represents if the current word is an adjective. During the training phase, we build up a list of adjectives for every language. This list is used during test phase to evaluate this feature. e.g.: *ekta, beshi, good, nice*

- Is Verb

  This feature represents if the current word is a verb. During the training phase, we build up a list of verbs for every language. This list is used during test phase to evaluate this feature. e.g.: *hoy, lage, be, will*

- Is Pronoun

  This feature represents if the current word is a pronoun. During the training phase, we build up a list of pronouns for every language. This list is used during test phase to evaluate this feature. e.g.: *tomar, tumi, you, I*

- Is Conjunction

  This feature represents if the current word is a conjunction. During the training phase, we build up a list of conjunctions for every language. This list is used during test phase to evaluate this feature. e.g.: *kintu, and, to, but*

---

[4] https://taku910.github.io/crfpp/\# download

- Is Adverb

  This feature represents if the current word is an adverb. During the training phase, we build up a list of adverbs for every language. This list is used during test phase to evaluate this feature. e.g.: *ekhon, takhon, just, very*

- Is Determiner

  This feature represents if the current word is a determiner. During the training phase, we build up a list of determiners for every language. This list is used during test phase to evaluate this feature. e.g.: *the, this, a*

- Is Dollar

  This feature represents if the word represent any numerical measure. e.g.: *1st, 26th, one, two*

- Is Q

  This feature represents if the word represent any quantitative measure. e.g.: *enuf, more, many, khub*

- Is U

  This feature represents if the word is website link e.g.: *pdf2fb.net*

- Is X

  This feature represents if the word is a non-classified token or if it has no meaning. e.g.: *geetamroadpi*

During the training phase, we train the CRF model using all the above features. Four language models are built, corresponding to the four dominant languages English, Bengali, Hindi and Tamil. In the test phase, we use the generated models to tag the words with their appropriate part-of-speech tags.

4.3.3 Post-processing

All the words belonging to the four dominant languages were tagged by the CRF model. The acronyms, named entities and the universal words were tagged by consulting the lists built during training. All the words which could not be tagged by our model were subjected to a post-processing module. For every language tag (acro, univ, ne), we found out the most frequent part-of-speech tag. Also, we used some logical reasoning to tag the words which were not tagged by our tagger models. For example, any untagged word which contains www, http or .com in it is allotted the U tag. Similarly, we use a smiley list to tag the smileys as E. Punctuations and hash-tags were tagged likewise. Finally, we combine all the words (which were chunked in initially) to obtain the output files.

5 Results and Observations

We evaluated the POS-tagging done by our baseline model (Stanford Parser) and the CRF model. The results are presented in Table 3.

Language Pair	Baseline (Stanford Model)	CRF Model
Bengali-English	60.05	75.22
Hindi-English	50.87	73.2
Tamil-English	61.02	64.83

Table 3: Accuracy of the system.

The results of Tamil-English are less than that of Bengali-English and Hindi-English. The primary reason for lower accuracy is the variation in tag used in gold standard files of Tamil-English.

6 Conclusion

In this paper, we have addressed the POS tagging of mixed script social media text. The texts contained two or three languages, with English being one of the three languages. The other languages were Hindi, Bengali and Tamil. We have trained Stanford POS Tagger to build a baseline model. Our final model used Conditional Random Field for part-of-speech tagging. Our results are encouraging and the performance deterioration of Tamil-English mixed text can be attributed to the mismatch of POS-tags.

Currently, there is a lack of quality training data. In the absence of sufficient training data, performance deteriorates using neural network based models or deep learning methods. In future, we would love to explore the effectiveness of Deep learning based features. Word2vec models can also be used to find out words which are semantically similar. We would also like to use of ensemble learning by using various models and combining their results to arrive at the final result. A step in that direction would be to collect more mixed script data from social media and building gold standards using that data. Building an efficient normalization system and disambiguating between similar tags should also improve the accuracy of the system.

Acknowledgment

We are thankful to the organizers of the Twelfth International Conference on Natural Language Processing (ICON-2015)[5] for the dataset which we have used in our work.

References

Himanshu Agarwal and Anirudh Mani. 2006. Part of speech tagging and chunking with conditional random fields. In *the Proceedings of NWAI workshop*.

Akshar Bharati, Vineet Chaitanya, Rajeev Sangal, and KV Ramakrishnamacharyulu. 1995. *Natural language processing: a Paninian perspective*. Prentice-Hall of India New Delhi.

Eric Brill. 1992. A simple rule-based part of speech tagger. In *Proceedings of the workshop on Speech and Natural Language*, pages 112–116. Association for Computational Linguistics.

Eric Brill. 1995a. Transformation-based error-driven learning and natural language processing: A case study in part-of-speech tagging. *Computational linguistics*, 21(4):543–565.

Eric Brill. 1995b. Unsupervised learning of disambiguation rules for part of speech tagging. In *Proceedings of the third workshop on very large corpora*, volume 30, pages 1–13. Somerset, New Jersey: Association for Computational Linguistics.

Md Shahnur Azad Chowdhury, NM Minhaz Uddin, Mohammad Imran, Mohammad Mahadi Hassan, and Md Emdadul Haque. 2004. Parts of speech tagging of bangla sentence. In *Proceeding of the 7th International Conference on Computer and Information Technology (ICCIT), Bangladesh*.

Doug Cutting, Julian Kupiec, Jan Pedersen, and Penelope Sibun. 1992. A practical part-of-speech tagger. In *Proceedings of the third conference on Applied natural language processing*, pages 133–140. Association for Computational Linguistics.

Sandipan Dandapat and Sudeshna Sarkar. 2006. Part of speech tagging for bengali with hidden markov model. *Proceeding of the NLPAI Machine Learning Competition*.

Sandipan Dandapat. 2007. Part of specch tagging and chunking with maximum entropy model. In *Proceedings of the IJCAI Workshop on Shallow Parsing for South Asian Languages*, pages 29–32.

Evangelos Dermatas and George Kokkinakis. 1995. Automatic stochastic tagging of natural language texts. *Computational Linguistics*, 21(2):137–163.

Steven J DeRose. 1988. Grammatical category disambiguation by statistical optimization. *Computational linguistics*, 14(1):31–39.

V Dhanalakshmi, M Anandkumar, MS Vijaya, R Loganathan, KP Soman, and S Rajendran. 2008. Tamil part-of-speech tagger based on svmtool. In *Proceedings of the COLIPS International Conference on natural language processing (IALP), Chiang Mai, Thailand*.

V Dhanalakshmi, G Shivapratap, and Rajendran S Soman Kp. 2009. Tamil pos tagging using linear programming.

Martin Eineborg and Björn Gambäck. 1994. Tagging experiment using neural networks. *Eklund (ed.)*, pages 71–81.

Asif Ekbal, S Mondal, and Sivaji Bandyopadhyay. 2007. Pos tagging using hmm and rule-based chunking. *The Proceedings of SPSAL*, 8(1):25–28.

Spandana Gella, Jatin Sharma, and Kalika Bali. 2013. Query word labeling and back transliteration for indian languages: Shared task system description. *FIRE Working Notes*, 3.

Jesús Giménez and Lluis Marquez. 2004. Fast and accurate part-of-speech tagging: The svm approach revisited. *Recent Advances in Natural Language Processing III*, pages 153–162.

Kevin Gimpel, Nathan Schneider, Brendan O'Connor, Dipanjan Das, Daniel Mills, Jacob Eisenstein, Michael Heilman, Dani Yogatama, Jeffrey Flanigan, and Noah A Smith. 2011. Part-of-speech tagging for twitter: Annotation, features, and experiments. In *Proceedings of the 49th Annual Meeting of the Association for Computational Linguistics: Human Language Technologies: short papers-Volume 2*, pages 42–47. Association for Computational Linguistics.

Barbara B Greene and Gerald M Rubin. 1971. *Automatic grammatical tagging of English*. Department of Linguistics, Brown University.

Muhammad Fahim Hasan, Naushad UzZaman, and Mumit Khan. 2007. Comparison of unigram, bigram, hmm and brill's pos tagging approaches for some south asian languages.

---

[5]ltrc.iiit.ac.in/icon2015/

Donald Hindle. 1989. Acquiring disambiguation rules from text. In *Proceedings of the 27th annual meeting on Association for Computational Linguistics*, pages 118–125. Association for Computational Linguistics.

Fred Karlsson, Atro Voutilainen, Juha Heikkilae, and Arto Anttila. 1995. *Constraint Grammar: a language-independent system for parsing unrestricted text*, volume 4. Walter de Gruyter.

John Lafferty, Andrew McCallum, and Fernando Pereira. 2001. Conditional random fields: Probabilistic models for segmenting and labeling sequence data. In *Proceedings of the eighteenth international conference on machine learning, ICML*, volume 1, pages 282–289.

Qing Ma and Hitoshi Isahara. 1998. A multi-neuro tagger using variable lengths of contexts. In *Proceedings of the 36th Annual Meeting of the Association for Computational Linguistics and 17th International Conference on Computational Linguistics-Volume 2*, pages 802–806. Association for Computational Linguistics.

Bernard Merialdo. 1994. Tagging english text with a probabilistic model. *Computational linguistics*, 20(2):155–171.

Marie Meteer, Richard Schwartz, and Ralph Weischedel. 1991. Studies in part of speech labelling. In *Proceedings of the workshop on Speech and Natural Language*, pages 331–336. Association for Computational Linguistics.

Tetsuji Nakagawa, Taku Kudo, and Yuji Matsumoto. 2001. Unknown word guessing and part-of-speech tagging using support vector machines. In *NLPRS*, pages 325–331. Citeseer.

Masami Nakamura, Katsuteru Maruyama, Takeshi Kawabata, and Kiyohiro Shikano. 1990. Neural network approach to word category prediction for english texts. In *Proceedings of the 13th conference on Computational linguistics-Volume 3*, pages 213–218. Association for Computational Linguistics.

Olutobi Owoputi, Brendan O'Connor, Chris Dyer, Kevin Gimpel, Nathan Schneider, and Noah A Smith. 2013. Improved part-of-speech tagging for online conversational text with word clusters. Association for Computational Linguistics.

Avinesh PVS and G Karthik. 2007. Part-of-speech tagging and chunking using conditional random fields and transformation based learning. *Shallow Parsing for South Asian Languages*, 21.

Christer Samuelsson and Atro Voutilainen. 1997. Comparing a linguistic and a stochastic tagger. In *Proceedings of the 35th Annual Meeting of the Association for Computational Linguistics and Eighth Conference of the European Chapter of the Association for Computational Linguistics*, pages 246–253. Association for Computational Linguistics.

Hinrich Schütze. 1993. Part-of-speech induction from scratch. In *Proceedings of the 31st annual meeting on Association for Computational Linguistics*, pages 251–258. Association for Computational Linguistics.

Md Hanif Seddiqui, AKMS Rana, Abdullah Al Mahmud, and Taufique Sayeed. 2003. Parts of speech tagging using morphological analysis in bangla. In *Proceeding of the 6th International Conference on Computer and Information Technology (ICCIT), Bangladesh*.

M Selvam and AM Natarajan. 2009. Improvement of rule based morphological analysis and pos tagging in tamil language via projection and induction techniques. *International journal of computers*, 3(4):357–367.

Fei Sha and Fernando Pereira. 2003. Shallow parsing with conditional random fields. In *Proceedings of the 2003 Conference of the North American Chapter of the Association for Computational Linguistics on Human Language Technology-Volume 1*, pages 134–141. Association for Computational Linguistics.

M Shrivastav, R Melz, Smriti Singh, K Gupta, and P Bhattacharyya. 2006. Conditional random field based pos tagger for hindi. *Proceedings of the MSPIL*, pages 63–68.

Manish Shrivastava and Pushpak Bhattacharyya. 2008. Hindi pos tagger using naive stemming: Harnessing morphological information without extensive linguistic knowledge. In *International Conference on NLP (ICON08), Pune, India*.

Thoudam D Singh, Asif Ekbal, and Sivaji Bandyopadhyay. 2008. Manipuri pos tagging using crf and svm: A language independent approach. In *proceeding of 6th International conference on Natural Language Processing (ICON-2008)*, pages 240–245.

Thamar Solorio and Yang Liu. 2008. Learning to predict code-switching points. In *Proceedings of the Conference on Empirical Methods in Natural Language Processing*, pages 973–981. Association for Computational Linguistics.

Kristina Toutanova, Dan Klein, Christopher D Manning, and Yoram Singer. 2003. Feature-rich part-of-speech tagging with a cyclic dependency network. In *Proceedings of the 2003 Conference of the North American Chapter of the Association for Computational Linguistics on Human Language Technology-Volume 1*, pages 173–180. Association for Computational Linguistics.

Yogarshi Vyas, Spandana Gella, Jatin Sharma, Kalika Bali, and Monojit Choudhury. 2014. Pos tagging of english-hindi code-mixed social media content. In *EMNLP*, volume 14, pages 974–979.

Part of Speech Tagging for Code Switched Data

Fahad AlGhamdi, Giovanni Molina[‡], Mona Diab, Thamar Solorio[‡],
Abdelati Hawwari, Victor Soto [†] and Julia Hirschberg [†]

Department of Computer Science, The George Washington University
{fghamdi,mtdiab,abhawwari}@gwu.edu
[‡]Department of Computer Science, University of Houston
[‡]gemolinaramos@uh.edu solorio@cs.uh.edu
[†]Department of Computer Science, Columbia University
[†]{julia,vs2411}@cs.columbia.edu

Abstract

We address the problem of Part of Speech tagging (POS) in the context of linguistic code switching (CS). CS is the phenomenon where a speaker switches between two languages or variants of the same language within or across utterances, known as intra-sentential or inter-sentential CS, respectively. Processing CS data is especially challenging in intra-sentential data given state of the art monolingual NLP technology since such technology is geared toward the processing of one language at a time. In this paper we explore multiple strategies of applying state of the art POS taggers to CS data. We investigate the landscape in two CS language pairs, Spanish-English and Modern Standard Arabic-Arabic dialects. We compare the use of two POS taggers vs. a unified tagger trained on CS data. Our results show that applying a machine learning framework using two state fof the art POS taggers achieves better performance compared to all other approaches that we investigate.

1 Introduction

Linguistic Code Switching (CS) is a phenomenon that occurs when multilingual speakers alternate between two or more languages or dialects. CS is noticeable in countries that have large immigrant groups, naturally leading to bilingualism. Typically people who code switch master two (or more) languages: a common first language (lang1) and another prevalent language as a second language (lang2). The languages could be completely distinct such as Mandarin and English, or Hindi and English, or they can be variants of one another such as in the case of Modern Standard Arabic (MSA) and Arabic regional dialects (e.g. Egyptian dialect– EGY). CS is traditionally prevalent in spoken language but with the proliferation of social media such as Facebook, Instagram, and Twitter, CS is becoming ubiquitous in written modalities and genres (Vyas et al., 2014; Danet and Herring, 2007; Cárdenas-Claros and Isharyanti, 2009) CS can be observed in different linguistic levels of representation for different language pairs: phonological, morphological, lexical, syntactic, semantic, and discourse/pragmatic. It may occur within (intra-sentential) or across utterances (inter-sentential). For example, the following Arabic excerpt exhibits both lexical and syntactic CS. The speaker alternates between two variants of Arabic MSA and EGY.

Arabic Intra-sentential CS:[1] wlkn AjhztnA AljnA}yp lAnhA m$ xyAl Elmy lm tjd wlw mEl-wmp wAHdp.

English Translation: Since our crime investigation departments are not dealing with science fiction, they did not find a single piece of information.

The speaker in the example switched from MSA to EGY dialect by using the word m$/not which is an Egyptian negation particle, while s/he could have used the MSA word lyst/not. The span of the CS in this example is only one token, but it can be more than one example. Such divergence

---

[1]We use the Buckwalter encoding to present all the Arabic data in this paper: It is an ASCII only transliteration scheme, representing Arabic orthography strictly one-to-one

Proceedings of the Second Workshop on Computational Approaches to Code Switching, pages 98–107,
Austin, TX, November 1, 2016. ©2016 Association for Computational Linguistics

causes serious problems for automatic analysis. CS poses serious challenges for language technologies, including parsing, Information Extraction (IE), Machine Translation (MT), Information Retrieval (IR), and others. The majority of these technologies are trained and exposed to one language at a time. However, performance of these technologies degrades sharply when exposed to CS data.

In this paper, we address the problem of part of Speech tagging (POS) for CS data on the intra-sentential level. POS tagging is the task where each word in text is contextually labeled with grammatical labels such as, noun, verb, proposition, adjective, etc. We focus on two language pairs Spanish-English (SPA-ENG) and Modern Standard Arabic-and the Egyptian Arabic dialect (MSA-EGY). We use the same POS tag sets for both language pairs, the Universal POS tagset (Petrov et al., 2011). We examine various strategies to take advantage of the available monolingual resources for each language in the language pairs and compare against dedicated POS taggers trained on CS data for each of the language pairs. Our contributions are the following:

- We explore different strategies to leverage monolingual resources for POS tagging CS data.

- We present the first empirical evaluation on POS tagging with two different language pairs. All of the previous work focused on a single language pair combination.

2   Related Work

Developing CS text processing NLP techniques for analyzing user generated content as well as cater for needs of multilingual societies is vital (Vyas et al., 2014). Recent research on POS for Hindi-English CS social media text conducted by Vyas et al. (2014), whereby social media text was proved to pose different challenges apart from CS, including transliteration, intentional and unintentional spelling differences, short and ungrammatical texts among others. Results indicated a significant improvement where language detection as well as translation were automatically performed. According to the study, accurate language detection as well as translation for social media CS text is important for POS tagging. However, they note that the juxtaposition of

two monolingual POS taggers cannot solve POS tagging for CS text. Barman et al. (2014) have also reported the challenge in POS tagging transliterated as well as CS social media text in Hindi English.

Solorio and Liu (2008) presents a machine learning based model that outperforms all baselines on SPA-ENG CS data. Their system utilizes only a few heuristics in addition to the monolingual taggers.

Royal Sequiera (2015) introduces a ML-based approach with a number of new features. The new feature set considers the transliteration problem inherent in social media. Their system achieves an accuracy of 84%.

Jamatia et al. (2015) uses both a fine-grained and coarse-grained POS tag set in their study. They try to tackle the problem of POS tagging for English-Hindi Twitter and Facebook chat messages. They introduce a comparison between the performance of a combination of language specific taggers and a machine learning based approach that uses a range of different features. They conclude that the machine learning approach failed to outperform the language specific combination tagger.

3   Approach

The premise of this work is that monolingual resources should be helpful in POS tagging CS data. We adopt a supervised framework for our experimental set up. Supervised POS taggers are known to achieve the best performance, however they rely on significant amounts of training data. In this paper, we compare leveraging monolingual state of the art POS taggers using different strategies in what we call a COMBINED framework comparing it against using a single CS trained POS tagger identified as an INTEGRATED framework. We explore different strategies to investigate the optimal way of tackling POS tagging of CS data. To identify the underlying framework we prepend all COMBINED frameworks with the prefix COMB, and all the INTEGRATED versions with the prefix INT. First we describe the monolingual POS taggers used in our set up. We consider the monolingual taggers to be our baseline systems.

3.1 Monolingual POS Tagging systems

We use a variant on the the publicly available
MADAMIRA tool (Pasha et al., 2014) for the Arabic MSA-EGY pair. MADAMIRA is a supervised
morphological disambiguator/tagger for Arabic text.
MADAMIRA extracts a wide variety of morphological and associated linguistic information from
the input, including (among other things) detailed
morphology and part-of-speech information, lemmas, fully-diacritized forms, and phrase-level information such as base phrase chunks and named entity
tags. MADAMIRA is publicly available in two versions, an MSA version and EGY version. However,
the publicly available version of MADAMIRA MSA
is trained on newswire data (Penn Arabic Treebanks
1,2,3) (Maamouri et al., 2004), while MADAMIRA
EGY is trained on Egyptian blog data which comprises a mix of MSA, EGY and CS data (MSA-EGY) from the LDC Egyptian Treebank parts 1-5
(ARZ1-5) (Maamouri et al., 2012). For our purposes, we need a relatively pure monolingual tagger per language variety (MSA or EGY), trained
on informal genres for both MSA and EGY. Therefore, we retrained a new version of MADAMIRA-MSA strictly on pure MSA sentences identified in
the EGY Treebank ARZ1-5. Likewise we created
a MADAMIRA-EGY tagger trained specifically on
the pure EGY sentences extracted from the same
ARZ1-5 Treebank.[2]

For the SPA-ENG language pair we created models using the TreeTagger (Schmid, 1994) monolingual systems for Spanish and English respectively
as their performance has been shown to be competitive. Moreover, as pointed out in (Solorio and Liu,
2008) TreeTagger has attractive features for our CS
scenario. The data used to train TreeTagger for English was the Penn Treebank data (Marcus et al.,
1993), sections 0-22. For the Spanish model, we
used Ancora-ES (Taulé et al., 2008).

3.2 Combined Experimental Conditions

**COMB1:LID-MonoLT: Language identification
followed by monolingual tagging** Given a sentence, we apply a token level language identification

---

[2]We are grateful to the MADAMIRA team for providing us
with the MADAMIRA training code to carry out our experiments.

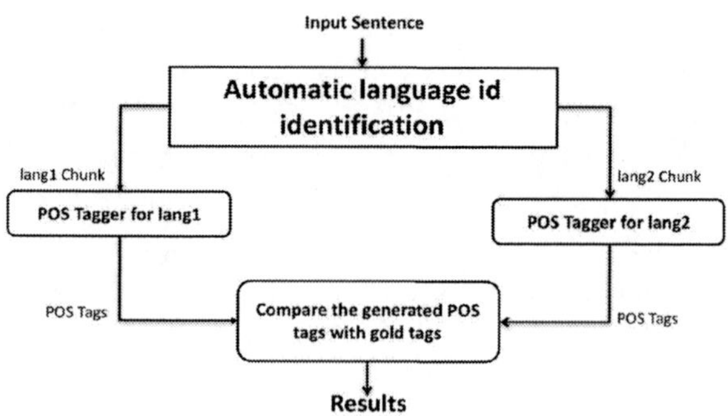

Figure 1: Graphic representation of the
COMB1:LID-MonoLT approach.

process to the words in the sentence. The chunks
of words identified as lang1 are processed by the
monolingual lang1 POS tagger and chunks of words
identified as lang2 are processed by the monolingual
lang2 POS tagger. Finally we integrate the POS tags
from both monolingual taggers creating the POS tag
sequence for the sentence. Figure-1 shows a diagram representing this approach for the MSA-EGY
language pair. For MSA-EGY, we used the Automatic Identification of Dialectal Arabic (AIDA2)
tool (Al-Badrashiny et al., 2015) to perform token
level language identification for the EGY and MSA
tokens in context. It takes plain Arabic text in Arabic UTF8 encoding or Buckwalter encoding as input
and outputs: 1) Class Identification (CI) of the input
text to specify whether the tokens are MSA, EGY,
as well as other information such as name entity,
foreign word, or unknown labels per token. Furthermore, it provides the results with a confidence
score; 2)Dialect Classification (DC) of the input text
to specify whether it is Egyptian. For SPA-ENG, we
trained language models (LM) on English and Spanish data to assign Language IDs to each token in context. We trained 6-gram character language models
using the SRILM Toolkit (Stolcke and others, 2002).
The English language model was trained on the AFP
section of the English GigaWord (Graff et al., 2003)
while the Spanish language model was trained on the
AFP section of the Spanish GigaWord (Graff, 2006).

**COMB2:MonoLT-LID: Monolingual tagging
then Language ID** Similar to Condition COMB1,
this experimental condition applies language ID
in addition to monolingual tagging, however the
order is reversed. In this condition we apply the

two monolingual language specific POS taggers to the input CS sentence as a whole, then apply the language id component to the sentence, and then choose the POS tags assigned by the respective POS tagger per token as per its language id tag. The difference between this condition and condition 1 is that the monolingual POS tagger is processing an entire sentence rather than a chunk. It should be highlighted that all four monolingual POS taggers (ENG, SPA, MSA, EGY) are trained as sequence taggers expecting full sentence data as input. Figure- 2 shows a diagram representing this approach

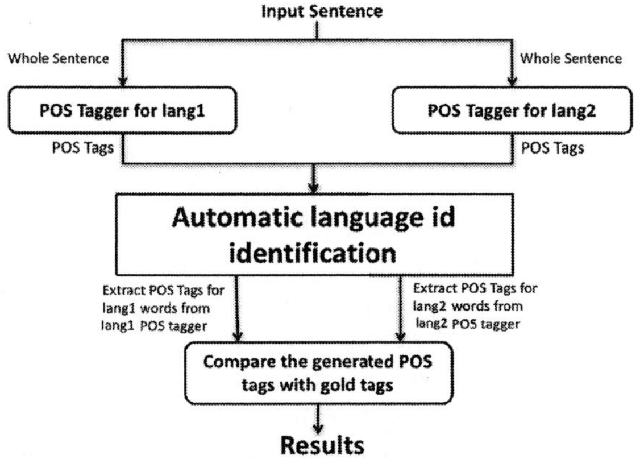

Figure 2: Graphic representation of the COMB2:MonoLT-LID approach.

COMB3:MonoLT-Conf In this condition, we apply separate taggers then use probability/confidence scores yielded by each tagger to choose which tagger to trust more per token. This condition necessitates that the taggers yield comparable confidence scores which is the case for the MADAMIRA-EGY and MADAMIRA-MSA pair, and the SPA-TreeTagger and EN-TreeTagger pair, respectively.

COMB4:MonoLT-SVM In this condition, we combine results from the monolingual taggers (baselines) and COMB3 into an ML framework such as SVM to decide which tag to choose from (MSA vs. EGY for example or SPA vs. ENG). By using an SVM classifier, we train a model on 10-fold cross-validation using the information generated by the monolingual POS taggers. The feature sets used for our model are the confidence scores and the POS tags generated by each tagger. Then, we evaluate

our model on a held-out test set.

3.3 Integrated Experimental Conditions

INT1:CSD In this condition, we train a supervised ML framework on exclusively code switched POS manually annotated data. In the case of Arabic, we retrain a MADAMIRA model exclusively with the CS data extracted from ARZ1-5 training data, yielding a MADAMIRA-CS model. For SPA-ENG, we trained a CS model using TreeTagger. This provides consistency to the experimental set up but also allows us to compare the COMB and INT approaches.

INT2:AllMonoData Similar to Condition INT1:CSD but changing the training data for each of the language pairs. Namely, we train a supervised ML framework on all the monolingual corpora that is POS manually annotated. For Arabic, we merge the training data from MSA and EGY, thereby creating a merged trained model. Likewise merging the Spanish and English corpora creating an integrated SPA-ENG model. The assumption is that the data in MSA is purely MSA and that in EGY is purely EGY. This condition yields an inter-sentential code switched training data set. None of the sentences reflect intra-sentential code switched data.

INT3:AllMonoData+CSD Merging training data from conditions "INT1:CSD" and "INT2:AllMonoData" to train new taggers for CS POS tagging.

4 Evaluation

4.1 Datasets

For MSA-EGY, we use the LDC Egyptian Arabic Treebanks 1-5 (ARZ1-5) (Maamouri et al., 2012). The ARZ1-5 data is from the discussion forums genre mostly in the Egyptian Arabic dialect (EGY). We refer to this data set as ARZ. Each part of the ARZ data set is divided into train, test and dev sets. According to AIDA2 (Al-Badrashiny et al., 2015), 38% of the data exhibits CS. In this paper we combined the annotated test and dev set to form a new Code Switching Test data set, we refer to as ARZTest. The total number of words in the test data ARZTest is 20,464 tokens.

As mentioned earlier, we created new baseline POS tagging models for MADAMIRA-EGY,

Dataset	# sentences	# Words	# Types	% CS
ARZ	13,698	175,361	39,168	40.78%
Spanglish	922	8,022	1,455	20.61%
Bangor	45,605	335,578	13,994	6.21%

Table 1: Data set details.

Dataset	Train/Dev Tokens	Test Tokens
ARZ	154,897	20,464
Spanglish	6,456	1,566
Bangor	268,464	67,114

Table 2: Data set distribution.

MADAMIRA-MSA and MADAMIRA-CS based on training data from ARZ1-5 training data portion. AIDA2 has a sentence level identification component that we used to identify the purity of the sentences from the training corpus ARZ1-5 training data. Specifically, we used the AIDA2 identified EGY sentences for training the MADAMIRA-EGY models, the MSA AIDA2 identified sentences for training the MADAMIRA-MSA models, and the CS identified AIDA2 sentences for training the MADAMIRA-CS models.

For SPA-ENG data, We used two SPA-ENG CS data sets, one is the transcribed conversation used in the work by Solorio and Liu (Solorio and Liu, 2008), referred to as Spanglish. The Spanglish data set has ~8K tokens and was transcribed and annotated by the authors of that paper. While this is a small data set we include it in our work since it allows us to compare with previous work.

The second SPA-ENG CS data is the Bangor Miami corpus, referred to as Bangor. This corpus is also conversational speech involving a total of 84 speakers living in Miami, FL. In total, the corpus consists of 242,475 words of text from 35 hours of recorded conversation. Around 63% of transcribed words are in English, 34% in Spanish and 3% in an indeterminate language. The transcriptions were carried out manually at the utterance level by a team of transcribers. They include beginning time and end time of utterance as well as language id for each word. Table 2 shows more details about the various data sets.

4.2 Part of Speech Tagset

The ARZ1-5 data set is manually annotated using the Buckwalter (BW) POS tag set. The BW POS tag set is considered one of the most popular Arabic POS tagsets. It gains its popularity from its use in the Penn Arabic Treebank (PATB) (Maamouri et al., 2004; Alkuhlani et al., 2013). It can be used for tokenized and untokenized Arabic text. The tokenized tags that are used in the PATB are extracted from the untokenized tags. The number of untokenized tags is 485 tags and generated by BAMA (Buckwalter, 2004). Both tokenized and untokenized tags use the same 70 tags and sub-tags such as nominal suffix, ADJ, CONJ, DET, and, NSUFF (Eskander et al., 2013) (Alkuhlani et al., 2013). Combining the sub-tags can form almost 170 morpheme sub-tags such NSUFF_FEM_SG. This is a very detailed tagset for our purposes and also for cross CS language pair comparison, i.e. in order to compare between trends in the MSA-EGY setting and the SPA-ENG setting. Accordingly, we map the BW tagset which is the output of the MADAMIRA tools to the universal tagset (Petrov et al., 2011). We apply the mapping as follows: **1)** Personal, relative, demonstrative, interrogative, and indefinite pronouns are mapped to Pronoun; **2)**Acronyms are mapped to Proper Nouns; **3)** Complementizers and adverbial clause introducers are mapped to Subordinating Conjunction; **4)**Main verbs (content verbs), copulas, participles, and some verb forms such as gerunds and infinitives are mapped to Verb; **5)**Adjectival, ordinal numerals and participles are mapped to Adjectives; **5)**Prepositions and postpositions are mapped to Adpositions; **6)**Interrogative, relative and demonstrative adverbs are mapped to Adverb; **7)**Tense, passive and Modal auxiliaries are mapped to Auxiliary Verb; **8)**Possessive determiners, demonstrative determiners, interrogative determiners, quantity/quantifier determiners, etc are mapped to Determiner; **9)** Noun and gerunds and infinitives are mapped to Noun; **10)**Negation particle, question particle, sentence modality, and indeclinable aspectual or tense particles are mapped to Particle.

The Bangor Miami corpus has also been automatically glossed and tagged with part-of-speech tags in the following manner: each word is automatically glossed using the Bangor Autoglosser (Donnelly and Deuchar, 2011).[3] Subsequently, tran-

---

102

scripts were manually edited to fix incorrect glosses. For the experiments presented here, the corpus went through two edition/annotation stages. In the first stage, a number of changes were performed manually: a) those tokens ambiguously tagged with more than one POS tag were disambiguated (e.g. that.CONJ.[or].DET); b) ambiguous POS categories like ASV, AV and SV were disambiguated into either ADJ, NOUN, or VERB; c) for frequent tokens like *so* and *that*, their POS tags were hand-corrected; d) finally, mistranscribed terms which were originally labeled as Unknown were hand-corrected and given a correct POS tag. The second stage consisted in mapping the Bangor corpus original POS tagset[4] to the Universal POS tagset (Petrov et al., 2011).[5] After a careful examination of both tagsets, the following mapping was applied: **1)** All those categories with an obvious match (like Nouns, Adjectives, Verbs, Pronouns, Determiners, Proper Nouns, Numbers, etc.) were automatically mapped; **2)** Exclamations and Intonational Markers were mapped to Interjections; **3)** As per the Universal POS tagset guidelines: Possessive Adjectives, Possessive Determiners, Interrogative Adjectives, Demonstrative Adjectives and Quantifying Adjectives were mapped to Determiner; **4)** Those tokens tagged as Relatives, Interrogatives and Demonstratives (with no specification to whether they were Determiners, Adjectives or Pronouns) were manually labeled; **5)** All possessive markers, negation particles, and infinitive *to* tokens were mapped to the PRT class; **6)** Conjunctions were mapped to Coordinating Conjunctions and Subordinating Conjunctions using word lists;

MSA-EGY Baseline		
Data set	MADAMIRA-MSA	MADAMIRA-EGY
ARZTest	77.23	72.22
SPA-ENG Baseline		
Dataset	TreeTagger SPA	TreeTagger ENG
Spanglish	44.61	75.87
Bangor	45.95	64.05

Table 3: POS tagging accuracy (%) for monolingual baseline taggers

7) Finally, a subset of English Verbs were mapped

to Auxiliary Verbs (could, should, might, may, will, shall, etc.).

Approach	Overall	CS	MSA	EGY
COMB1:LID-MonoLT	77.66	78.03	76.79	78.57
COMB2:MonoLT-LID	77.41	77.41	78.31	77.01
COMB3:MonoLT-Conf	76.66	77.89	76.79	76.11
COMB4:MonoLT-SVM	**90.56**	**90.85**	**91.63**	**88.91**
INT1:CSD	83.89	82.03	82.48	83.26
INT2:AllMonoData	87.86	87.92	86.82	86%
INT3:AllMonoData+CSD	89.36	88.12	85.12	87

Table 4: Accuracy (%) Results for ARZTest Dataset

Approach	Overall	CS	ENG	SPA
COMB1:LID-MonoLT	68.35	71.11	66.36	76.02%
COMB2:MonoLT-LID	65.51	69.66	64.44	71.32%
COMB3:MonoLT-Conf	68.25	68.21	71.93	65.03
COMB4:MonoLT-SVM	**96.31**	**95.39**	**96.37**	**96.60**
INT1:CSD	95.28	94.41	94.41	95.15
INT2:AllMonoData	78.57	78.62	81.85	76.53%
INT3:AllMonoData+CSD	91.04	89.59	92.00	89.48

Table 5: Accuracy (%) Results for Bangor Corpus

Approach	Overall	CS	ENG	SPA
COMB1:LID-MonoLT	78.73	77.81	80.18	73.99
COMB2:MonoLT-LID	73.52	73.80	73.60	71.57
COMB3:MonoLT-Conf	77.39	76.11	80.20	65.43
COMB4:MonoLT-SVM	**90.61**	**89.43**	**93.61**	**87.96**
INT1:CSD	82.95	83.03	85.95	77.26
INT2:AllMonoData	84.55	84.84	88.50	76.59
INT3:AllMonoData+CSD	85.06	84.70	90.15	76.59

Table 6: Accuracy (%) Results for Spanglish Corpus

To evaluate the performance of our approaches we report the accuracy of each condition by comparing the output POS tags generated from each condition against the available gold POS tags for each data set. Also, we compare the accuracy of our approaches for each language pair to its corresponding monolingual tagger baseline. We consistently apply the different experimental conditions on the same test set per language pair: for MSA-EGY we report results on ARZTest, and for SPA-ENG, we report results on two test sets: Spanglish and Bangor.

Baseline Results The baseline performance is the POS tagging accuracy of the monolingual models with no special training for CS data. Since we have four monolingual models, we consider four baselines. If CS data do not pose any particular challenge to monolingual POS taggers, then we shouldn't expect a major degradation in performance. Table 3 shows the performance of the 4 different baseline POS tagging systems on the test data. For Arabic, MSA monolingual performance for MADAMIRA-MSA, when tested on monolingual MSA test data, is around ~97% accuracy, and for MADAMIRA-EGY when tested in monolingual EGY data it is ~93%. We note here that the presence of CS data in the ARZ test data causes these systems to degrade significantly in performance (77% and 72% accuracy, respectively). For SPA-ENG, state of the art monolingual models achieve an accuracy of ~96% and ~93 on monolingual English and monolingual Spanish data sets, respectively. It is then clear that CS data poses serious challenges to monolingual technology. Other prior work has also reported similar drops in performance because of having mixed language data.

4.3   Results

Table 4, Table 5 and Table 6 show the results of all our experimental conditions. For all language pairs, we report four results, the accuracy results for only lang1 sentences, lang2 sentences, CS sentences, and all sentences. For example for MSA-EGY, we extract the MSA, EGY, and CS sentences, respectively, from each experimental setup to report the breakdown of the performance of the condition on the specific set, i.e. We calculate the accuracy for the MSA, EGY, CS, and All (MSA+EGY+CS) sentences. For MSA-EGY the highest accuracy is 90.56%. It is achieved when we apply condition "COMB4:MonoLT-SVM". All the INT conditions outperform the COMB conditions except for COMB4:MonoLT-SVM. Among the COMB conditions, we note that the MonoLT-SVM is the best COMBINED condition. In the SPA-ENG, the highest accuracies are achieved when we apply condition "COMB4:MonoLT-SVM". This finding of having the best POS tagging results when using the monolingual taggers output to train a machine learning algorithm confirms the concluded results in (Solorio and Liu, 2008). Our contribution is that we replicate these results using a unified POS tagging scheme using an additional, much larger data

set. The lowest accuracy in SPA-ENG is when we apply "COMB2:MonoLT-LID" condition. The accuracy reaches ~73% in the Spanglish dataset and ~65% for the Bangor corpus. In this language pair the INT conditions outperform all the COMB except the one that uses the stack-based approach (COMB4:MonoLT-SVM). It is interesting that we observe the same trends across both language pairs.

5   Discussion

Combined conditions For MSA-EGY, all the combined experimental conditions outperform the baselines. Among the combined conditions we note that applying language identification then applying language specific monolingual taggers yields worse results than applying the taggers on the input sentence then assigning tags as per the language ID tool. This is expected due to the fact that the taggers are expecting well formed sentences on input. Applying condition LID-MonoLT forces the taggers to tag chunks as opposed to sentences thereby leading to degraded performance. For the first two conditions COMB1:LID-MonoLT and COMB2:MonoLT-LID, the performance increases slightly from 77.41% to 77.66%. The results for MonoLT-SVM are the highest for the combined conditions for MSA-EGY. The worst results are for condition MonoLT-Conf. This might be relegated to the quality of the confidence values produced by the monolingual taggers, i.e. not being very indicative of the confidence scores for the tags chosen. For the SPA-ENG language pair, almost all the accuracies achieved by the combined conditions are higher than the Spanglish data set's baselines. The only combined condition that is lower than the baselines' of the Spanglish data set is "COMB2:MonoLT-LID" condition, where the accuracy is 73.52% compared to the monolingual English tagger that reached a baseline performance of 75.87%. This difference can be attributed to mistakes in the automated language identification that cause the wrong tagger to be chosen.

If we consider all accuracy results of the combined conditions for the Bangor corpus and its baselines, we see that the boosts in accuracy are of at least 2%. It is quite noteworthy that the trends seem to be the same between the two language pairs. Both language pairs achieve the highest performance with MonoLT-SVM and worse results with MonoLT-Conf. The gains in performance from using a learning algorithm are likely due to the fact that the learner is taking advantage of both monolingual tagger outputs and is able to go beyond the available tags for cases where there are errors in both. This result is also consistent with findings in the Spanglish dataset by (Solorio and Liu, 2008). The weaknesses of the MonoLT-Conf approach probably come from the fact that if the monolingual taggers are weak, their confidence scores are equally unreliable.

However the results are switched between conditions LID-MonoLT (condition 1) and MonoLT-LID (condition 2) for the two language pairs. Condition 1 outperforms condition 2 for MSA-EGY while we see the opposite for SPA-ENG. This is an indication of the quality and robustness of the underlying strength of the SPA and ENG monolingual taggers, they can handle chunks more robustly compared to the Arabic taggers. It is worth noting that the underlying Language id component for Arabic, AIDA2, achieves a very high accuracy on token and sentence level dialect id, F1 92.9% for token identification, and an F1 of 90.2% on sentence level dialect identification. Also compared to manual annotation on the TestDev set for dialect identification, we note an inter-annotator agreement of 93% between human annotation and AIDA2.

All COMB conditions use either out of context or in context chunks as an input for the monolingual taggers. We believe that the out of context chunks especially in the MSA-DA language pair contributed heavily in the noncompetitive results yielded.

Integrated conditions The rather simple idea of throwing the monolingual data together to train a model to label mixed data turned out to reach surprisingly good performance across both language pairs. In general, except the "COMB4:MonoLT-SVM" condition all the INT conditions outperformed the COMB conditions and in turn the baselines for the MSA-EGY language pair. For this language pair we note that adding more data helps, INT2:AllMonoData outperforms INT1:CSD, but combining the two conditions as training data, we note that INT3:AllMonoData+CSD outperforms the other INT conditions. Applying the INT conditions on only the CS sentences yields the highest accuracy compared to the other sentences types. For SPA-ENG, the worse INT condition is INT2:AllMonoData for Bangor (accuracy 78.57%) and INT1:CSD for Spanglish (accuracy 82.95%), compared to the best performing condition for both SPA-ENG data sets, Spanglish (accuracy of 90.61%) and Bangor (accuracy 96.31%). The largest difference is in the Bangor corpus itself and this gap in performance could be due to a higher domain mismatch with the monolingual data used to train the tagger. Another notable difference between the two language pairs is the significant jump in performance for the Bangor corpus from the first three COMB conditions from 68.35% to 96.31%. While we observe a similar jump for the Spanglish corpus, the gap is much larger for the Bangor corpus. Here again, we believe the major factor is a larger mismatch with the training corpus for the monolingual taggers. It should be highlighted that even though the language pairs are very different, there are some similar trends between the two combinations. COMB4:MonoLT-SVM is the best among combined conditions and INT conditions for the two language pairs. Moreover, except for the COMB4:MonoLT-SVM condition, all the INT conditions outperform combined conditions across the board. The percentage of the CS sentences in the ARZ dataset is ~51%. Moreover, MSA and EGY share a significant number of homographs some of which are cognates but many of which are not. This could be contrasted to the SPA-ENG case where the homograph overlap is quite limited. Adding the CSD to the monolingual corpora in the INT3:AllMonoData-CSD condition for MSA-EGY improves performance (1.5% absolute increase in accuracy) allowing for more discriminatory data to be included comparing to the other INT conditions, while the results are not consistent across the SPA-ENG data sets. In general, our results point to an inverse correlation between language similarity and the challenge to adapt monolingual taggers to a language combination. MSA-EGY has higher average baseline performance than SPA-ENG and all approaches outperform by a large margin those baseline results. In contrast, the average baseline performance for SPA-ENG is lower and the improvements gained by the approaches explored have different degrees of success. Additional studies are needed to further explore the validity of this finding.

6 Conclusions

We presented a detailed study of various strategies for POS tagging of CS data in two language pairs. The results indicate that depending on the language pair and the distance between them there are varying degrees of need for annotated code switched data in the training phase of the process. Languages that share a significant amount of homographs when code switched will benefit from more code switched data at training time, while languages that are farther apart such as Spanish and English, when code switched, benefit more from having larger monolingual data mixed. All COMB conditions use either out of context or in context chunks as an input for the monolingual taggers. We believe that out of context chunks especially in the MSA-DA language pair contributed heavily in the noncompetitive results that we got for the COMB conditions. Therefore, our plan for the future work that process the out of context chunks to provide a meaningful context to the monolingual taggers. Also, we plan to extend our feature set used in the COMB4:MonoLT-SVM condition to include Brown Clustering, Word2Vec, and Deep learning based features.

References

Mohamed Al-Badrashiny, Heba Elfardy, and Mona T. Diab. 2015. AIDA2: A hybrid approach for token and sentence level dialect identification in arabic. In Afra Alishahi and Alessandro Moschitti, editors, *Proceedings of the 19th Conference on Computational Natural Language Learning, CoNLL 2015, Beijing, China, July 30-31, 2015*, pages 42–51. ACL.

Sarah Alkuhlani, Nizar Habash, and Ryan Roth. 2013. Automatic morphological enrichment of a morphologically underspecified treebank. In *HLT-NAACL*, pages 460–470.

Utsab Barman, Amitava Das, Joachim Wagner, and Jennifer Foster. 2014. Code mixing: A challenge for language identification in the language of social media. *EMNLP 2014*, 13.

Tim Buckwalter. 2004. Buckwalter arabic morphological analyzer version 2.0. ldc catalog no. ldc2004l02, linguistic data consortium.

Mónica Stella Cárdenas-Claros and Neny Isharyanti. 2009. Code-switching and code-mixing in internet chatting: Betweenyes,'yes' , 'ya' , and 'si' a case study. *The Jalt Call Journal*, 5(3):67–78.

Brenda Danet and Susan C Herring. 2007. *The multilingual Internet: Language, culture, and communication online*. Oxford University Press.

Kevin Donnelly and Margaret Deuchar. 2011. Using constraint grammar in the bangor autoglosser to disambiguate multilingual spoken text. In *Constraint Grammar Applications: Proceedings of the NODALIDA 2011 Workshop, Riga, Latvia*, pages 17–25.

Ramy Eskander, Nizar Habash, Ann Bies, Seth Kulick, and Mohamed Maamouri. 2013. Automatic correction and extension of morphological annotations. In *Proceedings of the 7th Linguistic Annotation Workshop and Interoperability with Discourse*, pages 1–10. Citeseer.

David Graff, Junbo Kong, Ke Chen, and Kazuaki Maeda. 2003. English gigaword. *Linguistic Data Consortium, Philadelphia*.

Dave Graff. 2006. LDC2006T12: Spanish gigaword corpus. *Philadelphia: LDC*.

Anupam Jamatia, Björn Gambäck, and Amitava Das. 2015. Part-of-speech tagging for code-mixed english-hindi twitter and facebook chat messages. *RECENT ADVANCES IN*, page 239.

Mohamed Maamouri, Ann Bies, Tim Buckwalter, and Wigdan Mekki. 2004. The Penn Arabic Treebank: Building a large-scale annotated Arabic corpus. In *NEMLAR conference on Arabic language resources and tools*, volume 27, pages 466–467.

Mohamed Maamouri, Ann Bies, Seth Kulick, Dalila Tabessi, and Sondos Krouna. 2012. Egyptian arabic treebank pilot.

Mitchell P. Marcus, Mary Ann Marcinkiewicz, and Beatrice Santorini. 1993. Building a large annotated corpus of english: The penn treebank. *Comput. Linguist.*, 19(2):313–330, June.

Arfath Pasha, Mohamed Al-Badrashiny, Mona T. Diab, Ahmed El Kholy, Ramy Eskander, Nizar Habash, Manoj Pooleery, Owen Rambow, and Ryan M. Roth. 2014. Madamira: A fast, comprehensive tool for morphological analysis and disambiguation of arabic. In *LREC*.

Slav Petrov, Dipanjan Das, and Ryan T. McDonald. 2011. A universal part-of-speech tagset. *CoRR*, abs/1104.2086.

Kalika Bali Royal Sequiera, Monojit Choudhury. 2015. Pos tagging of hindi-english code mixed text from social media: Some machine learning experiments. In *Proceedings of International Conference on NLP*. NLPAI, December.

Helmut Schmid. 1994. Probabilistic part-of-speech tagging using decision trees. In *International Conference on New Methods in Language Processing*, pages 44–49.

Thamar Solorio and Yang Liu. 2008. Part-of-speech tagging for english-spanish code-switched text. In *Proceedings of the Conference on Empirical Methods in Natural Language Processing*, pages 1051–1060. Association for Computational Linguistics.

Andreas Stolcke et al. 2002. SRILM-an extensible language modeling toolkit. In *INTERSPEECH*, volume 2002, page 2002.

Mariona Taulé, M Antonia Martí, and Marta Recasens. 2008. Ancora: Multilevel annotated corpora for Catalan and Spanish. *Proceedings of the Sixth International Conference on Language Resources and Evaluation (LREC'08)*.

Yogarshi Vyas, Spandana Gella, Jatin Sharma, Kalika Bali, and Monojit Choudhury. 2014. Pos tagging of english-hindi code-mixed social media content. In *Proceedings of the 2014 Conference on Empirical Methods in Natural Language Processing (EMNLP)*, pages 974-979, Doha, Qatar, October. Association for Computational Linguistics.

The George Washington University System for the Code-Switching Workshop Shared Task 2016

Mohamed Al-Badrashiny and Mona Diab
Department of Computer Science, The George Washington University
{badrashiny,mtdiab}@gwu.edu

Abstract

We describe our work in the EMNLP 2016 second code-switching shared task; a generic language independent framework for linguistic code switch point detection (LCSPD). The system uses characters level 5-grams and word level unigram language models to train a conditional random fields (CRF) model for classifying input words into various languages. We participated in the Modern Standard Arabic (MSA)-dialectal Arabic (DA) and Spanish-English tracks, obtaining a weighted average F-scores of 0.83 and 0.91 on MSA-DA and EN-SP respectively.

1 Introduction

Linguistic Code Switching (LCS) is a common practice among multilingual speakers in which they switch between their common languages in written and spoken communication. In Spanish-English for example: "She told me that mi esposo looks like un buen hombre." ("She told me that my husband looks like a good man"). In this work we care about detecting LCS points as they occur intra-sententially where words from more than one language is mixed in the same utterance. LCS is observed on all levels of linguistic representation. It is pervasive especially in social media. LCS poses a significant challenge to NLP, hence detecting LCS points is a very important task for many downstream applications.

In this shared task(Molina et al., 2016), the participants are asked to identify the language type of each word in a large set of tweets. The shared task has two language pair tracks; MSA-DA and Spanish-English. For each language pair, the participants are required to identify each word in each tweet to be:

- lang1: if the word is related to the first language in each track (i.e. MSA or English) ;

- lang2: if the word is related to the second language in each track (i.e. DA or Spanish);

- ambiguous: if the word can be in both languages and can't decide which language should be picked based on the context;

- mixed: if the word is consisted of mixed morphemes from both languages (ex. prefix and suffix form MSA attached to a DA word);

- fw: if the word is related to any other language than the targeted language pair

- ne: if the word is named entity;

- other: if the word is number, punctuation, emoticons, url, date, starts with #, @, or contains underscore;

- unk: if can not be determined to by any of the above tags.

Relevant work on thhe LCS problem among different language pairs can be summarized in the following work.

3ARRIB (Al-Badrashiny et al., 2014; Eskander et al., 2014) addresses the challenge of how to distinguish between Arabic words written using Roman script (Arabizi) and actual English words in the same context/utterance. The assumption in this framework is the script is Latin for all words. It trains

Proceedings of the Second Workshop on Computational Approaches to Code Switching, pages 108–111,
Austin, TX, November 1, 2016. ©2016 Association for Computational Linguistics

a finite state transducer (FST) to learn the mapping between the Roman form of the Arabizi words and their Arabic form. It uses the resulting FST to find all possible Arabic candidates for each word in the input text. These candidates are filtered using MADAMIRA (Pasha et al., 2014), a state of the art morphological analyzer and POS disambiguation tool, to filter out non-Arabic solutions. Finally, it leverages a decision tree that is trained on language model probabilities of both the Arabic and Romanized forms to render the final decision for each word in context as either being Arabic or English.

Bar and Dershowitz (2014) addresses the challenge for Spanish-English LCS. The authors use several features to train a sequential Support Vector Machines (SVM) classifier. The used features include previous and following two words, substrings of 1-3 character ngrams from the beginning and end of each word thereby modeling prefix and suffix information, a boolean feature indicating whether the first letter is capitalized or not, and 3-gram character and word n-gram language models trained over large corpora of English and Spanish, respectively.

Barman et al. (2014) present systems for both Nepali-English and Spanish-English LCS. The script for both language pairs is Latin based, i.e. Nepali-English is written in Latin script, and Spanish-English is written in Latin script. The authors carry out several experiments using different approaches including dictionary-based methods, linear kernel SVMs, and a k-nearest neighbor approach. The best setup they found is the SVM-based one that uses character n-gram, binary features indicates whether the word is in a language specific dictionary of the most frequent 5000 words they have constructed, length of the word, previous and next words, 3 boolean features for capitalization to check if the first letter is capitalized, if any letter is capitalized, or if all the letters are capitalized.

On the other hand, for within language varieties, AIDA2(Al-Badrashiny et al., 2015) is the best published system attacking this problem in Arabic for the Arabic varieties mix problem. In this context, the problem of LCS is more complicated than mixing two very different languages since in the case of varieties of the same language, the two varieties typically share a common space of cognates and often faux amis, where there are homographs but the

words have very different semantic meanings, hence adding another layer of complexity to the problem. In this set up the assumed script is Arabic script. AIDA2 uses a complex system that is based on a mix of language dependent and machine learning components to detect the linguistic code switch between the modern standard Arabic (MSA) and Egyptian dialect (EGY) that are both written using Arabic script. It uses MADAMIRA(Pasha et al., 2014) to find the POS tag, prefix, lemma, suffix, for each word in the input text. Then it models these features together with other features including word level language model probabilities in a series of classifiers where it combines them in a classifier ensemble approach to find the best tag for each word.

In this paper we address this challenge using a generic simple language independent approach. We illustrate our approach on both language pair tracks.

2   Approach

The presented system in this paper is based on the idea we presented in (Al-Badrashiny and Diab, 2016). It is based on the assumption that each language has its own character pattern behaviors and combinations relating to the underlying phonology, phonetics, and morphology of each language independently. Accordingly, the manner of articulation constrains the possible phonemic/morphemic combinations in a language.

Accordingly, we use a supervised learning framework to address the challenge of LCS. We assume the presence of annotated code switched training data where each token is annotated as either Lang1 or Lang2. We create a sequence model using Conditional Random Fields (CRF++) tool(Sha and Pereira, 2003). For each word in the training data, we create a feature vector comprising character sequence level probabilities, unigram word level probabilities, and two binary features to identify if the word is named entity or not and is other or not . Once we derive the learning model, we apply to input text to identify the tokens in context. For the character sequence level probabilities, we built a 5-gram character language model (CLM) using the SRILM tool(Stolcke, 2002) for each of the two languages presented in the training data using the annotated words. For example, if the training data contains

	lang1	lang2	mixed	ne	ambiguous	fw	other	unk
MSA-DA-Training	127626	21722	16	21389	1186	0	13738	0
MSA-DA-Dev	6406	9326	2	3024	10	0	1888	0
EN-SP-Training	58844	27064	44	2364	252	11	20705	153
EN-SP-Dev	7067	5207	8	368	22	0	3912	58

Table 1: Language distribution (words/language) in the training and test data sets for all language-pairs

the two languages "lang1" and "lang2", we use all words that have the "lang1" tags to build a character 5-grams LM for "lang1" and the same for "lang2". We apply all of the created CLM to each word in the training data to find their character sequence probabilities in each language in the training data. To increase the difference between the feature vectors of the words related to "lang1" and those related to "lang2", we use a word level unigram LM for one of the two languages in the training data. In practice, we pick the language where large corpora exist in order to build the LM. Then we apply the unigram LM to each word in the training data to find their word level probability. For the "ne" feature, we use the tagged named entities words from the training data as a lookup table. Then we put one in this feature if the word in the input tweet can be found in that lookup table, otherwise it is zero. We use SPLIT (Al-Badrashiny et al., 2016) to check if the word is numbers, dates, urls, emoticons, sounds, or punctuation. Then if the word is found to be any of these types, we put one the "is other" feature, otherwise it is zero.

3 Experimental Setup

Table 1 shows the labels distribution of each language in the training and dev sets. The lang1, lang2 labels refer to the two languages addressed in the dataset name, for example for the language pair English-Spanish, lang1 is English and lang2 is Spanish, in that order.

We also used the English Gigaword (LDC, 2003b) to build the unigram word level LM for the English part in English-Spanish. And the Arabic Gigaword (LDC, 2003a) to build the unigram word level LM for the Arabic part in MSA-DA.

4 Evaluation

Table 2 shows the best results we got on the dev sets of both language-pairs. The best results we got

was by tuning the CRF classifier to use a window of 17 words (eight words before and after the current words).

	MSA-DA-Dev	EN-SP-Dev
lang1	81%	95%
lang2	83%	94%
mixed	0%	0%
ne	91%	70%
ambiguous	0%	0%
fw	0%	0%
other	99%	97%
unk	0%	12%
w-avg F-score	85%	94%

Table 2: Summary results of our system performance on the dev data of both language-pairs. For each group, the F-score is presented for all tags followed by the weighted average F-score for all tags.

Table 3 shows the results on the test set.

	MSA-DA-Test	EN-SP-Test
lang1	77%	81%
lang2	83%	95%
mixed	0%	0%
ne	83%	23%
ambiguous	0%	0%
fw	0%	0%
other	99%	95%
unk	0%	0%
w-avg F-score	83%	91%

Table 3: Summary results of our system performance on the test data of both language-pairs. For each group, the F-score is presented for all tags followed by the weighted average F-score for all tags.

The results show that the our system works better on the EN-SP data than the MSA-DA because, the words in the MSA and DA languages do not create disjoint sets, there is significant overlap hence they share significant character and word patterns. Hence, modeling more nuanced features is needed such as POS tags and morphological information to improve the performance on the MSA-DA data. The main tag that need some more improvement is the "ne". It needs some other sophisticated techniques other than just using a lookup table. We also misunderstood the "others" tag in the Spanish-English data. We gave any word that starts with # the "other" label as in the Arabic guidelines, which affected our final results.

The main advantage of the proposed system is that it is language independent since it does not require any language-dependent components. Finally, the simplicity of our system made it very fast. It can process up to 20,000 words/sec; which renders it very efficient and amenable to large scale processing especially if a language identification module is required as a preprocessing step in some other applications (ex. Machine translation)

References

Mohamed Al-Badrashiny and Mona Diab. 2016. Lili: A simple language independent approach for language identification. In *The 26th International Conference on Computational Linguistics (COLING 2016). Osaka, Japan.*

Mohamed Al-Badrashiny, Ramy Eskander, Nizar Habash, and Owen Rambow. 2014. Automatic Transliteration of Romanized Dialectal Arabic. In *Proceedings of the Eighteenth Conference on Computational Natural Language Learning*, pages 30–38, Ann Arbor, Michigan, June. Association for Computational Linguistics.

Mohamed Al-Badrashiny, Heba Elfardy, and Mona Diab. 2015. Aida2: A hybrid approach for token and sentence level dialect identification in arabic. In *Proceedings of the Nineteenth Conference on Computational Natural Language Learning*, pages 42–51, Beijing, China, July. Association for Computational Linguistics.

Mohamed Al-Badrashiny, Arfath Pasha, Mona Diab, Nizar Habash, Owen Rambow, Wael Salloum, and Ramy Eskander. 2016. Split: Smart preprocessing (quasi) language independent tool. In Nicoletta Calzolari (Conference Chair), Khalid Choukri, Thierry Declerck, Marko Grobelnik, Bente Maegaard, Joseph Mariani, Asuncion Moreno, Jan Odijk, and Stelios Piperidis, editors, *Proceedings of the Tenth International Conference on Language Resources and Evaluation (LREC 2016)*, Paris, France, may. European Language Resources Association (ELRA).

Kfir Bar and Nachum Dershowitz. 2014. The tel aviv university system for the code-switching workshop shared task. In *Proceedings of the First Workshop on Computational Approaches to Code Switching*, pages 139–143, Doha, Qatar, October. Association for Computational Linguistics.

Utsab Barman, Joachim Wagner, Grzegorz Chrupała, and Jennifer Foster. 2014. Dcu-uvt: Word-level language classification with code-mixed data. In *Proceedings of the First Workshop on Computational Approaches to Code Switching*, pages 127–132, Doha, Qatar, October. Association for Computational Linguistics.

Ramy Eskander, Mohamed Al-Badrashiny, Nizar Habash, and Owen Rambow. 2014. Foreign words and the automatic processing of arabic social media text written in roman script. *In Proceedings of the First Workshop on Computational Approaches to Code-Switching. EMNLP 2014, Conference on Empirical Methods in Natural Language Processing, October, 2014, Doha, Qatar.*

LDC. 2003a. Arabic Gigaword Fifth Edition LDC2011T11. Linguistic Data Consortium.

LDC. 2003b. English Gigaword LDC2003T05. Linguistic Data Consortium.

Giovanni Molina, Fahad AlGhamdi, Mahmoud Ghoneim, Abdelati Hawwari, Nicolas Rey-Villamizar, Mona Diab, and Thamar Solorio. 2016. Overview for the second shared task on language identification in code-switched data. In *Proceedings of The EMNLP 2016 Second Workshop on Computational Approaches to Linguistic Code Switching (CALCS).*

Arfath Pasha, Mohamed Al-Badrashiny, Mona Diab, Ahmed El Kholy, Ramy Eskander, Nizar Habash, Manoj Pooleery, Owen Rambow, and Ryan M. Roth. 2014. MADAMIRA: A Fast, Comprehensive Tool for Morphological Analysis and Disambiguation of Arabic. In *Proceedings of LREC*, Reykjavik, Iceland.

Fei Sha and Fernando Pereira. 2003. Shallow parsing with conditional random fields. In *Proceedings of Human Language Technology-NAACL*, pages 213–220, Edmonton, Canada.

Andreas Stolcke. 2002. Srilm an extensible language modeling toolkit. In *Proceedings of the International Conference on Spoken Language Processing (ICSLP).*

Columbia-Jadavpur submission for EMNLP 2016 Code-Switching Workshop Shared Task: System description

Arunavha Chanda
a.chanda@columbia.edu
Columbia University

Dipankar Das
dipankar.dipnil2005@gmail.com
Jadavpur University

Chandan Mazumdar
chandanm@cse.jdvu.ac.in
Jadavpur University

Abstract

We describe our present system for language identification as a part of the EMNLP 2016 Shared Task. We were provided with the Spanish-English corpus composed of tweets. We have employed a predictor-corrector algorithm to accomplish the goals of this shared task and analyzed the results obtained.

1 Introduction

Code-mixing, a phenomenon in linguistics, is exhibited by multi-lingual people. Any utterance in which the speaker makes use of the grammar and lexicon of more than one language is said to have undergone code-mixing or code-switching (Appel and Muysken, 2005).

English is considered the primary language of use, as well as the most widely used language on the internet, accounting for around 53.6% content language of websites (W3Techs, 2015). It may be a bit of surprise that the value isn't higher. However, the statistics on social media re-inforce this idea, since around half of the messages on Twitter are in non-English languages (Schroeder, 2010).

In contrast to English, multilingual people tend to communicate in several of the languages that they know. This is because of several reasons: some multilingual speakers feel higher level of comfort in their native language than in English; some conversational topics are more fluid in a particular language and some expressions convey the message properly only in one's native language.

In this paper, we describe our system based on predictor-corrector algorithm as part of the shared task of EMNLP 2016 Code-Switching Workshop. The system has been applied on the English-Spanish code-mixed corps of tweets. Several lexicons were employed along with some rules into the system, the results were obtained and discussed in detail.

Section 2 describes the conference task description, Section 3 deals with the tools and techniques we used, Section 4 describes the system functioning, Section 5 talks about the results obtained and finally, Section 6 closes with a discussion.

2 Task description

The EMNLP 2016 Code-Switching Workshop[1] included a Shared Task on two language pairs: (1) English-Spanish and (2) Modern Standard Arabic-Arabic dialects. In the present attempt, We worked only on the English-Spanish task. The task organizers provided a corpora composed from code-switched tweets on which annotation had to be done using the following labels:

1. **lang1**: Language 1 of the pair- English in our case. We use this if the word is undoubtedly used in English in the given context.

2. **lang2**: Language 2 of the pair- Spanish for us. It is same as lang1 and we use this as this word is undoubtedly used as Spanish.

3. **mixed**: Mixed words for the words that are composed of both the languages. An example given was "*Snapchateame*", in which "*Snapchat*" was used from English and "*-eame*" was from Spanish.

---

[1]http://care4lang1.seas.gwu.edu/cs2/call.html

Proceedings of the Second Workshop on Computational Approaches to Code Switching, pages 112–115,
Austin, TX, November 1, 2016. ©2016 Association for Computational Linguistics

4. **NE**: Named Entities- used for proper nouns like people, places, organizations, locations, titles and such.

5. **ambiguous**: Ambiguous words that exist in both English and Spanish and suh words are hard to be clarified based on the context given.

6. **FW**: Foreign words, which do not appear either in English or in Spanish, but exist in another language and used in that context.

7. **UNK**: Unknown words which do not fit any of the above categories and is unrecognizable.

8. **Other**: Numbers, symbols, emojis, URLs and anything else that is not a "word". However, the words beginning with a "hashtag" (#) are treated as other tag.

The tweets were provided in terms of sentences and we were asked to develop a system that would annotate every token in the entire corpus of tweets as one of the given eight labels.

3 Tools and Techniques Used

3.1 Lexicons used

The dictionaries we used are the following:

1. **English dictionary**: We use the Python Enchant library[2] for checking the English words and their existence in the dictionary. We also create a slang dictionary of our own containing colloquial English text words such as "LOL" and "gr8". We collected the lexicons from the works of researchers at the University of Melbourne and University of Texas at Dallas (Han et al., 2012; Liu et al., 2011; Liu et al., 2012).

2. **Spanish dictionary**: We use the Python Enchant library once again for checking of the words' existence in the Spanish dictionary.

3. **Foreign dictionaries**: We also use the Italian, French, Portuguese (Brazil), Portuguese (Portugal) and German dictionaries from Python Enchant to check for words' existence. Since the geographical spread is given, any person

with code-switching possibility between English and Spanish would most likely borrow words from one of these languages.

4. **Stanford Named Entity Recognizer**. For identifying the named entities, we used the Stanford NER (Named Entity Recognizer) (Finkel et al., 2005) and it's Python interface in the nltk library[3].

3.2 Algorithm

3.2.1 Word Slicing

For identifying the mixed words, we use a word-slicing algorithm. It consists of the following steps:

1. We keep slicing a word into two parts of varying lengths. For example, for "abcde", we would obtain four splits:

   - "a" and "bcde"
   - "ab" and "cde"
   - "abc" and "de"
   - "abcd" and "e"

2. For each of these splits, we check if one part is present in the English dictionary and one part appears in the Spanish dictionary. In such cases, it would be declared as a mixed word. For example, if "abc" was identified as an English word and "de" was a Spanish word, "abcde" would be declared a mixed word.

3.2.2 Predictor-Corrector algorithm

We use this algorithm for the words that are present in both the English and Spanish dictionaries.

- Prediction: During initial tagging, if a word is present in both the dictionaries, it is tagged as "both".

- Correction: During the second round, we return to the point of words that are tagged "both" and if both the words on either side (or the adjacent one if at the beginning or end) are in the same language, it is corrected to that language, otherwise marked as ambiguous.

This way, our predictor-corrector method helps us to achieve better accuracy for identifying the ambiguous words.

[2]https://pypi.python.org/pypi/pyenchant/

[3]http://www.nltk.org

4 System Description

We take every tweet at a time and come down to the word level tagging before moving to the next tweet.

4.1 Dictionary words

- For every word, we first strip it of a "hashtag" (#), if there. Next, we run the Stanford Named Entity Recognizer[4]. The words identified as a Named Entity are tagged **"NE"** within a sentence.

- Before adopting our dictionary checking module, we check whether the token is all-word or it contains any punctuation mark/special character or number in it or not. If it does, we label it as **other**. Otherwise, we advance to the next step.

- Next, we check for the word's presence in the English and Spanish dictionaries. Based on their presence or absence in either dictionary, we take action:

  - If the word is present in the English dictionary and absent in the Spanish dictionary or vice-versa, it is immediately tagged **lang1** or **lang2** respectively.
  - If the word is present in both the English and Spanish dictionaries, it is initially tagged as "both" and then returned to the Predictor-Corrector algorithm described in section 3.2.2. According to the results from that, we tag the word as **lang1**, **lang2** or **ambiguous**.
  - If it is not present in either of the dictionaries, we go through another list of processes described in section 4.2.

4.2 Non-dictionary words

If the word is not found in either the English or the Spanish dictionary, we use the following techniques:

- We check for the word's presence in the French, Spanish, Portuguese (Portugal), Portuguese (Brazil) and German dictionaries. If found, we label the word as a foreign word **(FW)**.

---

[4]http://nlp.stanford.edu:8080/ner/

Tweet type	No. of tweets	F-score
Monolingual	6090	0.83
Code-switched	4626	0.75
Total	10716	**0.79**

Table 1: Tweet-level results

Label	Tokens	Precision	Recall	F-score
lang1	16944	0.509	0.449	**0.478**
lang2	77047	0.813	0.597	**0.689**
ambiguous	4	0.000	0.000	0.000
mixed	4	0.000	0.000	0.000
ne	2092	0.139	0.169	0.153
fw	19	0.000	0.158	0.010
other	25311	0.500	0.431	0.466
unk	25	0.002	0.240	0.003

Table 2: Word-level results

- If the word is still not found, we use the word-slicing algorithm spoken about in section 3.2.1 to see if it is a mixed word or not. If it is, we tag it as **mixed**.

- If the word is not mixed, we have failed to find any of the given criteria in order to fit, we label it as **unk** or unknown.

5 Results

Tables 1 and 2 summarize the tweet-level and word-level results for the test data, while the overall accuracy was determined to be **0.536**.

The accuracies are a bit lower than on the training and development data (where we achieved a best F-score of 0.772) and there are quite a few scopes for improvement that we can think of:

- The Named Entity Recognizer works based only on the English language. If we ran both English and Spanish NERs, that might have helped to improve the accuracy for "ne".

- For ambiguous words, our existing predictor-corrector method would lead to tagging more ambiguous words than there actually would be, since a lot of the surrounding words would be unknown/other. Moreover, those are simply tagged as ambiguous, while they are not indeed. We expanded our search area on finding non-tagged words, it may have helped increasing the accuracy here.

- For identifying the foreign words, we have considered the potential loss of accents while typing and that might have helped us to increase our detection for foreign words a bit more.

- In case of identifying the mixed words, we check the presence of word slices in dictionaries. However, many of these slices would be morphemes and not complete words and thus, wouldn't be found in a dictionary. We would need to develop a way of detecting presence of morphemes in a language for this. An N-gram pruning technique may help, but in code-switched contexts, with more than 2 labels to classify words in, it may not be as helpful as in a binary situation.

- Certain misspellings, typos, abbreviations and contractions may not have carried and been wrongly classified. We would need more sophisticated algorithms for detecting these cases.

6   Conclusion

We have achieved a healthy level of accuracy and utilized a fully developed algorithm without any machine learning or classifiers and also discover and discuss some areas of improvement and potential correction. In future works, we would perhaps tweak our algorithms in those ways to achieve a better accuracy.

References

René Appel and Pieter Muysken, 2005. *Code Switching and Code Mixing.* Amsterdam University Press.

Jenny Rose Finkel, Trond Grenager, and Christopher Manning. 2005. Incorporating non-local information into information extraction systems by gibbs sampling. In *Proceedings of the 43nd Annual Meeting of the Association for Computational Linguistics*, pages 363–370.

Bo Han, Paul Cook, and Timothy Baldwin. 2012. Automatically constructing a normalisation dictionary for microblogs. In *Proceedings of the 2012 Joint Conference on Empirical Methods in Natural Language Processing and Computational Natural Language Learning*, pages 421–432, Jeju Island, Korea, July. Association for Computational Linguistics.

Fei Liu, Fuliang Weng, Bingqing Wang, and Yang Liu. 2011. Insertion, deletion, or substitution? normalizing text messages without pre-categorization nor supervision. In *Proceedings of the 49th Annual Meeting of the Association for Computational Linguistics (ACL 2011)*, pages 71–76.

Fei Liu, Fuliang Weng, and Xiao Jiang. 2012. A broad-coverage normalization system for social media language. In *Proceedings of the 50th Annual Meeting of the Association for Computational Linguistics (ACL 2012)*, pages 1035–1044.

Stan Schroeder. 2010. Half of messages on twitter aren't in english [stats].

W3Techs. 2015. Usage of content languages for websites.

The Howard University System Submission for the Shared Task in Language Identification in Spanish-English Codeswitching

Mario Piergallini, Rouzbeh Shirvani, Gauri S. Gautam, and **Mohamed Chouikha**
Howard University Department of Electrical Engineering and Computer Science
2366 Sixth St NW, Washington, DC 20059
mario.piergallini@howard.edu, Rouzbeh.asgharishir@bison.howard.edu
gaurishankar.gaut@bison.howard.edu, mchouikha@howard.edu

Abstract

This paper describes the Howard University system for the language identification shared task of the Second Workshop on Computational Approaches to Code Switching. Our system is based on prior work on Swahili-English token-level language identification. Our system primarily uses character n-gram, prefix and suffix features, letter case and special character features along with previously existing tools. These are then combined with generated label probabilities of the immediate context of the token for the final system.

1 Introduction & Prior Approaches

The internet and social media have led to the emergence of new registers of written language (Tagliamonte and Denis, 2008). One of the effects of this is the emergence of written codeswitching as a common occurrence (Cárdenas-Claros and Isharyanti, 2009). The First Workshop on Computational Approaches to Codeswitching brought increased attention to this phenomenon. This paper is our submission for the shared task in token-level language identification in codeswitched data for the second such workshop. Our submission is for the Spanish-English language pair.

Our approach was informed particularly by the submissions to the previous shared task in language identification in codeswitched data. Most, if not all, of the previous approaches to word-level language identification utilized character n-grams as one of the primary features (Solorio et al., 2014). Nguyen and Doğruöz (2013) and all but one of the systems

	Train	Dev	Test
# Tweets	11,397	3,011	17,723
# Tokens	139,539	33,276	211,474
Avg. tokens/tweet	12.2	11.1	11.9
% English words	56.5%	50.5%	15.3%
% Spanish words	24.1%	26.0%	58.6%
% Mixed	<0.1%	<0.1%	<0.1%
% Ambiguous	0.2%	0.2%	<0.1%
% Named Entities	2.1%	2.2%	2.1%
% Foreign words	<0.1%	0.0%	<0.1%
% "Other"	16.9%	20.6%	23.9%
% "Unknown"	0.1%	0.4%	<0.1%

Table 1: Data set statistics

submitted to the previous shared task used some form of context, several of which used conditional random fields. A number of other types of features have been utilized as well, including capitalization, text encoding, word embedding, dictionaries, named entity gazetteer, among others (Solorio et al., 2014; Volk and Clematide, 2014).

2 Data Description

Several thousand tweets were collected from Twitter and labeled by human annotators. Each token was labeled as being English, Spanish, ambiguous (words like *no* which are valid words in both languages and can't be disambiguated by context), mixed (tokens with elements from both languages), foreign (words from other languages), a named entity, "unknown" (tokens like "asdfhg") and "other". The "other" category includes numbers (unless they represent a non-numerical word, like <2> used for "to"), punctuation, Twitter @-mentions, URLs, emojis and emoticons. These tweets were divided

116

Proceedings of the Second Workshop on Computational Approaches to Code Switching, pages 116–120,
Austin, TX, November 1, 2016. ©2016 Association for Computational Linguistics

into train, development and test sets and released[1] to the participants in the shared task. Basic statistics about the train, development and test sets can be seen in Table 2. As can be seen, the proportion of English and Spanish is significantly different for the test set compared to the other two sets.

Systems were evaluated at the tweet level as well. For this purpose, tweets are considered as either monolingual or codeswitched. A codeswitched tweet must have tokens from at least two of the following categories: English, Spanish, mixed and/or foreign. All other tweets are considered monolingual.

3 Methodology

In another paper, also submitted to this conference, we experimented with a number of features for token-level language identification on mixed Swahili-English data (Piergallini et al., 2016). For this shared task, we modified our approach in a few ways due to the parameters of the task and also explored the use of a few new features. These are described below:

1) Word

2) Character n-grams (1- to 4-grams)

3) Word prefixes and suffixes (length 1 to 4)

For features 1-3, we filtered out words, n-grams, prefixes and suffixes that occurred less than 25 times for training our model. N-grams, prefixes and suffixes were also converted to lower-case at the three and four character length to reduce sparsity.

4) English-Spanish dictionary

The dictionary feature checks the token against the English and Spanish dictionaries used in the GNU Aspell package[2] and marked according to whether it was in one or both of the English or Spanish dictionaries, or neither.

5) English POS tag

6) Spanish POS tag

The part-of-speech tags were generated by the Stanford NLTK POS tagger (Toutanova et al., 2003). The Spanish tags were truncated at three characters to reduce sparsity.

7) Named entity tag

Tweets were labeled with the named entity recognition system described in Ritter et al. (2011). This system was developed for use on Twitter data.

8) Brown cluster and cluster prefixes

Brown clustering groups word types into a binary tree structure based on word context (Brown et al., 1992). Clusters tend to correlate with syntactical and semantic categories. They also correlate with language, since words of one language tend to co-occur with other words of the same language. To generate these clusters, we lower-cased all words and replaced all Twitter user names with "@username". We used 400 clusters based on the size of the data and the desire for some distinctions beyond basic word classes. Words that occur infrequently tend to be quite noisy in how they are clustered, so words that occurred less than 10 times were not given a cluster. To take advantage of the binary tree structure, we included features based on prefixes of the cluster. For example, in our clusters, nodes beginning with <0> were mostly Spanish words, while nodes beginning with <11> were mostly English words.

The remaining features are binary flags:

9) Is there a Latin alphabetic character?

10) Is there a Spanish-specific letter?

Spanish-specific characters are limited to accented vowels, <ü> and <ñ>. These are strong indicators of a word being Spanish, but they do not all occur equally frequently, so this feature reduces sparsity. For example, <ó> occurs approximately 40 times more frequently than <ü>. This is the most language-specific feature we use. These characters occur extremely infrequently in English text compared to Spanish text. A language-independent conceptualization of this would be whether the word contains a member of the relative complement of

---

[1]Data was released by providing tweet ID numbers. Participants scraped the text of the tweets themselves. Since Twitter users may delete or restrict access to their tweets, not all participants may have had the exact same subset of the full data.

[2]Available here: https://github.com/WojciechMula/aspell-python

the set of English letters in the set of Spanish letters. Such a feature would not be useful in the other direction since the 26 letters of the English alphabet are all used in Spanish, particularly in online usage (<w> and especially <k> are not limited to loanwords in internet Spanish writing).

11) Is there a number character?

12) Is the token a numerical expression?

Feature 12 is true for tokens which consist entirely of digits, mathematical symbols, and characters used for expressions of time ("12:00") or currency symbols (<$>), etc.

13) Is there an emoji Unicode character?

Since all tokens composed of emojis are labeled as "other", this feature does not rely on a particular emoji occurring in our training data to accurately classify tokens in the test data.

14) Does the token begin a tweet/sentence?

15) Is the first letter capitalized?

16) Are all of the other letters upper case?

17) Are all of the other letters lower case?

The last four features consider capitalization. These features was added particularly to account for named entities and abbreviations, acronyms, etc. which are typically capitalized or in all upper-case letters. Since words at the beginning of sentences are frequently capitalized, eliminating what is usually a distinction between proper and common nouns, feature 14 should reduce the weight towards labeling a word as a named entity.

Finally, we used logistic regression with L2-regularization to generate label probabilities on tokens using the various combinations of the first 14 features. The label probabilities of the previous and following tokens were then added to the feature vector for each token. Tokens at the beginning or end of a tweet were given all zero probabilities for the absent context. This was found to significantly improve performance in our work on Swahili-English codeswitching (Piergallini et al., 2016) and is simpler than CRF[3]. A second logistic regression model was then trained and applied to the final feature set.

---

[3]CRF using the same feature sets achieves improvements of only 0.05-0.2% on accuracy but is also much slower.

3.1 Results & Discussion

The results of various feature combinations on the development set are summarized in Table 3. Four of the labels are excluded from the table. None of our models ever predicted a token to be ambiguous, mixed or foreign because these categories were all very rare in the both the training and development data. Conversely, the other category was very easily predicted by even the baseline model and achieved F1 scores of about 99.8% for all configurations.

There is not a high variation in the accuracy based on the features used. What can be seen is that the addition of the label probabilities for the previous and following word consistently adds about 2% to the overall accuracy and improves performance on the English and Spanish categories. It seems that part-of-speech tags and Brown clusters are not especially helpful. It is possible POS tags they could be more useful with a coarser POS tag set, or that the Brown clusters could be more useful with different pre-processing. The use of the named entity recognizer does improve performance on the named entity category significantly, but it did not improve overall accuracy much.

For our predictions on the test data, we used features 2-7 and 9-14 with label probabilities on the word context. Results for our submitted predictions are summarized in Table 3.1. According to the released results, our system never correctly labeled a token as ambiguous or mixed. It also never labeled a token as foreign at all. There are two versions: one with the original test data, and one which excludes tweets which contained URLs. We overlooked URLs in designing our model since they never occurred in the training or development data, although our model likely would've labeled them correctly had they occurred in training. Nevertheless, we achieve an overall accuracy in line with other systems without correcting for this. When tweets containing URLs are excluded, we achieve the highest performance on several measures. Those measures which were highest among submitted systems are noted in bold.

To improve on our model, adding a feature or procedure for properly handling URLs would be the obvious first change to make. However, this does not account for all of the errors in our predictions.

Features Used		Baseline fts 1-3		+Dict +Binary fts 1-4, 9-14		+Brown clusters fts 2-4, 8-14		+POS/NER tags fts 2-7, 9-14		+Brown/NER fts 2-4, 7-14	
Label Prob.		none	w±1	none	w±1	none	w±1	none	w±1	none	w±1
English	P	93.1	95.7	93.4	96.1	93.4	96.1	94.0	96.1	93.5	96.4
	R	97.0	97.9	97.2	98.1	97.3	98.1	96.8	97.9	97.3	98.1
	F1	95.0	96.8	95.3	97.1	95.3	97.1	95.4	97.0	95.4	97.2
Spanish	P	91.6	94.0	92.7	94.4	92.7	94.4	91.7	94.2	92.8	94.5
	R	90.6	96.1	91.0	96.7	91.0	96.7	91.9	96.4	91.0	96.8
	F1	91.1	95.0	91.8	95.5	91.9	95.5	91.8	95.3	91.9	95.6
Named Entity	P	60.4	62.7	61.9	63.1	62.0	63.3	70.3	69.6	68.1	70.5
	R	26.6	29.7	33.5	32.3	33.1	32.6	38.4	39.9	38.7	41.6
	F1	37.0	40.3	43.5	42.7	43.2	43.0	49.7	50.7	49.3	52.3
Unknown	P	0	0	0	25.0	33.3	33.3	33.3	16.7	50.0	0
	R	0	0	0	0.8	0.8	0.8	0.8	0.8	0.8	0
	F1	–	–	–	1.5	1.5	1.5	1.5	1.4	1.5	–
Accuracy		93.8	95.7	94.1	96.0	94.1	96.0	94.3	96.0	94.3	96.2

Table 2: Word-level performance of language identification models on development set (given in percentages)

Token-level		Test	w/o URLs
Overall Accuracy		95.1%	**97.3%**
English	P	90.9%	93.6%
	R	92.9%	**94.1%**
	F1	91.9%	**93.8%**
Spanish	P	97.6%	**98.4%**
	R	**97.8%**	**98.4%**
	F1	**97.7%**	**98.4%**
Named Entity	P	48.9%	60.6%
	R	59.6%	59.9%
	F1	53.7%	60.3%
Other	P	**99.9%**	**99.9%**
	R	92.9%	99.3%
	F1	96.3%	**99.6%**
Unknown	P	1.3%	1.8%
	R	7.0%	8.0%
	F1	2.1%	2.9%
Tweet-level		Test	w/o URLs
Weighted F1		**89.0%**	**91.3%**

Table 3: Performance of the final system on the test data

Notably, our system does poorly with ambiguous, mixed and foreign words. This is largely due to there being very few instances of these categories. We also suspect that dealing with them would require some special approaches to account for their particular features. For example, a mixed language word would be expected to have some n-grams found in both English and Spanish, but logistic regression can't easily account for this type of pattern. A feature designed to represent the interaction between the English- and Spanish-like features of a mixed

word would be required. It is also possible that some tokens were mislabeled. In our examination, it seemed that the ambiguous and mixed categories were not consistently distinguished.

It is also evident that our system does much worse on named entities than on other large categories. It could be that the tool we used did not have a comprehensive list of named entities (we missed "Orange Is the New Black", for example). It was also only trained on English. Our case features may also be more powerful when combined rather than made into separate binary features. There is an interaction between whether the first letter or all letters are upper or lower case and whether the word is at the beginning of a sentence, and the algorithm we used cannot capture that easily. This could potentially slightly improve performance on named entities. We would also note that English and Spanish do not consider the same types of words to be proper nouns, and this may be the cause for some inconsistencies in the annotations that we noticed.

4 Conclusion

In this paper, we described our system for Spanish-English token-level language identification. We achieved the highest performance on several measures using only the token's immediate context. We also found that POS/NE tagging tools and Brown clusters did not significantly improve overall accuracy over using simpler features, but it is possible refinements could make them more useful.

References

Peter F. Brown, Peter V. deSouza, Robert L. Mercer, Vincent J. Della Pietra, and Jenifer C. Lai. 1992. Class-based n-gram models of natural language. *Computational Linguistics*, 18(4):467–479, December.

Mónica Stella Cárdenas-Claros and Neny Isharyanti. 2009. Code-switching and code-mixing in internet chatting: Between 'yes,' 'ya,'and 'si'-a case study. *The Jalt Call Journal*, 5(3):67–78.

Dong Nguyen and A. Seza Doğruöz. 2013. Word level language identification in online multilingual communication. In *Proceedings of the 2013 Conference on Empirical Methods in Natural Language Processing*, pages 857–862. Association for Computational Linguistics.

Mario Piergallini, Rouzbeh Shirvani, Gauri Gautam, and Mohamed Chouikha. 2016. Word-level language identification and predicting codeswitching points in Swahili-English language data. In *The Second Workshop on Computational Approaches to Code Switching*. Association for Computational Linguistics. To appear.

Alan Ritter, Sam Clark, Mausam, and Oren Etzioni. 2011. Named entity recognition in tweets: An experimental study. In *EMNLP*.

Thamar Solorio, Elizabeth Blair, Suraj Maharjan, Steve Bethard, Mona Diab, Mahmoud Ghoneim, Abdelati Hawwari, Fahad AlGhamdi, Julia Hirshberg, Alison Chang, and Pascale Fung. 2014. Overview for the first shared task on language identification in codeswitched data. In *Proceedings of The First Workshop on Computational Approaches to Code Switching*, pages 62–72. Association for Computational Linguistics.

Sali A. Tagliamonte and Derek Denis. 2008. Linguistic ruin? LOL! Instant messaging and teen language. *American Speech*, 83(1).

Kristina Toutanova, Dan Klein, Christopher D. Manning, and Yoram Singer. 2003. Feature-rich part-of-speech tagging with a cyclic dependency network. In *Proceedings of the 2003 Conference of the North American Chapter of the Association for Computational Linguistics on Human Language Technology - Volume 1*, NAACL '03, pages 173–180, Stroudsburg, PA, USA. Association for Computational Linguistics.

Martin Volk and Simon Clematide. 2014. Detecting code-switching in a multilingual Alpine heritage corpus. In *Proceedings of The First Workshop on Computational Approaches to Code Switching*, pages 24–33. Association for Computational Linguistics.

Codeswitching Detection via Lexical Features using Conditional Random Fields

Prajwol Shrestha

Verscend Technologies Pvt. Ltd.

`prajwol.shrestha@verscend.com`

Abstract

Half of the world's population is estimated to be at least bilingual. Due to this fact many people use multiple languages interchangeably for effective communication. At the Second Workshop on Computational Approaches to Code Switching, we are presented with a task to label codeswitched, Spanish-English (ES-EN) and Modern Standard Arabic-Dialect Arabic (MSA-DA), tweets. We built a Conditional Random Field (CRF) using well-rounded features to capture not only the two languages but also the other classes. On the Spanish-English(ES-EN) classification task, we obtained weighted F1-score of 0.88 on the tweet level and an accuracy of 96.5% on the token level. On the MSA-DA classification task, our system managed to obtain F1-score of 0.66 on tweet level and overall token level accuracy of 74.7%.

1 Introduction

It is very common to find people adept in two or more languages (Ansaldo et al., 2008). During interactions and conversations in real life as well as in social media, multilingual people tend to switch between languages in written as well as verbal communication. Hale (2014) found that over 10% of Twitter users tweet in multiple languages and they are in general more active users than their monolingual counterparts. Modupeola (2013), in his research of an effective way of teaching English to Nigerian students, finds codeswitching from English to Nigerian by teachers as a necessity for generating interest, elaborating word meanings and the transfer of knowledge of the secondary language in an efficient manner. Codeswitching phenomenon is more prevalent in multi-cultural societies, where means of communication is not primarily in a single language (Cheng and Butler, 1989; Auer, 2013). It can also be attributed to the huge amount of exposure to other languages due to social media, TV shows and movies. Codeswitched text identification is often the first step for text to speech translation, automatic speech recognition and sentiment analysis.

Our paper deals with the phenomenon of codeswitching between Spanish and English (ES-EN) words and Modern Standard Arabic to Dialect Arabic (MSA-DA). The main aim of this paper is to describe our system submitted to the Second Workshop on Computational Approaches to Code Switching shared task (Molina et al., 2016). We use Conditional Random Fields (CRF) based system to categorize the codeswitched text into eight different categories: *lang1*, *lang2*, *other*, *ne*, *mixed*, *unknown*, *ambiguous*, and *fw*(foreign words). The categories *lang1* and *lang2* refer to the two main language pairs, while *ne* refers to named entities. ES-EN classification uses all these labels whereas MSA-DA classification does not use the labels *unk* and *fw* labels. First we elaborate on the various features we chose to identify and distinguish one category from the other. Then we elaborate on our results and findings. Finally we will analyze the strengths and weaknesses of our system.

2 Related Work

Research into codeswitching and codeswitching detection is not new. There have been many studies on

Proceedings of the Second Workshop on Computational Approaches to Code Switching, pages 121–126,
Austin, TX, November 1, 2016. ©2016 Association for Computational Linguistics

codeswitching at socio-cultural level. According to Heredia and Altarriba (2001), the main reason multilingual people codeswitch is the lack of a single language proficiency and frequency/ease of use of word of one language than the other in given context. Eldin (2014) highlight other factors such as clarification, persuasion, effective interaction and current mood and expression of the person for codeswitching.

Recently many researchers have tried various computational methods for language identification in codeswitched text. Yu et al. (2012), Garrette et al. (2015) and Bacatan et al. (2014) use language models and word n-grams with position and frequency data as part of their system to identify codeswitched text. Both achieved an accuracy of over 80%. Maharjan et al. (2015) collected codeswitched tweets for Spanish-English and Nepali-English language pairs. They first figured out some seed users who codeswitched frequently and then followed him/her to collect more codeswitched tweets.They obtained an accuracy of 86% and 87% for Spanish-English and Nepali-English dataset using CRF GE algorithm.

CRF has been used for many different tasks, especially dealing with sequence labeling such as POS tagging (Lafferty et al., 2001a; Silfverberg et al., 2014) and named entity recognition (McCallum and Li, 2003; Settles, 2004). Similar to us, three out of seven participating teams also used CRF for codeswitching detection for the EMNLP 2014 language identification shared task (Solorio et al., 2014). Other participants used Support Vector Machines (SVM),k Nearest Neighbour (KNN), Extended Markov Models (eMM) and spell checker methods with external resources to tackle the problem. In the same year of the shared task, we used dictionaries to store and search prefix ngrams and further used a spell checker to identify wrongly spelled words from social media lingo so they can be classified correctly (Shrestha and Dhulikhel, 2014).

3 Methodology

Our system uses CRF for modeling the sequence of codeswitched tweets. CRF is a very popular sequence classifier for when constituents of a sequence are dependent upon their adjacent context. Rather than modeling for each part separately, it makes more sense to model for the whole sequence. CRF calculates the probability of a whole sequence of labels given a sequence of tokens (words) by using Equation 1. Here $\vec{s}$ represents a sequence of labels and $\vec{x}$ represents a sequence of tokens. $\vec{\phi}$ and $\vec{w}$ are the feature vector and the weights for the feature vector respectively.

$$p(\vec{s}|\vec{x};\vec{w}) = \frac{exp(\vec{w}.\vec{\Phi}(\vec{x},\vec{s}))}{\sum_{\vec{s'} \in S^m} exp(\vec{w}.\vec{\Phi}(\vec{x},\vec{s'}))} \quad (1)$$

Using a CRF with task-specific features, given a context can result in very robust systems for sequence labeling (Lafferty et al., 2001b; Ye et al., 2009). CRF fits the problem of codeswitching detection since frequent switching between languages is not very common. For example, if a token is in Spanish, it is very likely that the token before it and after it are also in Spanish. We describe our features in detail below.

3.1 Features

1. **Token**: The token itself is the biggest indicator of which language it might belong to. Fry and Kress (2012) estimate that the most frequent 1,000 words in the English language accounts for 89% of the text written in English. If the training data is large enough, even a dictionary based approach can provide a very good baseline to build upon. This feature is especially helpful for the tokens that are not shared between the two languages.

2. **Suffix**: Most languages have distinctive suffixes that tokens end in. For example: In English we add *ly* to adjectives to turn them into adverbs similarly in Spanish *-mente* is added to adjectives to turn them into adverbs. So *simply* in English is *simplemente* in Spanish. For the *ing* form of the verb in English there is a close representation in Spanish using the characters *ando,iendo*. English words ending in *-tion* have a Spanish word equivalent in *-cin*. Similarly English *ency, ancy* and Spanish *encia*, English *fic* and Spanish *fico,-fica* etc are some of the many equivalents. As there are many distinct suffixes in both language it is a very helpful feature. We use 1-4 letter suffixes as features.

3. **Prefix**: Although many common prefixes in English have identical prefixes in Spanish *(eg:anti,auto,inter)*, similar to suffixes, these languages also have distinctive prefixes. For example *pseudo* in English is *seudo* in Spanish. So *pseudoscience* in English is spelled as *seudociencia* in Spanish. Other examples include, words beginning in English with *s,ph,poly* generally begin in Spanish with *es,f,poli* respectively. To incorporate these distinct prefixes during classification, we use 1-4 letter prefixes as features.

4. **Prefix and Suffix bigrams**: Rather than just using prefixes and suffixes, we also used bigrams of prefixes and suffixes as features.

5. **Titlecase**: This feature can help catch named entities as the most characteristic attribute of a named entity in a properly written text is that it is in titlecase.

6. **Token is/has Punctuation(s)**: Punctuation tokens and tokens containing many punctuations are more likely to fall in the *other* category.

7. **has/all Unicode**: Spanish tokens contain accented Unicode characters, whereas English ones do not. Also, if the number of Unicode characters in a word is very high, the word is likely to be in the *other* category, for example, in emoticons.

8. **Number**: Tokens containing numbers do not belong to either language.

9. **Uppercase**: Token containing many uppercase characters are usually abbreviations, NE or slangs.

We use the same system with exactly the same features for both ES-EN and MSA-DA language pairs.

4 Implementation Details

We performed a very simple preprocessing step of removing the hashtags since hashtags do not have any significance for this task. The presence of hashtags might confuse the model instead. We also removed non-ASCII quotation marks since these

Evaluation Metric	ES-EN	MSA-DA
Monolingual F1	0.90	0.72
Codeswitched F1	0.86	0.34
Weighted F1	0.88	0.66

Table 1: Tweet level results for both Spanish-English and Modern Standard Arabic-Dialect Arabic.

Label	Recall	Precision	F1 score
ambiguous	0.000	0.000	0.000
lang1	0.919	0.919	0.919
lang2	0.981	0.975	0.978
mixed	0.000	0.000	0.000
ne	0.422	0.560	0.481
fw	0.000	0.000	0.000
other	0.993	0.994	0.994
unknown	0.000	0.000	0.000

Table 2: Recall, Precision and F1 score of token level results for Spanish-English.

would wrongly be accounted as unicode features. For CRF, we used the sklearn-crfsuite package (Korobov, 2015), which itself is a wrapper over CRFsuite (Okazaki, 2007). In order to obtain the best model, we experimented over all of the available algorithms in CRFsuite namely, *lbfgs, l2sgd, ap, pa,* and *arow*. Using the provided development set, we found the *pa* algorithm to perform the best among them. We also performed hyperparamter optimization by using randomized search over parameters specific to each algorithm. We obtained the highest accuracy on the development set with *pa_type=1* and *c=10.0*. We used these parameters to train a final model by combining both the training and the development datasets. We used this model to obtain our results on the test dataset.

5 Results

Tweet level results for both ES-EN and MSA-DA are shown in Table 1. For ES-EN, our F1 scores for both monolingual and codeswitched tweets are similar, although the results for monolingual tweets are slightly better. Our weighted F1 score is only 0.03 points below the system with the best weighted F1. The token level results broken down by labels for ES-EN are in Table 2. We could catch most of the *lang1, lang2* and *other* tokens. Both our precision and recall are very high for these classes. We also

Label	Recall	Precision	F1 score
ambiguous	0.000	0.000	0.000
lang1	0.959	0.551	0.699
lang2	0.586	0.943	0.722
mixed	0.000	0.000	0.000
ne	0.662	0.851	0.745
other	0.977	0.973	0.975

Table 3: Recall, Precision and F1 score of token level results for Modern Standard Arabic-Dialect Arabic.

catch nearly half of the name entities. Named entities are harder to capture with our system since we do not have a specialized system for named entities, apart from the features that check for titlecase and uppercase. Our system did not catch any of the *ambiguous*, *mixed*, *fw* or *unknown* tokens. The main reason behind this might be how sparse these types of tokens are in training. These comprised of only 0.408% and 0.652% of the total tokens in the training set the test set respectively. Most of the other systems in the shared task also failed to catch these tokens. Despite this, overall, our system was able to obtain good results in the ES-EN language pair codeswitching.

However, we did not fare as well for the MSA-DA language pair. The monolingual F1 is a lot higher at 0.72 than the codeswitched F1 at 0.34 and as such the weighted F1 also suffers. Our system has the propensity of predicting a high number of tokens as lang1, as evidenced by the token level results in Table 3. The recall for *lang1* is very high, while the recall for *lang2* is low. This might owe to the fact that the ratio of tokens in lang1 and *lang2* are reversed in training and test sets. In the training set, 68.74% of the tokens are lang1 and 11.70% of the tokens are *lang2*. Whereas in the test set, only 28.10% of the tokens are lang1 and 46.62% of the tokens are *lang2*. This might have led our model to predict high number of *lang2* tokens as lang1. Similar as in ES-EN, we again perform very well for *other* tokens. A surprising finding with the MSA-DA results is that we have a lot better results for named entities than for ES-EN in both precision and recall, although the system used for both language pairs are exactly the same. One reason might be that the model has a higher number of named entities to learn from in MSA-DA dataset than in the ES-EN dataset. Unfor-

State	Coefficient	Transition	Coefficient
prefix:@,other	2.0138	lang1 → lang1	0.2050
suffix:os,lang2	0.6566	lang2 → lang2	0.2034
is_number,other	0.5938	lang1 → ne	0.1629
has_punct,other	0.5831	unk → unk	0.1491
prefix:',lang1	0.5704	ne → ne	0.1087
suffix:as,lang2	0.5629	fw → fw	0.1048
all_punct,other	0.5563	ne → lang1	0.0896
suffix:o,lang2	0.4872	lang1 → amb	0.0843
suffix:t,lang1	0.4663	lang2 → mixed	0.0776
all_unicode,other	0.4488	lang2 → amb	0.0712
suffix:a,lang2	0.4436	lang2 → ne	0.0651
suffix:tion,lang1	0.4264	mixed → lang1	0.0455
prefix:th,lang1	0.4230	other → lang1	0.0413
suffix:ed,lang1	0.3837	amb → lang1	0.0412
suffix:ien,lang2	0.3830	unk → other	0.0403
suffix:ing,lang1	0.3726	mixed → lang2	0.0382
prefix:w,lang1	0.3517	unk → lang1	0.0373
suffix:oy,lang2	0.3511	lang1 → unk	0.0371
prefix:Th,lang1	0.3302	lang1 → mixed	0.0314
suffix:ly,lang1	0.3196	other → unk	0.0276

Table 4: Most likely states (state:feature,label) and transitions for the ES-EN model.

tunately, apart from that, we cannot provide any further intuition into this due to our lack of knowledge of Arabic. Overall, our results for the MSA-DA language pair could definitely use some improvement.

6   Analysis

To gain an insight into what our model might be learning, we look at the most likely states and transitions of our CRF model trained on the ES-EN language pair dataset. These are shown in Table 4. Most of the top likely states deal with prefixes and suffixes. The state with the highest coefficient is the one for tokens that have a prefix as @ being *other*. This is very intuitive as most of the tokens that start with @ are Twitter usernames and do indeed have *other* as their label. The suffixes *-os*, *as* and *a* have been associated with Spanish while *t*, *tion*, *ed*, *ing*, and *ly* have been taken as indicators of the token being English by our model. Similarly, the tokens that start with ' as the prefix having label *other* has high coefficient. This works for tokens such as *'s*, *'ll*, *'d*. Similarly most other top likely states are intuitive and are aligned our knowledge of Spanish and English. The associations of *is_number*, *has_punct* and *all_unicode* with other also have high weight. This reflects the data as numbers do not belong to either language and tokens with all unicode characters are mostly emoticons.

Four out of five most likely transitions are between the same two labels. This shows that language users do not switch between labels too often. The most likely transitions are from English to English and from Spanish to Spanish. The transition from English to Spanish or vice versa did not fall under the top 20 likely transitions. This might be because a person can only use so many *ne* or *other* tokens before switching back to a language but when a person switches from one language to another, there is no such constraint and people are likely to keep on using the other language rather than switching back.

We also looked at some of the instances in the development set where our system predicted the wrong label. We made the most number of mistakes for *ne*. Almost all of these mistakes were for tokens that were not in titlecase. Since this was our only feature specific to named entities, our model could not catch these. There were also some cases where our model did correctly label the tokens as named entities, such as *twitter*, *RT*, *iphones*, etc but the labels given to them in the dataset were different. The most confusion between English and Spanish were for words that are present in both languages such as *yo*, *a*, *no*, *senior*, etc. But this was rare and most of the time our model correctly labeled even these words.

7 Conclusion and Future Works

The task of codeswitching detection is highly suited to be solved using CRF as evidenced by our results. The performance of the system depends on the features chosen and in our case, these features worked for ES-EN and did not work too well for MSA-DA. Our lack of knowledge of Arabic definitely proved to be a hindrance in crafting sensible features for MSA-DA. Nonetheless, we were able to obtain competitive scores for both language pairs. We were also able to see the characteristics of both English and Spanish being captured by our model, especially the most common prefixes and suffixes of both languages. In our further research, we will work towards finding effective features for both ES-EN as well as MSA-DA language pairs. One of the shortcomings of our system is also not being able to capture named entities. In the future, we will also look into named entity recognition systems that work for codeswitched texts.

Acknowledgments

We would like to thank the organizers of the Computational Approaches to Code Switching shared task for providing us with this opportunity.

References

Ana Inés Ansaldo, Karine Marcotte, Lilian Scherer, and Gaelle Raboyeau. 2008. Language therapy and bilingual aphasia: Clinical implications of psycholinguistic and neuroimaging research. *Journal of Neurolinguistics*, 21(6):539–557.

Peter Auer. 2013. *Code-switching in conversation: Language, interaction and identity*. Routledge.

Arianna Clarisse R Bacatan, Bryan Loren D Castillo, Marjorie Janelle T Majan, Verlia F Palermo, and Ria A Sagum. 2014. Detection of intra-sentential code-switching points using word bigram and unigram frequency count. *International Journal of Computer and Communication Engineering*, 3(3):184.

Li-Rong Cheng and Katharine Butler. 1989. Code-switching: a natural phenomenon vs language deficiency. *World Englishes*, 8(3):293–309.

Ahmad Abdel Tawwab Sharaf Eldin. 2014. Socio linguistic study of code switching of the arabic language speakers on social networking. *International journal of English linguistics*, 4(6):78.

Edward B Fry and Jacqueline E Kress. 2012. *The reading teacher's book of lists*, volume 55. John Wiley & Sons.

Dan Garrette, Hannah Alpert-Abrams, Taylor Berg-Kirkpatrick, and Dan Klein. 2015. Unsupervised code-switching for multilingual historical document transcription. In *Proceedings of the 2015 Conference of the North American Chapter of the Association for Computational Linguistics: Human Language Technologies*, pages 1036–1041.

Scott A Hale. 2014. Global connectivity and multilinguals in the twitter network. In *Proceedings of the SIGCHI Conference on Human Factors in Computing Systems*, pages 833–842. ACM.

Roberto R Heredia and Jeanette Altarriba. 2001. Bilingual language mixing: Why do bilinguals code-switch? *Current Directions in Psychological Science*, 10(5):164–168.

Mikhail Korobov. 2015. sklearn-crfsuite.

John Lafferty, Andrew McCallum, and Fernando Pereira. 2001a. Conditional random fields: Probabilistic models for segmenting and labeling sequence data. In *Proceedings of International Conference on Machine Learning (ICML)*, pages 282–289.

John Lafferty, Andrew McCallum, and Fernando Pereira. 2001b. Conditional random fields: Probabilistic models for segmenting and labeling sequence data. In *Proceedings of the eighteenth international conference on machine learning, ICML*, volume 1, pages 282–289.

Suraj Maharjan, Elizabeth Blair, Steven Bethard, and Thamar Solorio. 2015. Developing language-tagged corpora for code-switching tweets. In *Proc. LAW IX at NAACL*.

Andrew McCallum and Wei Li. 2003. Early results for named entity recognition with conditional random fields, feature induction and web-enhanced lexicons. In *Proceedings of the seventh conference on Natural language learning at HLT-NAACL 2003-Volume 4*, pages 188–191. Association for Computational Linguistics.

Olagunju Robert Modupeola. 2013. Code-switching as a teaching strategy: Implication for english language teaching and learning in a multilingual society. *IOSR Journal of Humanities and Social Science*, 14(3):92–94.

Giovanni Molina, Fahad AlGhamdi, Mahmoud Ghoneim, Abdelati Hawwari, Nicolas Rey-Villamizar, Mona Diab, and Thamar Solorio. 2016. Overview for the second shared task on language identification in code-switched data. In *Proceedings of The Second Workshop on Computational Approaches to Linguistic Code Switching, held in conjunction with EMNLP 2016*.

Naoaki Okazaki. 2007. Crfsuite: a fast implementation of conditional random fields (crfs).

Burr Settles. 2004. Biomedical named entity recognition using conditional random fields and rich feature sets. In *Proceedings of the International Joint Workshop on Natural Language Processing in Biomedicine and its Applications*, pages 104–107. Association for Computational Linguistics.

Prajwol Shrestha and Nepal Dhulikhel. 2014. Incremental n-gram approach for language identification in code-switched text. *EMNLP 2014*, page 133.

Miikka Silfverberg, Teemu Ruokolainen, Krister Linden, Mikko Kurimo, et al. 2014. Part-of-speech tagging using conditional random fields: Exploiting sub-label dependencies for improved accuracy. In *ACL (2)*, pages 259–264.

Thamar Solorio, Elizabeth Blair, Suraj Maharjan, Steve Bethard, Mona Diab, Mahmoud Gonheim, Abdelati Hawwari, Fahad AlGhamdi, Julia Hirshberg, Alison Chang, and Pascale Fung. 2014. Overview for the first shared task on language identification in code-switched data. In *Proceedings of the First Workshop on Computational Approaches to Code-Switching. EMNLP 2014, Conference on Empirical Methods in Natural Language Processing*, Doha, Qatar.

Nan Ye, Wee S Lee, Hai L Chieu, and Dan Wu. 2009. Conditional random fields with high-order features for sequence labeling. In *Advances in Neural Information Processing Systems*, pages 2196–2204.

Liang-Chih Yu, Wei-Cheng He, and Wei-Nan Chien. 2012. A language modeling approach to identifying code-switched sentences and words. *CLP 2012*, page 3.

Language Identification in Code-Switched Text
Using Conditional Random Fields and Babelnet

Utpal Kumar Sikdar and **Björn Gambäck**

Department of Computer and Information Science
Norwegian University of Science and Technology
Trondheim, Norway
`{sikdar.utpal,gamback}@idi.ntnu.no`

Abstract

The paper outlines a supervised approach to language identification in code-switched data, framing this as a sequence labeling task where the label of each token is identified using a classifier based on Conditional Random Fields and trained on a range of different features, extracted both from the training data and by using information from Babelnet and Babelfy.

The method was tested on the development dataset provided by organizers of the shared task on language identification in code-switched data, obtaining tweet level monolingual, code-switched and weighted F1-scores of 94%, 85% and 91%, respectively, with a token level accuracy of 95.8%. When evaluated on the unseen test data, the system achieved 90%, 85% and 87.4% monolingual, code-switched and weighted tweet level F1-scores, and a token level accuracy of 95.7%.

1 Introduction

Today many short messages contain words from different languages and it is a challenging task to identify which languages the different words are written in. Often the messages contain text snippets from several languages, that is, showing code-switching. Sometimes the messages even contain code-mixing, where there is a mix of the languages inside a single utterance or even inside a token itself.

The first code-switching data challenge was organized at EMNLP 2014 (Solorio et al., 2014). The task was to identify the language for each word in a text, classifying the words according to six labels: 'Lang1', 'Lang2', 'Mixed', 'NE', 'Other', and 'Ambiguous'. The first two labels identify tokens from the main languages that are mixed in the text, while the third is for tokens with word-internal mixing between these languages; 'NE' for named entities; 'Other' for language independent tokens (punctuation, numbers, etc.) and tokens from other languages, and 'Ambiguous' denotes tokens that cannot safely be assigned any (or only one) of the other labels. This shared task was organized again this year (Molina et al., 2016), with new datasets and slightly different labels, adding 'Unk' for unknown tokens.[1]

Work on developing tools for automatic language identification was initiated already in the 1960s (Gold, 1967), and although analysing code-switched text is a research area which has started to achieve wide-spread attention only in recent years, the first work in the field was carried out over thirty years ago by Joshi (1982), while Bentahila and Davies (1983) examined the syntax of the intra-sentential code-switching between Arabic and French. They claimed that Arabic-French code-switching was possible at all syntactic boundaries above the word level.

Das and Gambäck (2013) give a comprehensive overview of the work on code-switching until 2015. Notably, Solorio and Liu (2008) trained classifiers to predict code-switching points in Spanish and English, using different learning algorithms and transcriptions of code-switched discourse, while Nguyen and Doğruöz (2013) focused on word-level language identification (in Dutch-Turkish news commentary). Nguyen and Cornips (2016) describe

---

[1]An eighth label 'FW' was included for foreign words, but no words in the English-Spanish corpora were tagged with it.

127

Proceedings of the Second Workshop on Computational Approaches to Code Switching, pages 127–131,
Austin, TX, November 1, 2016. ©2016 Association for Computational Linguistics

work on analyzing and detecting intra-word code-mixing by first segmenting words into smaller units and later identifying words composed of sequences of subunits associated with different languages in *tweets* (posts on the Twitter social-media site).

The paper is organized as follows: Section 2 provides a description of the language identification method, whereby a supervised model was built using Conditional Random Fields to classify each token in a tweet into one of the seven categories based on different features, most of which are extracted from the training data, as described in Section 3. Results are then presented and discussed in Section 4, while Section 5 addresses future work and concludes.

2 Language Identification Method

The language identification system was built around a Conditional Random Field (CRF) classifier. We used the C^{++}-based CRF^{++} package (Kudo, 2013), a simple, customizable, and open source implementation of Conditional Random Fields for segmenting or labelling sequential data. Conditional Random Fields (Lafferty et al., 2001) are conditional, undirected graphical models that can easily incorporate a large number of arbitrary, non-independent features while still having efficient procedures for non-greedy finite-state inference and training.

Conditional Random Fields calculate the conditional probability of values on designated output nodes given the values of (other) designated input nodes. The conditional probability of a state sequence $s = < s_1, s_2, \ldots, s_T >$ given an observation sequence $o = < o_1, o_2, \ldots, o_T >$ is calculated as in Equation 1 (McCallum, 2003):

$$P_\wedge(s|o) = \frac{1}{Z_o} \exp(\sum_{t=1}^{T} \sum_{k=1}^{K} \lambda_k \times f_k(s_{t-1}, s_t, o, t))$$

$$(1)$$

where $f_k(s_{t-1}, s_t, o, t)$ is a feature function whose weight λ_k, is to be learned via training. The feature function values may range from $-\infty$ to $+\infty$.

To make all the conditional probabilities sum up to 1, the normalization factor Z_o is calculated in the same fashion as in HMMs (Hidden Markov Models), that is, as given by Equation 2.

$$Z_o = \sum_{s} \exp(\sum_{t=1}^{T} \sum_{k=1}^{K} \lambda_k \times f_k(s_{t-1}, s_t, o, t)) \quad (2)$$

To train a CRF, the objective function to be maximized is the penalized log-likelihood of the state sequences given the observation sequences:

$$L_\wedge = \sum_{i=1}^{N} \log(P_\wedge(s^{(i)}|o^{(i)})) - \sum_{k=1}^{K} \frac{\lambda_k^2}{2\sigma^2} \quad (3)$$

where $\{< o^{(i)}, s^{(i)} >\}$ is the labelled training data. The second sum corresponds to a zero-mean, σ^2-variance Gaussian prior over parameters, which facilitates optimization by making the likelihood surface strictly convex. Here, we set the parameter λ to maximize the penalized log-likelihood using Limited-memory BFGS (Sha and Pereira, 2003), a quasi-Newton method that is highly efficient, and which results in only minor changes in accuracy due to changes in λ.

2.1 Features based on training data

Two sets of features were developed to train the model: one extracted from the training data and the other based on information from Babelnet (Navigli and Ponzetto, 2012) and Babelfy (Moro et al., 2014), with most of the features and their settings being based on the training data. The complete set of features induced from training data was as follows:

Local context. Local contexts play an important role for identifying the languages. Here the two preceding and two succeeding words were used as local context.

Word suffix and prefix. Fixed length characters stripped from the beginning and ending of the current word. Up to 4 characters were removed.

Word length. Analysis of the training data showed that the Spanish words on average were shorter than the English words. Words with 1–4 characters were flagged with a binary feature.

Word previously occurred. A binary feature which checks if a word already occurred in the training data or not.

Initial capital. In general, proper nouns tend to start with capital letters, so this feature checks whether the current word has an initial capital.

All capitals. A binary feature which is set if the current word contains only capital letters. The feature is very helpful for identifying named entities (since, e.g., abbreviations often refer to named entities).

Single capital letter: checks if the word contains a single capital letter or not.

All digits: set to 1 if the word contains only numerical characters. This is helpful for identifying tokens belonging to the 'Other' category.

Alphanumeric: a binary feature which flags if the word contains only digits and alphabetical characters together.

All English alphabet: checks if all a word's characters belong to the English alphabet.

Special Spanish character: a flag which is set if the current word contains any Spanish-specific letters (á, é, etc.).

Hash symbol: set to 1 if a word contains the symbol '#', otherwise 0.

Rate symbol: set to 1 if the current word contains the symbol '@'.

Word with single letter. Many single letter words were observed to belong to Spanish, so this flag is set if the word length is exactly 1.

Two consecutive letters. Some words repeat two character sequences several times (e.g., *ha-haha, jaja*). Each token is split into two character sequences and this binary feature is set if each two letter character sequences matches.

Same letter occurred multiple times. Many words in tweets contain sequences of the same character repeated many times (e.g., ewww, yaaaas). The feature is set if a letter occurred in a word more than two times consecutively.

Gazetteer NE list. A list of named entities (NE) was collected from the training data. This flag is set if a token matches an item on the NE list.

Special character list. A list of special characters (e.g., emojis) was collected from the training data. If a tokens contains any character which is on the list, the binary feature is set.

2.2 Babelnet and Babelfy features

Three further features were developed from external resource, Babelnet (Navigli and Ponzetto, 2012) and Babelfy (Moro et al., 2014):

Dataset	Number of	
	tweets	tokens
Training	11,400	140,745
Development	3,014	33,743
Test	18,237	218,138

Table 1: Statistics of the tweet datasets

WordNet feature: Every token is passed to the Babelnet database for checking whether the token exists in the English WordNet or not. If the token appears in the database, the feature is set to 1, otherwise to 0.

Multilingual WordNet: The Babelnet Multilingual WordNet is checked for Spanish, by passing each token to the Babelnet database and checking whether the token is present in the database or not.

Babelfy Named Entity: Named entities are extracted from Babelfy and used as a feature, which is utilized for identification of the 'NE' category tokens.

3 Datasets

We used the datasets provided by the organizers of the EMNLP 2016 code-switching workshop shared task on language identification in code-switched data (Molina et al., 2016).[2]

Three types of data were provided: training, development and test. In the training and development datasets, the total number of tweets are 11,400 and 3,014, respectively, with language identification offsets given for each category. In the test data, the total number of tweets is 18,237 without annotations.

The number of tweets and the number of tokens in each of the three datasets are given in Table 1.

4 Results

We developed a supervised model for language identification using the CRF++ classifier, implemented the different features described above, and trained the CRF++ classifier using these features. Initially, the classifier was trained using the training data and tested on the development data for Spanish-English.

---

[2]`care4lang1.seas.gwu.edu/cs2/call.html`

System setup	Mono-lingual			Code-switched			Weighted	Token-level
	P	R	F_1	P	R	F_1	F_1	Accuracy
Without external resources	0.94	0.92	0.93	0.82	0.85	0.83	0.904	0.943
With external resources	0.95	0.93	0.94	0.82	0.87	0.85	0.911	0.952

Table 2: System performance on the development data, with and without the external resources (Babelnet and Babelfy)

Team	Accuracy
IIIT Hyderabad	0.961
NepSwitch	0.958
NTNU	0.957
HHU-UH-G	0.953
Howard U	0.951
McGill U	0.941
UW group	0.926
GWU*	0.918
Arunavha Chana	0.527

Team	Mono-lingual	Code-switched	Weighted
Howard U	0.90	0.87	0.890
IIIT Hyderabad	0.90	0.86	0.886
HHU-UH-G	0.90	0.85	0.878
NTNU	0.90	0.85	0.874
NepSwitch	0.89	0.85	0.870
McGill U	0.86	0.78	0.820
UW group	0.78	0.78	0.780
Arunavha Chana	0.80	0.71	0.760
GWU*	0.93	0.54	0.740

Table 3: Token level accuracy (left) and tweet level F_1 scores (right) on the test data for all participating systems

There were two types of evaluation, at tweet level and at token level. The tweet level precision (P), recall (R) and F_1-scores obtained on the monolingual part of the development data were 95%, 93% and 94%, respectively. On the code-switched part of that data, the precision, recall and F_1-scores were 82%, 87% and 85%, giving a weighted, total F_1-score of 91.1%. For token level evaluation, the development data accuracy was 95.2%, as shown in Table 2.

Table 2 also gives the development data scores for a system trained without the second feature set, i.e., without the Babelnet and Babelfy features. As can be seen in the table, the contribution from those features is small but useful, adding 0.9% to the token-level accuracy and 0.7% to the tweet-level weighted F_1 score, with the main contribution (2%) being on recall for the tweets containing code-switching.

Applying our system (NTNU) to the test data, the tweet level monolingual, code-switched and weighted F_1-scores were 90%, 85% and 87.4%, with a token level accuracy performance of 95.7%.

A comparison of the results of the different systems participating in the shared task is given in Table 3, for both token level and tweet level evaluation, with the performance of our system marked in bold face. For token level evaluation, the NTNU system achieved third place in the shared task, with an accuracy difference between our system and the best performing system (IIIT Hyderabad) of only 0.4%.

At the tweet level, the NTNU system performed on par with the best systems on the monolingual tweets, while it scored 2% lower on the tweets that contained some code-switching, giving it fourth place on weighted F_1-score. However, as can be seen from the tables, the top-5 teams actually obtained very similar performance on all measures, and both at token and tweet level.

5 Conclusion

For this shared task, we have outlined an approach using a CRF based system for language identification in code-switched data, implementing a range of different features and achieving state-of-the-art results. Most of the features are extracted directly from training data, while some are induced by using Babelnet and Babelfy as external resources.

In future, we will aim to optimize these features using grid search and evolutionary algorithms, as well as generate different models using several classification algorithms and utilize the predictions of ensembles of such machine learners in order to enhance the overall system performance.

References

Abdelâli Bentahila and Eirlys E. Davies. 1983. The syntax of Arabic-French code-switching. *Lingua*, 59:301–330.

Amitava Das and Björn Gambäck. 2013. Code-mixing in social media text: The last language identification frontier? *Traitement Automatique des Langues*, 54(3):41–64.

E. Mark Gold. 1967. Language identification in the limit. *Information and Control*, 10(5):447–474.

Aravind K. Joshi. 1982. Processing of sentences with intra-sentential code-switching. In *Proceedings of the 9th International Conference on Computational Linguistics*, pages 145–150, Prague, Czechoslovakia, July. ACL.

Taku Kudo. 2013. CRF++: Yet another CRF toolkit. `http://taku910.github.io`.

John D. Lafferty, Andrew McCallum, and Fernando C. N. Pereira. 2001. Conditional Random Fields: Probabilistic models for segmenting and labeling sequence data. In *Proceedings of the 18th International Conference on Machine Learning*, pages 282–289, Williamstown, Maryland, USA, June.

Andrew McCallum. 2003. Efficiently inducing features of Conditional Random Fields. In *Proceedings of the 19th Conference on Uncertainty in Articifical Intelligence*, pages 403–410, Acapulco, Mexico, August. Association for Uncertainty in Artificial Intelligence.

Giovanni Molina, Fahad AlGhamdi, Mahmoud Ghoneim, Abdelati Hawwari, Nicolas Rey-Villamizar, Mona Diab, and Thamar Solorio. 2016. Overview for the second shared task on language identification in code-switched data. In *Proceedings of the 2016 Conference on Empirical Methods in Natural Language Processing*, Austin, Texas, November. ACL. 2nd Workshop on Computational Approaches to Linguistic Code Switching.

Andrea Moro, Alessandro Raganato, and Roberto Navigli. 2014. Entity linking meets word sense disambiguation: a unified approach. *Transactions of the Association for Computational Linguistics*, 2:231–244.

Roberto Navigli and Simone Paolo Ponzetto. 2012. BabelNet: The automatic construction, evaluation and application of a wide-coverage multilingual semantic network. *Artificial Intelligence*, 193:217–250.

Dong Nguyen and Leonie Cornips. 2016. Automatic detection of intra-word code-switching. In *Proceedings of the 14th Annual SIGMORPHON Workshop on Computational Research in Phonetics, Phonology, and Morphology*, pages 82–86.

Dong Nguyen and A. Seza Doğruöz. 2013. Word level language identification in online multilingual communication. In *Proceedings of the 2013 Conference on Empirical Methods in Natural Language Processing*, pages 857–862, Seattle, Washington, October. ACL.

Fei Sha and Fernando C. N. Pereira. 2003. Shallow parsing with Conditional Random Fields. In *Proceedings of the 2003 Human Language Technology Conference of the North American Chapter of the Association for Computational Linguistics*, pages 134–141, Edmonton, Alberta, May. ACL.

Thamar Solorio and Yang Liu. 2008. Learning to predict code-switching points. In *Proceedings of the 2008 Conference on Empirical Methods in Natural Language Processing*, pages 973–981, Honolulu, Hawaii, October. ACL.

Thamar Solorio, Elizabeth Blair, Suraj Maharjan, Steven Bethard, Mona Diab, Mahmoud Ghoneim, Abdelati Hawwari, Fahad AlGhamdi, Julia Hirschberg, Alison Chang, and Pascale Fung. 2014. Overview for the first shared task on language identification in code-switched data. In *Proceedings of the 2014 Conference on Empirical Methods in Natural Language Processing*, pages 62–72, Doha, Qatar, October. ACL. 1st Workshop on Computational Approaches to Code Switching.

Codeswitching language identification using Subword Information Enriched Word Vectors

Meng Xuan Xia
McGill University
3480 University, Rm. 318
Montreal, Quebec H3A 0E9, Canada
`meng.xia@mail.mcgill.ca`

Abstract

Codeswitching is a widely observed phenomenon among bilingual speakers. By combining subword information enriched word vectors with linear-chain Conditional Random Field, we develop a supervised machine learning model that identifies languages in a English-Spanish codeswitched tweets. Our computational method achieves a tweet-level weighted F1 of 0.83 and a token-level accuracy of 0.949 without using any external resource. The result demonstrates that named entity recognition remains a challenge in codeswitched texts and warrants further work.

1 Introduction

Codeswitching (CS) is a widely observed phenomenon in social media. Solorio et al. (2014) define CS broadly as a communication act, whether spoken or written, where two or more languages are being used interchangeably. Codeswitching is common among bilingual speakers, both in speech and in writing. Identifying the languages in a codeswitched input is a crucial first step before applying other natural language processing algorithms.

The second shared task, like the previous one (Solorio et al., 2014), challenges the participants to develop computational method for identifying the language of each word in a dataset of codeswitched tweets. For each word in the source, the goal is to identify whether the word is *lang1*, *lang2*, *mixed*, *other* (punctuation, emotion and everything that is not a word in neither *lang1* nor *lang2*), *ambiguous*,

Token	Gold standard label
Hay	lang2
Dios	ne
,	other
I	lang1
'm	lang1
tired	lang1

Table 1: Example of label assignments for a English-Spanish codeswitched tweet

ne (named entity), *unknown* or *fw* (foreign word). *Lang1* and *lang2* are the two languages presented in a codeswitched language pair. There are two language pairs available in this shared task: Modern Standard Arabic-Arabic Dialects (MSA-DA) and English-Spanish (EN-ES). An example of token language identification is shown in Table 1.

Our work covers only the EN-ES language pair. We use FastText (Bojanowski et al., 2016) to train a subword information enhanced word vectors model from the datasets of the shared task. We then use these vectors and, in addition, custom features extracted from the words to train a linear-chain Conditional Random Field model that predicts the language label of each word. Our system requires only the dataset provided by the shared task, without any external resource. The final model scores 0.83 in weighted tweet-level F1 and 0.949 in overall token-level accuracy.

2 Related Work

Seven systems were submitted for the previous shared task. The system with the highest prediction result for the EN-ES language pair scores 0.822 in F-measure (Bar and Dershowitz, 2014). Solorio

Proceedings of the Second Workshop on Computational Approaches to Code Switching, pages 132–136,
Austin, TX, November 1, 2016. ©2016 Association for Computational Linguistics

et al. (2014) shows that Conditional Random Field (CRF) and Support Vector Machines (SVM) are the most popular supervised machine learning algorithms used for this task. Similar approach have been found outside of the share tasks, including Nguyen and Dogruoz (2013). All of these systems rely on external resources, while our system relies only on data prepared by the shared task.

Aside from the last shared task, previous work on identifying languages emphasizing on word-level identification includes Yamaguchi and Tanaka-Ishii (2012; VRL (2014; Zubiaga et al. (2015). There are also studies on multilingual documents, focusing on inter-sentential codeswitching (King and Abney, 2013; Singh and Gorla, 2007).

Previous work on language models that encode syntactic constraints from codeswitching theory includes Li and Fung (2013; Li and Fung (2014). These models require a parser for the codeswitched input, while our work only requires word-level tokenization.

3 System Description

Our system contains two steps to identify tokens in a codeswitched input.

In the first step, we use FastText (Bojanowski et al., 2016) to train a subword information enhanced skipgrams word vectors model, using the tweets presents in the train and the dev dataset. Word vectors are vector representations of the words learned from their raw form, using models such as Word2Vec (Mikolov and Dean, 2013). When used as the underlying input representation, word vectors have been shown to boost the performance in NLP tasks (Socher et al., 2013). FastText word vectors are used instead of standard word2vec because Fast-Text can obtain representations of out-of-vocabulary words by summing the representations of character n-grams. This feature is particularly useful because the size of the training data is relatively small. We expect the test dataset to contain words not found in the training dataset. Another motivation for using FastText word vectors is for its ability to take into account morphological information. We trained a skipgram FastText word vector representation model from the train datasets, using the default parameters provided by FastText (size of word vectors: 100, size

of the context window: 5, number of epochs 5, minimal number of word occurences: 5, max length of word ngram: 1 and loss function: ns)[1].

In the second step, We use supervised machine learning to train a Linear-Chain Conditional Random Field (CRF) (Lafferty et al., 2001) classifier that predicts the label of every token in the order given by the EN-ES token assigner. CRF is naturally suited for sequence labeling tasks and it has been shown to perform well in previous work on language identification tasks (King and Abney, 2013; Chittaranjan et al., 2014; Lin et al., 2014). We use CRFsuite(Okazaki, 2007) in our experiment.

3.1 Feature Extraction

For each token, we extract three types of features: word features, spelling features and intra-word features.

3.1.1 Word features

Word features contain the word vector representation of the current token and that of the token directly before and after the current one. We use the word vector model trained in the first step to obtain the word vector of each token. Word vectors of out-of-vocabulary tokens are automatically predicted in FastText by summing up the vector representations of character n-grams.

3.1.2 Spelling features

The following boolean features are extracted from the current token and that of the token directly before and after the current one:

- whether the token capitalized

- whether the token is all uppercase

- whether the token is all lowercase

- whether the token contains an uppercase character anywhere but in the beginning

- whether the token is alphanumeric

- whether the token contains any punctuation

- whether the token ends by an apostrophe

---

[1] https://github.com/facebookresearch/fastText#full-documentation

- whether the token contains no roman alphabets

- whether the token is in the beginning of the sentence

- whether the token is in the end of the sentence

Capitalization is a strong indicator of a proper noun, hence a named entity. However, this is not always the case with social media texts, where grammatical rules are not always followed. The boolean feature of the lack of roman alphabets is added because of our observation on the training data – most tokens classified as *other* do not have roman alphabets.

We also considered adding a boolean feature of whether the token contains Spanish-only accented characters (i.e. í, ú, é). However, it did not positively impact the prediction performance when tested against the dev dataset. This is possibly due to that social media users are more casual with spelling and replace accented characters with their non-accented counterpart. For example, both the correct spelling *así como*[2] and the incorrect spelling *asi como* are found in the training data.

3.1.3 Intra-word features

In contrast to English, Spanish is a morphologically rich language, demonstrating a complicated suffixed-based derivational morphology (Bar and Dershowitz, 2014). To capture repeating prefixes and suffixes that characterize each language, we extract the first 1-3 and the last 1-3 characters of each token as intra-word features. These features have also been shown to help predicting named entities and tokens labelled as *other*. For example, hashtags (tokens that begin with a # sign) are often named entities; twitter handles always begin with an @ sign.

4 Experiment

The shared task maintains three sets of dataset: a training dataset, a development dataset and a testing dataset. Each dataset contains rows of token extracted from EN-ES codeswitched tweets and the respective gold standard label for each token. We train an unsupervised FastText word vectors model

using the training dataset. Then we train a supervised CRF model using the same dataset. The supervised model is validated on the development dataset by evaluating standard metrics: precision, recall and F-measure of the predictions (Powers, 2011). We make hyper-parameter tuning to the CRF classifier using grid search.

To verify that all our features were contributing to the model's performance, we also did an ablation study, removing one group of features at a time.

Using the final model which consist of all the features, we compute predictions for the tokens in the testing dataset and submit the result to the workshop as final result.

5 Result and Analysis

5.1 Feature ablation

Table 2 shows the F1 scores on the dev dataset resulting from training with each group of feature removed. Note that although the removal of word features has no impact on the overall average F1, we decide to keep it because of the extra boost in performance it provides for named entities.

5.2 Final model performance

Our final model, when evaluated on the test dataset, has a tweet-level performance of 0.83 in weighted F1 as shown in Table 3. In terms of token-level performance, our model has an overall token accuracy of 0.949. The detailed metrics for each label are shown in Table 4.

We observe that the model is not able to predict mixed, foreign word, ambiguous and unknown labels. This is due to the lack of sufficient training data for these labels.

Our model has relatively low precision and recall with the NE labels. This suggests that our system is weak in recognizing named entities. While Bar and Dershowitz (2014) describe improvements of name entity recognition by using a gazetteer of proper nouns, our system did not benefit from having such a gazetteer. In fact, when validating on the development set, having such a gazetteer feature introduces over-fitting and decreases the overall accuracy of the model. The result suggests that named entity recognition remains a challenge in the context of codeswitched text.

---

[2]Meaning *as well as* in English

Features	lang1	lang2	ne	other	unk	Average
All	**0.965**	**0.945**	**0.355**	0.995	0.095	**0.946**
– Word features	**0.965**	0.944	0.331	**0.997**	0.058	**0.946**
– Intra-word	0.957	0.936	0.228	0.981	**0.126**	0.936
Spelling	0.963	0.944	0.353	0.989	0.093	0.944

Table 2: Feature ablation study. F1 on dev dataset after training with individual feature groups removed. The F1 for *mixed, fw* and *ambiguous* are all 0, hence omitted in this table. The average F1 is micro-averaged, taking into account all eight labels. The number of tokens for each label are the following: lang1: 16813, lang2: 8653, ne: 740, mixed: 14, ambiguous: 70, unk: 133, other: 6853 and fw: 0

Monolingual F1	Codeswitched F1	Weighted F1
0.86	0.79	0.83

Table 3: Tweet-level performance – there are in total 4626 codeswitched tweets and 6090 monolingual tweets.

Label	Recall	Precision	F1
lang1	0.879	0.866	0.873
lang2	0.968	0.962	0.965
other	0.993	0.994	0.993
ne	0.313	0.421	0.359
mixed	0	0	0
fw	0	0	0
ambiguous	0	0	0
unknown	0	0	0

Table 4: Token-level performance – the number of tokens for each label are the following: ambiguous: 4, lang1: 16944, lang2: 77047, mixed: 4, ne: 2092, fw: 19, other: 25311, unknown: 25, Total : 121446.

6 Conclusion

We participated in the shared task of the second codeswitching workshop by creating a supervised machine learning model that identifies the languages given a English-Spanish codeswitched input. Our model uses FastText to train a subword information enhanced word vectors model from the shared task datasets. In addition to these vectors, we add custom features extracted from the words to train a linear-chain Conditional Random Field model that predicts the language label of each word. Our system uses only the training data provided by the shared task and requires no external resource. The final model scores 0.83 in weighted tweet-level F1 and 0.949 in overall token-level accuracy. Our result suggests that named entity recognition remains difficult for codeswitched text and warrants future work.

Acknowledgment

The author thank Jackie Chi Kit Cheung for mentoring and the two anonymous reviewers for providing detailed constructive feedback.

References

Kfir Bar and Nachum Dershowitz. 2014. The Tel Aviv university system for the Code-Switching Workshop Shared Task. *EMNLP 2014*, page 139.

Piotr Bojanowski, Edouard Grave, Armand Joulin, and Tomas Mikolov. 2016. Enriching Word Vectors with Subword Information. *arXiv preprint arXiv:1607.04606*.

Gokul Chittaranjan, Yogarshi Vyas, and Kalika Bali Monojit Choudhury. 2014. Word-level language identification using CRF: Code-switching shared task report of MSR India system. In *Proceedings of The First Workshop on Computational Approaches to Code Switching*, pages 73–79.

Ben King and Steven P Abney. 2013. Labeling the Languages of Words in Mixed-Language Documents using Weakly Supervised Methods. In *HLT-NAACL*, pages 1110–1119.

John Lafferty, Andrew McCallum, and Fernando Pereira. 2001. Conditional random fields: Probabilistic models for segmenting and labeling sequence data. In *Proceedings of the eighteenth international conference on machine learning, ICML*, volume 1, pages 282–289.

Ying Li and Pascale Fung. 2013. Improved mixed language speech recognition using asymmetric acoustic model and language model with code-switch inversion constraints. In *2013 IEEE International Conference on Acoustics, Speech and Signal Processing*, pages 7368–7372. IEEE.

Ying Li and Pascale Fung. 2014. Code switch language modeling with functional head constraint. In *2014 IEEE International Conference on Acoustics, Speech and Signal Processing (ICASSP)*, pages 4913–4917. IEEE.

Chu-Cheng Lin, Waleed Ammar, Lori Levin, and Chris Dyer. 2014. The CMU submission for the shared task on language identification in code-switched data. In *Proceedings of the First Workshop on Computational Approaches to Code Switching*, pages 80–86.

T Mikolov and J Dean. 2013. Distributed representations of words and phrases and their compositionality. *Advances in neural information processing systems.*

Dong-Phuong Nguyen and A Seza Dogruoz. 2013. Word level language identification in online multilingual communication. Association for Computational Linguistics.

Naoaki Okazaki. 2007. Crfsuite: a fast implementation of conditional random fields (crfs).

David Martin Powers. 2011. Evaluation: from precision, recall and F-measure to ROC, informedness, markedness and correlation.

Anil Kumar Singh and Jagadeesh Gorla. 2007. Identification of languages and encodings in a multilingual document. In *Building and Exploring Web Corpora (WAC3-2007): Proceedings of the 3rd Web as Corpus Workshop, Incorporating Cleaneval*, volume 4, page 95. Presses univ. de Louvain.

Richard Socher, John Bauer, Christopher D Manning, and Andrew Y Ng. 2013. Parsing with Compositional Vector Grammars. In *ACL (1)*, pages 455–465.

Thamar Solorio, Elizabeth Blair, Suraj Maharjan, Steven Bethard, Mona Diab, Mahmoud Ghoneim, Abdelati Hawwari, Fahad AlGhamdi, Julia Hirschberg, Alison Chang, et al. 2014. Overview for the first shared task on language identification in code-switched data. In *Proceedings of The First Workshop on Computational Approaches to Code Switching*, pages 62–72. Citeseer.

NICTA VRL. 2014. Accurate language identification of twitter messages. In *Proceedings of the 5th Workshop on Language Analysis for Social Media (LASM)@ EACL*, pages 17–25.

Hiroshi Yamaguchi and Kumiko Tanaka-Ishii. 2012. Text segmentation by language using minimum description length. In *Proceedings of the 50th Annual Meeting of the Association for Computational Linguistics: Long Papers-Volume 1*, pages 969–978. Association for Computational Linguistics.

Arkaitz Zubiaga, Iñaki San Vicente, Pablo Gamallo, José Ramom Pichel, Iñaki Alegria, Nora Aranberri, Aitzol Ezeiza, and Víctor Fresno. 2015. TweetLID: a benchmark for tweet language identification. *Language Resources and Evaluation*, pages 1–38.

Author Index

Association for Computational Linguistics
209 N. Eighth Street
Stroudsburg, Pennsylvania 18360

ISBN 978-1-5108-3147-6